The Politics of Literature in a Divided 21st Century

How does literature matter politically in the 21st century? This book offers an ecocritical framework for exploring the significance of literature today. Featuring a diverse body of texts and authors, it develops a future-oriented politics embedded in those transgressive realities which our political system finds impossible to tame. This book re-imagines political agency, voices, bodies and borders as transformative processes rather than rigid realities, articulating a 'dia-topian' literary politics. Taking a contextual approach, it addresses such urgent global issues as biopolitics, migration and borders, populism, climate change, and terrorism. These readings revitalize fictional worlds for political enquiry, demonstrating how imaginative literature seeds change in a world of closed-off horizons. Prior to the pragmatics of power-play, literary language breathes new energy into the frames of our thought and the shapes of our affects. This book shows how relation, metamorphosis and enmeshment can become salient in a politics beyond the conflict line.

Dr. Katharina Donn is a teacher, lecturer and author in 20th century and contemporary literature. She specializes in memory and trauma studies, ecocriticism, feminism, and the politics of literature. Her first monograph *A Poetics of Trauma after 9/11* (Routledge, 2016) explores the entanglement of intimate vulnerability and virtual spectacle that is typical of the globalized present. Katharina has taught at the Universität Augsburg in Germany and the University of Texas at Austin in the US, and has held research fellowships at the UCL Institute of Advanced Studies and the Eccles Centre for American Studies at the British Library.

Routledge Studies in Contemporary Literature

Reading Contingency
The Accident in Contemporary Fiction
David Wylot

Death-Facing Ecology in Contemporary British and North American Environmental Crisis Fiction
Louise Squire

Poetry and the Question of Modernity
From Heidegger to the Present
Ian Cooper

Apocalyptic Territories
Setting and Revelation in Contemporary American Fiction
Anna Hellén

Displaced
Literature of Indigeneity, Migration, and Trauma
Edited by Kate Rose

Masculinities in Austrian Contemporary Literature
Strategic Evasion
Matthias Eck

Transcending the Postmodern
The Singular Response of Literature to the Transmodern Paradigm
Edited by Jean-Michel Ganteau and Susana Onega

The Politics of Literature in a Divided 21st Century
Katharina Donn

For more information about this series, please visit: www.routledge.com

The Politics of Literature in a Divided 21st Century

Katharina Donn

NEW YORK AND LONDON

First published 2021
by Routledge
52 Vanderbilt Avenue, New York, NY 10017

and by Routledge
2 Park Square, Milton Park, Abingdon, Oxon, OX14 4RN

Routledge is an imprint of the Taylor & Francis Group, an informa business

© 2021 Taylor & Francis

The right of Katharina Donn to be identified as author of this work has been asserted by her in accordance with sections 77 and 78 of the Copyright, Designs and Patents Act 1988.

All rights reserved. No part of this book may be reprinted or reproduced or utilised in any form or by any electronic, mechanical, or other means, now known or hereafter invented, including photocopying and recording, or in any information storage or retrieval system, without permission in writing from the publishers.

Trademark notice: Product or corporate names may be trademarks or registered trademarks, and are used only for identification and explanation without intent to infringe.

Library of Congress Cataloging-in-Publication Data
A catalog record for this title has been requested

ISBN: 978-0-367-22251-2 (hbk)
ISBN: 978-1-003-04848-0 (ebk)
ISBN: 978-0-367-45746-4 (pbk)

Typeset in Sabon
by Apex CoVantage, LLC

Contents

	Introduction: Towards a Diatopian Politics of Literature	1
1	Unmappable Gestures: Politics of Literature in the Age of Donald Trump	18
	Gestural Selfhood: From Addressability to Response-ability 26	
	Writing From the Ruins: Politics of Literary Form 29	
	Rhizomatic Space: De-territorializing the Nation 34	
	From Stratifying Systems to Writ(h)ing Vipers: Literary Politics in Populist Times 37	
2	Uncontainable Bodies: Posthuman Biopolitics	41
	Cyberpunk Breakdowns 48	
	Beginning Breakthroughs: Schizo-Analysing the Posthuman 52	
	Bodies Beyond Control: Transcorporeal Cyborg Feminism 57	
	Conclusion: Cells Interlinked 66	
3	Transversing the Event: Beyond the Trauma of Terrorism	70
	Transnational Scars: Uncontainable Bodies 76	
	From Traumatic Certainties to Virtual Possibilities 85	
	Gyres of Time: Subverting the Logic of Pre-emption 90	
	Conclusion: A Politics of Wounded Relation 98	
4	Emergence, Submergence, Insurgence: Politics on Liquid Ground	102
	Literature – Ecology – Politics: Unravelling the Knot 110	
	Voices Unbound 114	

*Immersed Agencies Along Thresholds of
    Sustainability 122*
Monstrous Freedom 127
Watery Politics as Queering? 132

5   **Unravelling the Nation State: Openwork Lives in
    Migrant Graphic Narratives**   138
    Weaving as Diatopian Metaphor 140
    Unfixability: Migrant Graphic Narratives 142
    *"We are the granddaughters of the witches that you
        could not burn": Embroidery as Rhizomatically
        Rooted Feminism 145*
    *Woven Voices: Intertextual Patterns of
        Disorientation 150*
    *Weaving Tails: Fantastical Migrations Through Folded
        Space 153*
    Conclusion: Processual Space, Relational Politics 155

Index   161

Introduction
Towards a Diatopian Politics of Literature

On January 3, 1919, the socialist minister-president of the Bavarian Soviet Republic, Kurt Eisner, proclaimed his political philosophy to the provisional national assembly: politics, as he saw it, was art, and art was politics. A true statesman, he continued, should feel himself to be more closely aligned with artists, writers and dramatists than his own fellow politicians. And his vision was ambitious; if dramatists were to carry the seeds of the revolution even into the remotest village, if each and every writer was to liberate the anarchist of the highest moral order hidden deep inside, and to create at the hazard of their lives, then this sedate Bavarian people sheltering in the Alpine shade could celebrate its new soul as the pioneer of one of the few successful (if short-lived) revolutions in German history. The revolution, Eisner believed, was mainly a question of disposition, ideally of an anti-militarist, socialist and emancipatory nature; and such a disposition art could shape in the revolutionary interest.

What had happened to trigger such utopian hopes? On November 7, 1918, the first anniversary of the Russian revolution, theatre critic Kurt Eisner, farmer-revolutionary Ludwig Gandorfer and poets including Ernst Toller and Erich Mühsam had brought the energies of a mass movement of workers and soldiers, exhausted from war and inspired by Soviet ideas, to a tipping point. They proclaimed the People's State of Bavaria, as King Ludwig II fled the country. The first Bavarian Republic was in the power of poets.

The poets' revolution died in bitter street fights on May 6, 1919, crushed by reactionary forces. So why hark back to this idea of a literary politics now? There is little doubt that the literary politics Eisner envisioned was of a propagandist nature, such as none of the texts I will explore in this book would ever let themselves be harnessed to. The equation of politics with art sounds as tempting as it proved naïve, making it easy to dismiss the Bavarian revolutionaries as dreamy actors in a socialist carnival (Schulze 1982, 329). Easy, yet premature. What remained, after all, was not only the democratic republican structure initiated by the poets' revolution. It has also left the aftertaste of a lingering connect between art and radical politics. A century later, such yearning for a wilder political thought returns, though it needs to be sought out in the depths of texts rather than at the forefront of mass demonstrations. Its impact might be none the less vibrant.

Nevertheless, there is no denying that the beginning of the 21st century was marked by a skepticism about the political significance of the aesthetic sphere. This is particularly apparent as regards the neoliberalisation of the anglophone West, in which literary critique seemingly "capitulates" (Huehls 2016, 6) to the all-encompassing and pervasive force of a competitive, profit-driven and individualized free market ideology. After all, if there is no 'outside' space to step into, no refuge into which to escape from the din of self-improvement and efficient self-management, how can it be possible to gain the critical distance necessary to de-familiarize this "soul-sucking" (Huehls 2016, 6) reality? There is no simple answer to this; this book, however, makes it its project to re-vitalise critique differently, and proposes that this is possible when understood immanently and without relying on the pre-given presence of such outside spaces. On a side-note, such surrender to the allegedly all-encompassing neoliberal triumphant march is also based on a limited perspective; Terry Eagleton bitingly satirized the "extraordinary irony" that postmodern theorists declared that "the ideological party is over" whilst "American Evangelicals, Egyptian fundamentalists, Ulster Unionists or British fascists" continue to inhabit a world "gripped by powerful, sometimes death-dealing ideologies" (1994, 18). The same seems true for any universalizing pronouncement that 'the world' has become neoliberal and thus, for some obscure reason, impossible to inhabit differently.

Quite to the contrary, an energized literary politics is as urgent than ever. In 1994, Mario Vargas Llosa warned against the "mental slavery" we would submit to, were we to allow what he termed – in what now seems almost an endearing anachronism – "the kingdom of the audiovisual" (3) to take over the democratic public sphere. If anything, the recent re-invention of politics as a twitter-based shouting match is beyond what Llosa feared. Given the dominance of such acerbic political speech, the violence of language is once more de-limiting horizons of possibility and restricting imaginations of the future. Populists bordering on the demagogical have re-discovered the performative power of the speech act, and use it to construct oppressive realities under the guise of common sense. Their words become sites of exclusion, and are thus all the easier to instrumentalize, as refusing to differentiate can engender an equally un-differentiated anger. After all, calling refugee settlements a 'jungle' is uncannily close to a colonial rhetoric of wilderness versus civilization, and thus serves to create a discourse of civilized nations under threat from those who, in a bitter irony, only demand the very human rights which supposedly were introduced to uphold this 'civilization' in the first place. Words matter. At its best, the written word reveals a "stubborn resistance against being enslaved" (Llosa 1994, 2) filled with uncontainable bodies, metaphors opening into new horizons of meaning and blossoming relations between the seemingly distinct. At its worst, though, this literary imagination can become looted by a language which chooses to "forgo," as Toni Morrison warned in her 1993 Nobel Speech, "its nuanced, complex, mid-wifery properties for menace and subjugation." Turned oppressive, such language exerts violence when it "drinks blood, laps vulnerabilities, tucks its fascist boots under crinolines of respectability and patriotism" (Morrison 1993). This is the kind of political speech we see dominating the Anglophone world. Privileging the entrapment of the 'fake,' not the freedom of the fictional, it polices mutual exchange and shuts down emergent ideas. Instead, it unleashes destruction in the fire of mass shootings and unchecked ecological exploitation.

With Donald Trump or Boris Johnson as its pioneers, political language has begun, once more, to perpetuate mental slavery, or "thoughtlessness" as Hannah Arendt (1971, 4) termed it. This is chilling because it forces us to accept that decades of democracy, and in some countries centuries, have not made us immune to the neo-fascist and nationalist temptations which many hoped had been buried with the dead of World War II. Yet the refusal to think from the position of another, a key dimension of Arendt's critique, has once more become embedded in an undemocratic political language which brands as traitors those who attempt to hold power to account. Horizons of possibility have become limited enough, in what seems like an endless replay, century after century, of what a line of philosophers, from Spinoza to Wilhelm Reich and Gilles Deleuze, saw as the fundamental problem of political philosophy: "Why do men fight for their servitude as stubbornly as though it were their salvation?" (1983, 29). Instead of taking back control, what is needed is an opening of the imagination to make a future possible which is not merely a 21st century replay of past oppression. Literature can offer a space of doubt, as Michael Keren suggests, a hypothetical stance which can serve as an antidote to the affirmative mode of a politics that insists rather than enquires, and emphasizes rather than explores (2015, 10). Yet doubt is a positive phenomenon, opening rigid structures to more creative solutions; it is also more sustainable. The absolute confidence of a politics manifested in concrete walls, historically, has been known to splinter and fragment sooner than the constructors of said walls can envisage. Doubt acknowledges complexity and responds to it with a democratic flexibility that is less provocative as a slogan on a bus or baseball bat, but ultimately more durable.

"It matters what ideas we use to think other ideas with," as Donna Haraway proposes together with Marilyn Strathern (2016, 12); similarly, Audre Lorde suggests that "the quality of light by which we scrutinize our lives has direct bearing upon the product which we live" (1984), forming ideas to be birthed and realized. The politics of literature which

I am interested in developing, therefore, addresses the frameworks of our political thought and the most politically salient pre-conditions and experiences. While the narratives of the ultra-right employ a male, competitive and capitalist logic to coerce a complex world into the straight lines of war and conquest, predators and prey, fictional texts acknowledge one fundamental truth: linearity deceives. After all, symbiosis, partnership and cohabitation are fundamental realities of the earth's history and its present, whereas the political cult surrounding strength and autonomy only seeks to render absolute a partial truth. Such simplicity is not only deceptive, but also already disempowered by the enmeshed realities of human life within an ecology in turmoil, against which no tweet or rally will hold out. Powerful as such oppressive language might seem, its anthropocentrism, if nothing else, will be its downfall. Imaginative literature can offer different ideas to think politics with; more responsive to those nomadic and ecological realities which are proving disobedient to a nation-state-based model of the world, it is also, paradoxically, closer to the truth of current life conditions than the crumbling certainties promised by concrete border walls. Fiction not only makes the imperceptible perceptible, the invisible visible, and the noiseless heard. It also experiments with better ways to inhabit the interconnected, affective, inter-relational, and transgressive realities that our current political system finds impossible to tame, seeding change in a world of seemingly closed-off horizons.

In seeking out the politics inherent in 21st century literature even when and particularly if, at first glance, it seems de-politicized, I am therefore interested in a literary practice which "scoops out," as Michael Mack puts it, "the mental space in which we can rethink what it means to be human and to live in our world" (2014, 15). Yet while Mack is focused on an ethics of resilience by which we can find more future-oriented alternatives to the perpetuation of recurring harmful practices, I propose a more explicitly ecocritical vision of literary politics. Instead of searching for more resilient and flexible human practices, I argue that the human itself, with its related political notions of agency, voice, or bodily delimitation, needs to be re-visited and newly envisioned. Finding ways to resist exclusion or stereotyping is therefore only one step when approaching the politics of literary texts. Ultimately, their fictional worlds suggest a more radical transformation: instead of coping with change, human life in and of itself needs to transform from alleged master to participant, from bounded individual to interrelated being, from root to rhizome, in order to become future-oriented.

Of course, poets do not make the best politicians, as literature neither institutionalizes, orders nor prescribes. The politics of literature, after all, is neither a question of how literary texts communicate political ideas, nor is it restricted to exposing grievances. As a political phenomenon distinct, though by no means detached, from the institutionally or discursively constituted political sphere, it was perhaps in the antechamber of the revolution that the true impact of poetic thought unfolded. Throughout this book, I explore the premise that literary politics is a proto-politics and not program, situated both in the 'before' and in the 'more than' of politics. Prior to the pragmatics of power-play, literary language breathes new energy into the frames of our thought and the shapes of our affects, re-vitalising politically salient concepts such as voice, space, border or body. Once (and if) institutionalised politics moves through this experimental space, it will come out changed, shot through with ideas of a wilder and more liberated kind. As the 'more than' of politics, literature creates a space for the marginalized and repressed dimensions of human life; the visceral, emotional or erotic impulses of such sensual modes can become politically salient once they enter into the public sphere, a presence which literary language ensures by performing and pre-senting, rather than re-presenting or smoothly translating them. Readers will notice immediately that I am sidestepping the notion of literature as a form of critique which might hold a mirror up to power. This is because a 21st century literary politics is not merely reactive; to the contrary, as Judith Fetterley has argued powerfully from a feminist perspective, a "new understanding of our literature" can "make possible a new effect of that literature on us," in turn providing "the conditions for changing the culture that the literature reflects" (2011, 95). An updated politics of literature, indeed, is not primarily a question of content, but of form, and thus demands new modes of reading and thinking about politics from us.

Although literature certainly provides "a sensorium for what goes wrong in a society, for the biophobic, life-paralyzing implications of one-sided forms of consciousness and civilizational uniformity," as Hubert Zapf argues (2016, 91), these taboo-breaking energies of the literary imagination are not the major drive of its political force. In Zapf's cultural ecology, they are accordingly situated within a broader process of "constant cultural self-renewal" (2016, 91), a future-bound impulse which evokes vital life-cycles in a literary ecology but which, in a literary politics, heralds the possibility of change. The literary 'more-than,' therefore, promises to us the opportunity to leave into the new wordings and world-ings of imaginary texts, in order to return, changed, to a reality freshly de-familiarised. Free from the patterns of societal order, literature is a way of bursting beyond the brain's schemata, opening new pathways for thought and feeling. As Jacques Rancière noted, the "politics of literature is not the same thing as the politics of writers" (2011, 3); it does not require an author's personal agenda, but occurs through the workings of the text itself, which is not a vehicle for ideas but uses the creative innovations of metaphor to envisage change. I would certainly be cautious about tracing this back to an alleged "purity" (2011, 3) of the art of writing, as Rancière proposes; indeed, the texts I read in this book often suggest the opposite, delving straight into the darkness and dirt or our lives to find new political seeding ground. Yet I share the focus on the texts itself, unbound from (though not unaware of) the politics of their authors.

Yet if literature infuses with the potential for change the preconditions of politics, such as agency, voice, or power, this occurs without a preconceived telos in mind. Unlike the logic of the revolution, the literary politics of 21st century texts, for the most part, do not pursue an idealized and ultimate aim. As such they have long departed from the doctrinal certainties of the early and mid-20th century, when Georg Lukács smelled the scent of imperialist corruption in poetic ambivalence and revolutionary fervor drove the dramatic innovations of Bertolt Brecht. Although I will discuss the relation between literature, politics and ideology in more detail further on in this introduction and in the chapters to follow, this is neither the time nor the place for a misled nostalgia for lost certainties. Suffice it to say for now that the end of the 20th century brought neither the end of ideology, nor did the decades preceding it speak with any unified political confidence. Even Bertolt Brecht's Marxist assuredness becomes infused with tenderness, doubt and desire in his poetry, which cannot be contained in doctrine alone. The 'more than' of literary politics already pervades even such openly political art, and it is perhaps no coincidence that it is these poems' eros, more than anything else, which marks the difference between art as a vehicle for political ideas, and a truly literary politics. "Desire in the guise of sexual desire is the irrepressible reality which challenges the totalitarian state in all three of the great dystopias" (2011, 213), Ruth Levitas finds in her analysis of *We*, *Brave New World*, and *Nineteen Eighty-Four*. This embodied dimension will remain key throughout the analyses I offer in this book, as literary textualities complexify politics beyond the restraints of programmatic agendas, embedding them in sensual life.

Yet just because such literary politics does not have a recognizable political program does not mean no politics is there, and neither does it indicate indifference, right-wing complicity or a nihilistic 'anything goes.' Literature, after all, occupies its own cultural space, which in clear contrast to political speech seeks neither to persuade nor to be smoothly translatable into real-world applications. Imaginative worlds gain their visceral creativity from friction and insist on difference. The literary politics I am interested in unearthing, therefore, proposes change, but not towards a preconceived aim or in a manner tangible in the simplistic coherence of a manifesto. Its movement is more akin to a metamorphosis than a revolution; it is a branching out, an opening into precariousness and porosity through which different bodies, borders, voices and agency can emerge. As such it is a post-ideological politics, not because it falsely assumes the end of belief systems but, to the contrary, because it acknowledges the extent to which we as 21st century human beings are implicated in ideological, political and ecological power patterns. Such implicated political conditions cannot be shaped by assuming the purity of any counter-ideology, which would only serve to shadow-box the surface phenomena of a problem that runs deeper. Trump, after all, is a symptom of a neoliberal power pattern gone rogue, not an instigator or creator. Only gestures that are equally embedded and relational can respond to such complexities, and inhabit them subversively. Instead of consolidating power in complex financial patterns, such literary enmeshments seek to suffuse bodies of humans or nations with otherness, becoming intractable to the oppressive dualism between self and other, the powerful and the powerless. Unlike the clear-cut lines of nation-state borders, literary paths disseminate and cross, disobedient to the tyrannical imperative of the straight line.

Working from this literary perspective, I therefore have a specific conception of politics in mind. The manifestations of the political which are most obviously decisive in our everyday lives, such as politics as it concerns the state, the exercise of power, conflict and conflict resolution, are not at the forefront of my thinking here. Instead, I am interested in politics as it presents itself in the struggle over the meaning of key concepts, in a discursive approach aligned with a reading methodology interested in the metaphoric and conceptual innovations of imaginative worlds, rather than exploring writers' motivations or pursuing a more ideas-and content-based critique. "Reading a text," as Gilles Deleuze and Félix Guattari note, is "never a scholarly exercise in search of what is signified," but an exercise that "extracts from the text its revolutionary force" (1983, 106). Literature, in this sense, is a form of political theory because it thinks the political and shifts what we mean by political.

Explicitly intended as an alternative to the equation of politics with manifest law or power struggles, this book traces how imaginative literary innovations can re-shape the conditions of our political existence and experience. Whereas Jacques Rancière notes, not without some bitterness, that "all political activity is a conflict aimed at deciding what is speech or mere growl" (2011, 4), I am interested in how politics can be re-configured not as a competition for presence and legitimacy, but as a relational activity that privileges the gesture over the victory; not as a "carving up of space and time, the visible and invisible, speech and noise" (Rancière 2011, 4), but as a process of shared creation. When I acknowledge that not all politics need be defined by disagreement, such a vision, perhaps paradoxically, involves more, not less, friction. A gesture can carry both conflict or desire in several dimensions simultaneously. What is more, my focus on the pre-conditions of political experience seeks to delve beneath the sheen of orderly appearances, down to the questions hidden by the simple answers which the straight lines marking national territory, the boundaries of skin delineating unitary individuals, the powerfuls' clarity of purpose are so adept at giving.

One prominent effect of this is to re-vitalize both the embodied and the emotional side of human life for political readings. Kyle Scott criticises modern political science for having "segregated" the rational and the emotional "while promoting the supremacy of rationalism" (2016, xi). Alarmingly, the darkness lurking within such enlightened lucidity first came to prominence as the topic of Theodor W. Adorno's and Max Horkheimer's dialectics of instrumental reason; whilst their interpretation of the regression into fascism as the paradoxical outcome of societal over-rationalization remains firmly rooted in the early 20th century historical context, it should nevertheless remain of note that the ease with which a Donald Trump can sow and harvest an emotionality of anger and resentment stands symptomatic for the political consequence of the irrational. The current unleashing of emotions into politics, however, is also a de-limitation. However virulent and dangerous, the ranges of emotions in current politics remain reductive, as any broader horizon of affect is drowned out by the fury and triumph of thoughtless crowds. I hope to unearth more subtle affective currents and more varied feelings, driven by the belief that a politics that is not reduced to conflict might allow a broader scope of feeling and embodied sensation, and thus – despite the fictionality of the worlds through which I think – become better anchored in 21st century lived realities.

Articulating this literary politics, therefore, is a challenge because imaginative texts ask of us to grasp agency, transformation, and an ethics of relation as political, but in terms that do not obey the norms of current political practice. The texts which I will discuss in this volume are not openly political in a utopian, dystopian or socialist realist sense. Yet they are politically salient, and to acknowledge their politics requires a departure from the reductive terms of a politics only acknowledged as such when it presents itself as a conflict between discernible interests. Rather than working with the premise of a subject affecting change, these texts unsettle the position of such an agentic subject per se, and warn against falling back on the myths of anthropocentrism or an enlightenment rationality that posit free will and suggest autonomy. 21st century human beings, as the current climate crisis amply shows, are not autonomous, and have long since spent the hope that human free will could rise above a wounded earth. Enmeshed, the primary political transformation these texts propose involves the human being herself with her voice, body and agency.

Given that horizons of imagination and possibility have become de-limited, we need a renewed understanding of literary politics which opens our vision, sensations and concepts, without merely falling back into the trap of a fixed dualism between power and opposition, self and other, 'us' versus 'them.' The series of readings in this book develops what I term a politics of the Diatopian as a way beyond such double-binds. The Diatopian carries both the hopes of utopia and the fears of dystopia within its syllabic make-up, retaining their future-oriented, critical thrust. Etymologically, the diatopic already exists as a term in phonetics used to describe linguistic changes occurring over or with space, and both the spatial aspect, as well as the idea of change, will remain key in my literary adaptation of it, too. However, let me begin to delineate its difference from these more conventional terms of political writing by establishing the relevant field of tension between two modes of subversive thought:

On the one hand, picture Thomas More's utopian insula. A crescent-shaped isle centered around the capital right in its middle, and consolidated by symmetrically arranged towns, this perfect imaginary world breathes balance. Nevertheless, More's titular pun infuses this self-sufficient isle with playful ambivalence; he coined the word 'utopia' from the Greek *ou-topos*, suggesting a 'no place,' yet this 'nowhere' is also pregnant with the almost identical Greek word *eu-topos*, meaning 'a good place.' At the heart of this utopia, therefore, resides a question: can a perfect world ever be realized, or is it, as Paul Ricœur suggests, an otherworldly fiction creating a space from which to cast an "exterior glance" on our reality, opening the field of the possible to "alternative ways of living" (1986, 16)?

In his 2008 "Map of Nowhere," Grayson Perry takes this to the extreme by revisiting utopia, yet this time as an island of doubt. Centered around a satirically enlarged body of the artist himself instead of the communal space of a city, this map questions the concept of utopia not because of political feasibility, but because of human nature itself; the print features small figures whose halos of virtues – truth, beauty, or peace – are clearly unsettled by the inscriptions on the body itself – madness, ignorance or darkness. For a best-possible society to become reality, Perry seems to suggest, human beings themselves need to transform. This focus on the situation of humanity per se is key for a Diatopian reading, but in both Perry's and More's vision, the idea of a mappable and orderly isle remains, even if as a tool for critique. Despite the ambiguity between perfection and impossibility which characterizes the utopian, such imaginary worlds, "free from the difficulties that beset us in reality" (Levitas 2011, 1), remain one of the foremost modes of political literature, although the recent turn towards the dystopian demonstrates such imagination in reverse; instead of exposing shortcomings of lived realities by contrasting with perfection, Margaret Atwood's *Handmaid's Tale* and other dystopias take current tendencies to their apocalyptic extreme. Both, however, work by a similar logic. Holding the mirror up to present society, they remain embedded in origin and destination myths, whether that destination be salvation or damnation. Both also share the impulse of the universal, an aspect which Ruth Levinas foregrounds in her analysis of utopias (2011, 214), which in the dystopian often manifests as the violence of totalitarian rule or total ecological collapse. This universal thrust might be the reason why the utopian has become politically compromised, as the utopias currently infusing our political realities might seem "uncongenial" (Levitas 2011, 215) to utopists. The most powerful utopias, after all, today belong to the far-right and describe an homogenous and orderly land which fits the mould of the utopian symmetrical isle, with a bloody underbelly of exclusion. Incontrovertible, therefore, is what Paul Ricœur describes as the common origin of utopia and ideology. What differentiates both is the future-oriented thrust of the former, which seeks to insert difference and to open up imaginations of possible worlds. The link between both, however remains uncomfortable.

Leaving such symmetries aside for a moment, let's move towards a different shape of political thought: Gilles Deleuze and Félix Guattari open *A Thousand Plateaus* with the score of Sylvano Bussoti's "Piece Four" from the cycle "Five Piano Pieces for David Tudor" (1987, 3). There are no individualized notes on this script. Criss-crossing across several dimensions of clefs, once jagged and once curling tightly together, the traces unsettle the staff lines and transform them into lines of flight, entraining their pre-given linearity into a whirl of multi-dimensional and multi-directional musical thresholds. Nodal points, connections, intensities and movement define this visual; as an introduction to Deleuze and Guattari's rhizome, however, this is more than a rhythmic abstraction. It describes a mode of thinking, reading and writing that is as political as Thomas More's utopia, but follows a fundamentally different logic. Instead of delineating a pre-given idea in the shape of an orderly fictional world, these lines continuously explore. They do not contain, but transgress. They do not exclude or trace the clear boundaries of an isle, but relate and connect in unexpected and protean patterns. Thought, in this mode, does not move towards an idea, an end-purpose to be grasped or an apocalypse to succumb to. It is immanent in movement itself, not a mirror up to nature but an intensity radiating and vibrating from within reality itself, which, symbolized by the suddenly energized staff lines, begins to transform. Taken further, this suggests a politics without a center or a leader.

The Diatopian combined impulses from both the modes of thought I have just outlined: it retains the interest of the utopian (or dystopian) in a *topos*, understanding this not merely as a theme, but also and more literally as a place in all its physical materiality and visceral embodiment. The *topos* in Diatopian, therefore, is more akin to Donna Haraway's generative, rotting and recreating humus in which humans can "wallow" in a "multispecies muddle" (2016, 31), than to More's cultivated isle. As such it puts more explicit focus on the material than Zapf's "discursive heterotopia" (2016, 27), and is not mappable but an amalgamation of biotic life, a complex matter of human and non-human organic tissue and non-organic flux. Crucially, though, it is not soil, with its connotations of agriculture and patriotic blood. This is because its matter is both transgressive and de-territorialized. It is not a place for roots to solidify in, but a space of joyful or friction-laden encounters between critters, creatures and life forms travelling through it, heterogeneous and fluctuating. Its porosity entails both generative creativity and vulnerability. This transgressive nature is why I changed the pre-fix of a 'nowhere' space to a 'dia' space, which charges the *topos* with motions of a 'passing through,' a 'going apart' or even being 'opposed in moment' as in diamagnetism. This is a literary politics that replaces the utopian 'elsewhere' with a becoming-with: immanent, situated yet interconnected, the Diatopian offers a proto-politics which enquires into the preconditions of our political existence, engaging in new configurations of concepts including voice, body, agency and border. It offers the potential of perpetual renewal instead of a petrified vision of a mapped-out good life. As such, it changes the operating rules of the political, positing interbleeding and reciprocal transformation as an alternative to a politics of unitary power-players pitted against each other in disagreement. Disenchanted, it does not recognize a Garden of Eden, and neither does it seek salvation. It describes a mode of participating, co-shaping and co-creating a future on a planet in crisis.

Such a Diatopian literary politics has five core dimensions: it challenges notions of the political subject and their voice, the body, the border, agency and the solid territory, and seeks to re-imagine them as transversal and transgressive processes, rather than rigid and petrified realities. This conceptual scaffold already makes tangible how my approach to literary politics differs from more programmatic readings, which might suggest gender or race as points of focus. Both these concerns, along with topics such as populism, climate change or neoliberalism, infuse my readings and give this book's chapters a more succinct topicality. However, my focus remains on the preconditions which shape any such politics, and each chapter in this book retains a primary focus on one of these.

Firstly, a Diatopian reading unearths a political subject that is fundamentally different from the assuredness of the *zoon politicon*. The fractured and exposed selfhood that speaks from Claudia Rankine's *Citizen*, Douglas Kearney's poetry or Colson Whitehead's *Underground Railroad* re-imagines the politico-poetic voice as a gesture of address, speaking from a position of the utmost vulnerability. "Unmappable Gestures: Politics of Literature in the Age of Donald Trump" is situated in the present moment of the Trump presidency and the white supremacist discourse it has encouraged; this opening chapter thus focuses on a writing from the ruins. Deep within the fragmentation of such texts, however, lies a search for a renewed ability to be addressed and to respond. These texts explore a transversal subjecthood and create the open-ended and participatory space in which such gestures can be acted upon. Such political voices do not primarily seek the stage of conflict and disagreement, but explore the kind of subjecthood that might make possible a future that does not perpetuate racial violence. These voices' demands are both more radical and more tender for operating in a performative mode rather than representing a cause.

Gestural voices inhabit uncontainable bodies. More's utopia strove towards an organic whole, symbolized in the healthy body of its citizenry; yet whereas related notions of the body politic seem anachronistic today, the underlying norms that bodies should be honed to health in the interests of a smoothly functioning economical or political system certainly are not. Chapter 2, "Uncontainable Bodies: Posthuman Biopolitics," explores fictional configurations of the posthumanly monstrous as the flip side of neoliberal fantasies of biopolitical perfection. I develop a vision of human bodies which, instead of relying on the skin as a border to be proofed at all cost, immerse themselves in the interlinked cells of human and non-human organic matter. Envisioned as an alternative to a biopolitics that demands discipline and docility, such uncontainable bodies embed the human into the multiplicity of life, rescuing it from the need to immunize until life becomes mere survival. I trace the political agency emergent from such bodies through readings of the cyberpunk that is dominant in contemporary pop culture, such as *Bladerunner* or William Gibson's *Peripheral*. It is in Larissa Lai's feminist biopunk and postcolonial science fiction, however, that posthuman figures explore new forms of political agency. Inhabiting bodies which, nourished by multiplicity, seek connection instead of transcendence, these figures become politically salient when they establish subversive connections. Instead of paying credence to the premise of unitary one-ness and singularity, such multiple personhood becomes untameable to (bio)power in an ecological re-imagining of the posthuman politics.

The question of agency continues into chapter 3, "Transversing the Event: Beyond the Trauma of Terrorism." Working from within the context of post-9/11 trauma and terrorism, this chapter explores how affect can become politically salient. Focusing on atmospheres of affect and currents of implication creates an alternative vision to the notion of the traumatic event, which, puncturing boundaries, only unleashed a politics of revenge and violent pre-emption. Writers including Ruth Ozeki, Kamila Shamsie and Thomas Pynchon negotiate ways of coexisting, sustainably and in empathy, with each other's lives as they are rendered precarious by shared histories of violence; I propose that the horizons of possibility inherent in the virtual, whether they manifest in Pynchon's digital spaces or in Ozeki's gyres of time, offer relational time-spaces which might counteract the repetition compulsion on a nation-state level, with its seemingly inevitable re-run of suicide soldiers. Acting from within their implicated subject positions, these scarred and resistant figures initiate a relationally created present because they offer a narrative that is de-centered from the absoluteness of the injured 'I,' be it individual or that of a nation state, which reduced emotional horizons to victimization and vengeance in the war on terror.

Chapter 4, "Emergence, Submergence, Insurgence: Politics on Liquid Ground," makes explicit the ecological premises which inform all these Diatopian readings. I explore the possibility of a more sustainable politics, concurring with Val Plumwood that this would require us to let go of the tendency to "hyperseparate" (2002, 9) ourselves from nature. On "liquid ground" (Irigaray 1991, 37), texts by Lutz Seiler, Rita Indiana or Linda Hogan enable me to conceive of politics not as disagreement, but as whirl. Their imaginations of hybrid bodies in flux uproot identity politics, offering a vision of transversing and transversed voices, agency, and borderlines. In a darkly comedic rather than tragic mode, they expose the "fragile states where man strays on the territories of animal" (Nixon 2011, 55), challenging the white, cis-gendered, territorialized and hierarchical consensus that underpins the socio-political order. In this politics of di- and re-fraction, the "agentic entanglement" (Iovino and Oppermann 2014, 10) of world and text changes the preconditions of our politics, which we have seen to be ecologically destructive precisely because the interleaving of human and non-human life is to often obscured.

What politics can emerge when we imagine global space not as a pre-given set of territorial lines, but to be constantly created in the threads-being-woven of human passages and relations? This question is at the heart of my final chapter, "Unravelling the Nation State: Openwork Lives in Migrant Graphic Narratives." This not a thought experiment, as migrant paths are already re-defining and traversing the spaces so carefully territorialized by post-war diplomats and so diligently measured by their cartographers. Working with migrant graphic narratives, I seek to turn this forcefully repressed reality into a seeding round for a different conception of citizenship, re-inscribing change and movement into the core of human life. Understanding space not as defined by endpoints and borders, but as a shifting ground of passages and transformative nodal relays, I articulate a notion of nomadic rootedness. The textures of braiding and open lacework in graphic narratives by Marjane Satrapi, Shaun Tan, or Hamid Sulaiman are both literal and figurative; yet all their aesthetic languages activate existent, lived spaces, energizing realities that are at best casually ignored and at worst violently repressed. Instead of resulting from the violence of the trenches, they generate political space as a participatory process. Whereas bird's eye cartographies operate on normative codes of ethnic exclusivity, economic profitability or military strategy, which are hidden beneath the apparent clarity of the borderline, woven maps dismantle such codes.

In positing the concept of the Diatopian, I also seek to respond to and further develop current critical tendencies in the field of political literature. Firstly, this contribution is intended to move beyond the idea of a 'use' of the literary, often understood as an individual moral journey. In *The Moral Laboratory*, for instance, Jēmeljan Hakemulder suggests that stories are instruments for socialization (2000, 5), which can enhance our ability to make inferences about the emotions, thoughts or motives of others, train us to acknowledge the complexity of ethical problems, or produce awareness of repressed emotions. Hakemulder is careful to caution against over-zealous claims that literature somehow makes us better human beings; yet while I find myself re-stating some of these arguments to teenagers and their parents when, inevitably, the question of the purpose of a literary education arises in the classroom, this is ultimately a reductive vision. It serves a tangible purpose when promoting literary learning to sceptical 15-year-olds, and as such I value it without reserve. This, however, is also its limit. Yes, Toni Morrison's *Beloved* can help them articulate a more complex and nuanced evaluation of the impact of slavery. The 'tree' of whiplashes on the fugitive slave's back, however, has a metaphoric richness that innovates meaning beyond such contextual critique. As Derek Attridge rightly warns, treating a text as a "as a means to a predetermined end" is ultimately doomed by literature's own "resistance to such thinking" (2004, 7). The quality of a 'more than' in literary politics is decisive here, and often emerges in the embodied, material and sensual dimensions of life which the Diatopian, with its ecological focus on bios, is particularly attuned to. A noteworthy and ambitious contribution in this area is Rita Felski's 2008 *Uses of Literature*, a self-described manifesto for a different mode of engagement with literature. Felski sets out to explore "what is lost when we deny a work any capacity to bite back" (2008, 7), replacing the alleged 'otherness' of literary worlds with a more deeply embedded connectedness, and turning, too, against the notion of text as a symptom of social structures or political causes to be "diagnosed rather than heard" (2008, 6). She traces four dimensions of reading, which include a logic of recognition, a sense of enchantment, the potential of literature to reconfigure social knowledge and its capacity to shock readers. Her approach is deeply embedded in textual readings, yet overall, it remains loyal to the humanist frame of literature as a tool for the *Bildung* of the individual. Beyond the notion of 'use,' in contrast, I am interested in how literature affects not the individual reader but challenges broader societal and political conceptual frames. In many ways Martha Nussbaum's approach offers a bridge between this book's political project and the individual dimension of literary experience. After all, understanding the literary imagination as part of what she terms "public rationality" (1995, xvi) is a precondition to any literary politics; from her focus on empathetic imagining, too, speaks an impulse of reciprocity which gestures across distance, implying a relational approach which the Diatopian imagination makes explicit and politicizes.

Secondly, though, the Diatopian also proposes an alternative to the idea of literature as resistance; after all, not all literary texts are subversive, and whilst there might always be ways of reading subversively, certainly not all imaginative worlds pull on one string when it comes to political agendas – or indeed, pull on any such discernible string at all.

Jacqueline Rose's thesis of literature as the "last resistance," therefore, is undeniably appealing and succinctly relevant in the context of the Israel-Palestine conflict, in which her readings are situated. I wonder, however, whether her equation of literature's "power to unsettle [. . .] all idealised, official rhetorics, whether of nationhood, race, religion or state" with its "powers of resistance" (2017, 12) does not inadvertently limit the scope of the literary politics she describes. Resistance is a reactive term, which too often remains mired in a duality of the powerful and the powerless, and which opposes, rather than creates. Such a movement is undeniably necessary, and part of any literary politics. Rose's psychoanalytical approach, however, means that resistance is linked not to the emergence of the new but to "one of the mind's best defences," immunizing the subject from "the pain and mess of the inner life" (2017, 5), thus also blocking the psyche's passage into freedom. Literature certainly exposes such unconscious barriers of nations and of individuals; however, dissidence is a politically one-dimensional concept, requiring forms and contents that can be contained with some coherence and clarity in a two-sided situation of disagreement. I wonder whether the 'pain and mess of the inner life' does not revolt against such delineation, asking for a differently conceived platform to make known the voices of bodies, psyches and non-human beings in pain.

This caution about reverting into a dualism between the powerful and the powerless is also why the Diatopian proceeds in a manner that is more akin to minor readings, responsive to, but ultimately diverging from discourses of the subaltern or the marginal. Minor Literature, as defined by Gilles Deleuze and Félix Guattari, is performative rather than representational when it "constructs within a major language" (1986, 16) a new, heterogeneous form of articulation, instead of merely exposing a minor position; it de-stratifies the strata which bind and imprison the human, such as the self-contained organism or distinguishable languages, and taps into the energies of that which does not fit. As such is through and through political, as all individual concerns and spaces within it immediately short-circuit back to politics, producing "an active solidarity in spite of scepticism" (1986, 17). Both the performative aspect and the resistance to the dual are key for the literary politics of the 21st century, but it is the last point of a resilient solidarity which, perhaps, is the most striking. I have already situated the Diatopian within a *topos* that I described in terms of Donna Haraway's humus, an earthly multi-species ground for the seedings of different modes of life. This, however, is not merely a frolicking of the anything-goes, but an ethical stance that celebrates relationality, enmeshment and the implication in each other's lives. I would not go quite as far as Deleuze and Guattari, however, in positing that there is no subject in such a literature, only enunciative assemblages; in the readings that follow, I will demonstrate how subjecthood remains, though in a transformed, porous and much more posthuman manner than the enlightened view of (hu)man-kind expects. Literary politics challenges the notion of the agentic subject; it does not and cannot relinquish it altogether.

Overall, therefore, literary politics render rigid realities fluid and imbue them with relationality and transformative energies; moving beyond the idea of literature as a sensorium for grievances, a medium to expose taboos or a form of resistance, my readings explore the configurations of alternative realities inherent in imaginative texts, and make them available for political enquiry. Ethical challenges are a necessary element of such politics, unsettling preconditions and preconceptions prior to the pragmatized sphere of activism or institutionalized decision-making. In a Diatopian literary politics, metamorphosis is the destination. It is focused on process and becoming, not on the telos of a utopia to be attained. Understanding the artwork as a "living forcefield of transformative energies" (Zapf 2016, 14) entails a politics that occurs when the world is being co-shaped and co-inhabited. This is a politics not of radical change or revolutionary eventhood, as such change would require externalised and autonomous actors taking effect on an objectified real. Its activism is a participation, an opening, and an enmeshment that is not passively suffered but actively offered. In a world prescribing rigidity, porosity is political; in a political order based on sedentary citizens, movement is subversive. In the wake of the totalitarianism of Nazi Germany, Theodor W. Adorno stated in his 1951 *Minima Moralia* that "the whole is the false" (2005, 50), inverting Hegel. In this book, I ask whether it is indeed not the fragment, but the transversally crossing and perpetually moving that offers any hope of such truth.

References

Adorno, Theodor W. 2005 [1951]. *Minima Moralia: Reflections on a Damaged Life*. Translated by E. F. N. Jephcott. London and New York: Verso.
Arendt, Hannah. 1971. *The Life of the Mind: The Groundbreaking Investigation on How We Think*. San Diego and London: Harcourt.
Attridge, Derek. 2004. *The Singularity of Literature*. London and New York: Routledge.
Deleuze, Gilles, and Félix Guattari. 1983. *Anti-Oedipus. Capitalism and Schizophrenia*. Translated by Robert Hurley, Mark Seem, and Helen R. Lane. Minneapolis: University of Minnesota Press.
Deleuze, Gilles, and Félix Guattari. 1986. *Kafka: Toward a Minor Literature*. Translated by Dana Polan. Minneapolis: University of Minnesota Press.
Deleuze, Gilles, and Félix Guattari. 1987. *A Thousand Plateaus: Capitalism and Schizophrenia*. Translated and edited by Brian Massumi. Minneapolis: University of Minnesota Press.
Eagleton, Terry, ed. 1994. *Ideology*. London and New York: Longman.
Felski, Rita. 2008. *Uses of Literature*. Hoboken, NJ: Blackwell Publishers.

Fetterley, Judith. 2011. "On the Politics of Literature." In *The History of Reading. A Reader*, edited by Shafquat Towheed, Rosalind Crone, and Katie Halsey, 94–98. London and New York: Routledge.
Hakemulder, Jēmeljan. 2000. *The Moral Laboratory: Experiments Examining the Effects of Reading Literature on Social Perception and Moral Self-Concept.* Amsterdam and Philadelphia: John Benjamins Publishing Company.
Haraway, Donna. 2016. *Staying with the Trouble: Making Kin in the Chthulucene.* Durham, NC: Duke University Press.
Huehls, Mitchum. 2016. *After Critique: Twenty-First Century Fiction in a Neoliberal Age.* Oxford: Oxford University Press.
Iovina, Serenella, and Serpil Oppermann, eds. 2014. *Material Ecocriticism.* Bloomington and Indianapolis: Indiana University Press.
Irigaray, Luce. 1991. *Marine Lover of Friedrich Nietzsche.* Translated by Gillian C. Gill. New York: Columbia University Press.
Levitas, Ruth. 2011. *The Concept of Utopia.* Oxford: Peter Lang.
Llosa, Mario Vargas. 1994. *Literature and Freedom.* St Leonards, Australia: The Center for Independent Studies.
Lorde, Audre. 1984. *Sister Outsider: Essays and Speeches.* Trumansburg, NY: Crossing Press.
Mack, Michael. 2014. *Philosophy & Literature in Times of Crisis: Challenging Our Infatuation with Numbers.* London: Bloomsbury.
Michael, Keren. *Politics and Literature at the Turn of the Millennium.* Calgary and Alberta: University of Calgary Press, 2015.
Morrison, Toni. 1993. *Nobel Lecture.* Nobelprize.org. Last accessed on March 1, 2020.
Nixon, Rob. 2011. *Slow Violence and the Environmentalism of the Poor.* Cambridge, MA: Harvard University Press.
Nussbaum, Marta C. 1995. *Poetic Justice: The Literary Imagination and Public Life.* Boston: Beacon Press.
Plumwood, Val. 2002. *Environmental Culture: The Ecological Crisis of Reason.* London and New York: Routledge.
Rancière, Jacques. 2011. *The Politics of Literature.* Translated by Julie Rose. Cambridge: Polity Press.
Ricœur, Paul. 1986. *Lectures on Ideology and Utopia*, edited by George H. Taylor. New York: Columbia University Press.
Rose, Jacqueline. 2017. *The Last Resistance.* London and New York: Verso.
Schulze, Hagen. 1982. *Weimar. Deutschland 1917–1933.* München: Siedler Verlag.
Scott, Kyle. 2016. *The Limits of Politics: Making the Case for Literature in Political Analysis.* London: Lexington Books.
Zapf, Hubert. 2016. *Literature as Cultural Ecology: Sustainable Texts.* London: Bloomsbury.

1 Unmappable Gestures
Politics of Literature in the Age of Donald Trump

The dystopian is the new real. As the name of the president of the United States flares on hotel towers over Chicago's riverbanks and gleams above mid-town Manhattan, it seems that the finance- and data-flows of late capitalism are suffocating the democratic public sphere. Like "monstrous and mutant algae," as Félix Guattari (2008, 29) described Donald Trump's particular brand of invasive real estate development, patterns of political, capital and information-driven power have becomes so intricately entwined as to form a pervasive parasitical presence on democratic life.

Meanwhile, in 2015: 23-year-old Johari Osayi Idusuyi settles into her seat on the podium at a Trump rally. She takes out a book she was carrying in her bag, holds it up for the camera to catch the cover and starts reading. It is not just any book; the cover now displayed on TV screens features the black hood of Claudia Rankine's *Citizen*, a documentation of the piercing pain inflicted by systemic racism. Her act of resistance, savvy in its insouciance, proves why reading matters today. It enthused *Huffington Post* writer Claire Fallon in November 2015 to hail a new movement: "Political protest through pointed book-reading." Yet this protest is not of the traditionally oppositional kind; indeed, Idusuyi's ambivalent position is simultaneously complicit and subversive, which is precisely why it symbolizes the challenges of literary politics in a 21st century reality. As democracy itself has become shot through with autocratic and oligarchic elements, politics has lost the clear-cut conflict lines which existed at least on the surface of the 20th century. Now entangled in nodes that threaten implication, the position of democratic agents is unsettled. The challenge they face is not a binary choice between complicity or opposition, but the need for a differently articulated position that is as dynamic and complex as the political realities they face. Politics, as Guattari notes with significant foresight, "is no longer a question of creating an unequivocal ideology" but necessitates the "reconstruction of human praxis" (23) lest we revert to the reductionist outlooks on which charismatic leaders thrive. This requires a re-worlding of political subjecthood and the space it positions itself in per se, as only such an alternative positioning might provide a vision for a more future-oriented, less entangled existence.

'Is there a kind of thought that does not turn into tyranny?' ("Gibt es ein Denken, das nicht tyrannisch wird?") is a question Hannah Arendt noted in her *Denktagebuch* in the 1950s. It captures precisely our current dilemma. Where, after all, is the place for utopian thought in a public sphere so deeply entwined in largely invisible powers? It seems desperately needed, as utopia offers the kind of imagination that "makes the actual world seem strange," as Paul Ricœur claimed in 1986, 299f, shattering the seemingly obvious with doubt and affirming the possibility of living differently from the way we presently do. A century earlier Oscar Wilde went even further, asserting that "A map of the world that does not include Utopia is not worth even glancing at, for it leaves out the one country where Humanity is always landing" (2001, 141). It is worth noting that, in contrast to today's ambivalent positionality as exemplified by Johari Osayi Idusuyi, utopia here is defined by its unequivocal mappability despite retaining a certain lure of the beyond. It offers an 'other' place from which to critique the present, ensuring a safe space for the imagination even as it develops worlds and narratives that are potentially wildly oppositional to the consensus of their time. Utopia, in Wilde's sense, thus is a side effect of the map of the world and akin to the flip side of a coin. It appears as a foil, yet is already integrated into the system.

Despite the enticing sheen of Google Earth, though, 21st century worlds are becoming un-mappable to the conventional means of clear-cut boundaries and differentiated territories. The forces of what Guattari calls "de-territorialisation" (2008, 30), the power of which the Trump towers unapologetically symbolize, easily transverse the illusory bounds of mappable territory. Yet this de-territorialisation, as a pattern that defines contemporary life, is politically disinterested. However globalized the slow violence (Nixon 2011) of climate change and economic exploitation might be, terrorist networks and refugee migrations are all equally de-territorialized, too. Politically, thus, this issue cannot be grasped by a simple juxtaposition of neoliberal rightwing globalization versus leftwing thought. Re-territorialisation, manifested in the clarity of de-limited nation states, has historically engendered and continues to enforce violence, as Donald Trump's 2017 inauguration speech made blatantly clear when his affirmation that "we all bleed the same red blood of patriots" awoke ideologies of soil-and-blood from their graves.

Unmappability, thus, is a Ianus-faced phenomenon, but it also offers new opportunities to articulate a more humane agency elsewhere. This search for what it means to be, live and act humanely, though, requires a departure from the kind of thinking that moves along maps. Utopias might have entered the public imagination in the shape of territorialized visions, countries to be travelled to, most famously in Thomas More's eponymous 1516 satire. Yet this de-limitation also opens the genre to charges of frozen perfection, costuming "a will to power over all those individuals for whom you are plotting an ironclad happiness" (Jameson 2000, 383) in the seductive garments of visions of a better life. This raises questions not about the nature or ideological content of the utopian as such, but addresses a more fundamental dilemma between a politics of motion versus the rigidity of ideological end points; how can the velocity and energy of the initial creative impetus be retained without inadvertently being channelled into a petrified utopian ideal? An open society can paradoxically become set in stone; Saint-Simon's early 19th century socialist utopia, for example, begins with passionate revolutionary activity but ends in a final diagram which inscribes the symmetries and hierarchies of his utopian rule into the brickworks of a metaphoric house. Used with scathing clarity by Ricœur to exemplify how utopian thinking might carry the seeds of its own failure when it "becomes a picture; time has stopped. [. . .] Everything must comply with the model" (1986, 295), this also indicates a conceptual difference between a politics in motion, and one that seeks fulfilment. It is the former, dynamic conception that interests here, as it offers an opportunity to translate the utopian impulse into the 21st century in an updated, Diatopian form.

After all, Jameson's premature denunciation of all utopian thought, as cited above, was articulated on the basis of the traditional canon's obsession with accurate symmetries and mappable societies, and is thus based on a reductive notion of the genre. The utopian desire to infuse current reality with doubt plays out much more openly in what Sean Austin Grattan (2017) terms the "critical utopias" of the 1970s, in which authors such as Ursula LeGuin, Octavia Butler, Margaret Atwood, JP Delaney, or Marge Piercy create alternative worldings without becoming trapped in monolithic answers. Contrary to the returning declarations of the end of utopia, the end of mappability, thus, does not entail the end of the utopian impulse – it just cannot be located on Oscar Wilde's map anymore. When Karl Mannheim declared such an end of utopia in 1929 in *Ideologie und Utopie* (1995), his argument that society was disintegrating into piecemeal approaches that left no opportunity for larger visions proved to be astonishingly blind to the totalitarian near future of the first half of the 20th century. Yet it can be argued that Mannheim's notion of circularity, which renders any evaluative standpoint impossible, has returned in a neoliberal era. Indeed, Mitchum Huehls voiced similar concerns when he noted in 2016 that "[G]iven neoliberalism's omnipresence, the position you hold will be just as neoliberal as the position you're against" (5). At the end of the 20th century, Zygmunt Baumann had equally observed that the liquidation of modernity, rendering fluid all that was solid, would flatten out visions of change; and frustrated with the state of Western capitalism, Slavoj Žižek took a similarly apocalyptic standpoint when he declared that "nobody seriously considers possible alternatives to capitalism any longer . . . it seems easier to imagine 'the end of the world' than a far more modest change in the mode of production" (1994, 1). Yet even if this list could be continued even further, reading these late 20th century and early 21st century voices with and against Mannheim also opens up a host of perspectives on how to escape this circle and to re-instate critique. After all, Mannheim himself sees the historical process and emergent correlations in history as a way beyond this very doublebind.

This pattern of capitulations to ideological entrapment can be traced back to Mannheim's view of ideology as a vicious circle which, by virtue of being engrained in every aspect of thought and life, undermines any possibility of critical evaluation. Yet this is, ultimately, politically reactionary, submitting to the sense that "we cannot put our social life into radical question precisely because we are the products of it, because we bear in our bones and fibres the very traditions we are foolishly seeking to objectify," as Terry Eagleton (1994, 3) phrases it. Recent political U-turns, for instance by Žižek when, in an interview with the *New Statesman* in January 2019, he endorsed Donald Trump in the hope of a "crack appear[ing] in the liberal centrist hegemony" demonstrate that this apocalyptic view of an ideological entrapment, allegedly only to be breached by violently populist white supremacism, is a dead end. Paul Ricœur's claim that "the only way to get out of the circularity in which ideologies engulf us is to assume a utopia, declare it, and judge an ideology on this basis" (1986, 172), in contrast, insists on both the possibility and need for an 'outside' to current realities. The gesture of declaration here is particularly interesting, as it enacts a performative impulse rather than prescribing an alternative normative order. Yet just as the ideological landscape has changed since he wrote this in 1986, ideas of what such an 'outside' might entail need to change and adjust, too. In the 21st century, imagining change needs to take a different shape.

As I am tracing the development of utopian literature into what I will propose as the Diatopian impulse, I have already repeatedly referenced the performative qualities of a politics in motion. Ideas, as Terry Eagleton emphasizes in *Ideology* (1994), are an "active force," and however virulent ideologies of patriarchy, racism, neo-colonialism, or free-marketeering remain, they are never fully internalized nor accepted "without a struggle" (19). Literary politics does not require a utopian idea to be rendered absolute, yet neither is it purely experimental play with configurations. It rather proposes a non-representational mode of thought, seeking not analogy or any correspondence between word and a pre-existing world, but free movement from the interior to the exterior, riding difference.

While the border wall, as erected between the United States and Mexico, seems to be the emblem of a world order defined by unsurmountable dual opinions, this violent clarity is actually misleading. The issue of a politics of literature in a convoluted, unmappable present, thus, cannot be approached in terms of the traditional differentiation of the political sphere into 'left' and 'right,' and neither can the de-territorialized, transversal currents shaping our reality be made to stop. Driving beneath such partisan divides, literature drills through to the deeper conditions of our agency, positionality and voice. The recurrent rhetoric of border walls only marks the deadly absurdity of retaining the need for clear-cut distinctions, be they nationalist, racist, or normative, proving the impotence of wall constructions which can destroy lives, but, driven by a mistaken nostalgia for sedentary rigidity, cannot reshape the world into a fixity it most likely never had.

When attempting to explain this seeming paradox of political forces seeking fixed, territorialised positions in a de-territorialised world, Italian philosopher Roberto Esposito approaches our contemporary condition through the ongoing negations of 'community' and 'immunity' – a sense of exemption and protection that is in continuous friction with the responsibility of care for one another in our coexistences and cohabitations. This negotiation, as such, is not exclusive to the present-day but can be traced through the history of humankind. What Esposito identifies in our present-day condition, though, is the key to current political challenges. According to Esposito, this immunitary dispositif has become the "rotating axis around which is constructed both the practices and the imaginary of an entire civilization" (2008, 4). The contact of the globalized self with different forms of contagion and responsivity, ranging from cyber viruses to AIDS and globalized terrorist grooming, has increased the perceived sense of risk to such an extent that self-immunization has morphed into the core ideological tenet of our times. Yet when he argues that it is precisely the tearing down of walls such as the Berlin Wall, "a wall both real and symbolic," which engenders the construction of new walls until it "perverted the very idea of community into the form of a fortress under attack" (2008, 6) he puts his finger on the dangerous paradox this entails: "immunization at high doses is the sacrifice of the living, which is to say, every form of qualified life, to simple survival" (2008, 7). A politics of literature that retains the political impulses of the Diatopian, but shies away from the rigidity of fixed orders, can address this double-blind by creating imaginative realities as worlds performed and enacted in constant motion.

To explore what such a literary politics of transversality and unmappability can entail, let's return to what Osayi Idusuyi was reading at that fateful rally:

> "The wrong words enter your day like a bad egg in your mouth and puke runs down your blouse, a dampness drawing your stomach in toward your rib cage. [. . .] You are reminded of a conversation you had recently, comparing the merits of sentences constructed implicitly with "yes, and" rather than "yes, but." You and your friend decided that "yes, and" attested to a life with no turn-off,

no alternative routes: you pull yourself to standing, soon enough the blouse is rinsed, it's another week, the blouse is beneath your sweater, against your skin, and you smell good."

(Rankine 2014, 8)

Searching for a language that says "yes, but": this is what thinking about political speech today entails. Against the limping untruths of ideological non-thought, poetic speech engenders the kind of thought that dares to imagine new ways of inhabiting our world. Yet these sentences starting with "but" do not people an alternate land of utopian hope or dystopian demise. Rankine's writing is Diatopian because it addresses a "you," a poetic gesture that traces the scars of racist violence. Cutting across time, skin and mind, it is also deeply embedded in bodies, implicated in the ideological stratosphere of systemic racism it strives against but cannot fully escape. In her ecological feminism, Stacy Alaimo describes this double-bind as a core principle shaping practices of resistance, noting that "[I]f we are all constituted by discourses implicated in oppressive systems, there is never any untainted path to liberation" (2000, 9).

Physically sick from taking every-day blows, of friends confusing the names of the only two black people they know, of teachers who do not even consider that a white girl might be copying the answers of a black student, the outcry that should follow never does. The blouse is tucked back in and the hurt banished inside. Being a citizen in *Citizen* means being engulfed in a desperate conflict between insult and survival instinct in which the sentence that begins with "but" taunts and evades you. "Every day your mouth opens and receives the kiss the world offers, which seals you shut." Flows, parameters, patterns of dis-and re-assembly increasingly shape not merely Guattari's de-territorialized globalized capitalism, but also define the working of ideologies such as the "stratifying system of difference" of racism, requiring constant upkeep, "[Y]ou have to build something, a machine to maintain the cruel, ridiculous institution of it" (Kearney 2015, 28). The question of transversal thought, thus, affects not merely anticapitalistic politics. The search for ways to re-appropriate such systems, and to regain agency and voice in them, motivates the literary resistance to white supremacist narratives which the authors in this chapter pursue. In this sense, it is deeply responsive to the idea of "transversality" as developed by Félix Guattari in *Chaosmosis*. Engendering "unprecedented, unforeseen and unthinkable qualities of being" (106), such diagonally traversing lines contaminate seemingly autopoietic domains with each other. This transversal impulse describes the role of art in a capitalist system. It celebrates process instead of what Guattari calls "inert facticity" (1995, 109). It moves freely from mind to matter. And most importantly, it is part of Guattari's vision of chaotization that throws compositions into relation with each other, altering them, spinning and unwinding complexities (1995, 114).

This chaosmotic transversality is political because it is anti-dogmatic; celebrates the creation of the new, the search for the unknown, laughing in the face of a need for consensus or reassurance. However, in so doing it also flees the body, not in its conceptual sense, but in its material, wounded, scarred experience. Claudia Rankine challenges transversality with the coded, vomiting, hurting body. It is this tension that the Diatopian imagination seeks to negotiate.

To understand how the contemporary literary imagination becomes political requires leaving behind any notion of utopian purity, accepting (which does not mean succumbing to) the taintedness of resistance, of the allegedly "wrong words" and their nauseating smell. Rankine's gesture for connectivity, and its embodied situatedness, are thus central features of the contemporary political imagination. "Tried rhyme, tried truth, tried epistolary untruth, tried and tried," is how Rankine describes this search for a different kind of engaged speech. Disillusioned with and disinterested in the grand narratives of utopia, the Diatopian is a way of apprehending the cry of the human in and through its entanglements.

The lack of alternative, utopian master narratives in contemporary literature, therefore, should not be misread as a shying away from critique. Mitchum Huehls' "hunch" that "many contemporary authors who at first glance might appear to be abandoning politics are actually entirely rethinking what politics looks like in our neoliberal age" (2016, xi) is thus a more perceptive acknowledgement of the politics of the 21st century literary imagination than the Žižekian diagnosis of capitulation. In his assessment of critique, motions of re-configuration, re-shaping geographies of inclusion, re-arranging the positioning of bodies in physical and discursive spaces replace the clarity of traditional oppositional resistance in order to make themselves un-hijackable by the dominant neoliberal ideology.

> In a world in which neoliberalism touches everything but the barest of life, you can certainly make critiques, challenge norms, and offer competing representations of the world, but given neoliberalism's omnipresence, the position you hold will be just as neoliberal as the position you're against.
>
> (Huehls 2016, 5)

Such a constellational approach certainly captures the multidirectionality of the phrase "yes, but," which differs from the simple "no" as it is subversive rather than purely oppositional. Yet at the same time, the affective intensity of Rankine's writing demonstrates how such a politics, which works via re-configuration, is also driven by sharp ethical clarity. Huehls is fascinated by the protagonist in Colson Whitehead's *Zone One*, who, caught up within a gruelling zombie apocalypse, decides to "fuck it; "let's see what happens when we swim with the zombies" (2016, x). There is no "fuck it" in Rankine's prose. It is an intentional gesture towards inhabiting the world differently, not by unwilled experiment, but by a willed resistance to having one's own existence be co-opted by dominant (racist) narratives. Rankine doesn't assume re-configurations of isolated begins; her beings inter-bleed.

Instead of succumbing to the forces of right-wing deterritorialization merely because the symmetrical diagrams of 19th century utopias crumble, contemporary literature abounds with criticism of present social, political and economic arrangement, and teems with desires to imagine alternatives. It is just that these alternatives are not mapped out as lands to be travelled to. They play out in gestures demanding response, networks to be traversed, bodies seeking connectivity, in ways that subvert conventional hierarchies and ideological frameworks alike. These Diatopian impulses are nomadic where the utopian was insular, and embodied where the utopian sought enlightened abstraction. Instead of mapping imagined spaces, they are exploratory, tracing a narrative line that evolves and unfolds to engender alternative visions. A de-territorialized reality requires an equally "transversal" (Guattari 2008, 29) counter-imagination. This is the fluid habitat that political literature learns to inhabit and re-code, resisting its take-over by the man in the blue suit and red tie.

In this context it would be easy to dismiss reading a book at a right-wing rally as a singular gesture, poignant perhaps, but unlikely to have any lasting effect. Easy, but misleadingly shortsighted. Fictional resistance has long seeped into our realities, shadowboxing with fake news in the contested space of the cultural imaginary. One man behind the mask, for sure, is very much alive. Each November people gather for the Million Mask March, inspired by V, Alan Moore and David Lloyd's unsettling protagonist who nurtures his resistance to the authoritarian darkness of his dystopian universe with the works of Shakespeare, the Divine Comedy, and a Motown-playing jukebox, in a library that is also a labyrinth and as such has no track with the violent single-mindedness of Norsefire rule. As V claims (quoting William Butler Yeats), "the centre cannot hold." As the ruthlessness of late capitalism merges with the thoughtlessness of neofascist politics, it is the labyrinthine, the rhizomatic, and the nodal that feeds notions of political resistance in the literary imagination.

Ideology, as Ricœur defined it, is not an act of reason, but of the imagination. Yet the ideological leap of faith deprives the imagination of its wings. Pedestrian, it shuffles and begrudges. It is the imagination of enmity. It builds a bridge from unrealistic claim to unconditional belief. Yet not all imagination is ideological. In the era of fake news, we need to develop critical instruments and alternate political sensibilities to celebrate an open-ended, interconnected and process-based imagination that does not exist, as its ideological counterpart does, merely to shut down resistant thought. To counteract ideological leaps of faith, authors such as Claudia Rankine refuse to play into the oppositional logic of an ideological clash, proving more interested in developing a poetics that gestures towards an 'other,' searching for ways to respond, to become responsive and responsible. To think poetically and politically, in this sense, makes violence in the name of the one and the true impossible, as it gestures for connection but denies closure.

Gestural Selfhood: From Addressability to Response-ability

Claudia Rankine's auto-fictive prose replaces the traveller journeying towards enlightenment in the lands of utopia with a fractured, participatory, exposed self. She writes in the mode of the "you," and this indeed captures the first dimension of how literature speculates, confabulates, re-creates poetically the conditions of our political thinking and experience. Her "you" is the poetic first-person "I" stepped out of itself, refusing to be, as Adorno would put it, "at home in one's home" (2005, 39). Rankine herself presents tennis player Serena Williams' claim that she had to "split herself of from herself and create different personae"(2014, 36) as the double consciousness that racism enforces and which becomes a self-destructive survival strategy to persist without exploding in anger every time the sense of being a black player on a white playing field becomes too glaringly exposed. In this sense Rankine's "you" is in a line with W. E. B. DuBois' premises in *The Souls of Black Folk* (1903). This "peculiar sensation," as DuBois writes, of "always looking at one's self through the eyes of others," forced to measure "one's soul by the tape of a world that looks on in amused contempt and pity" makes dissociation the symptom of being subjected to systemic racism, entailing such "two-ness" – "an American, a Negro; two souls, two thoughts, two unreconciled strivings" (1903, 563). Yet beyond this psycho-political diagnosis, looking to Adorno's notion of an exiled self opens up an additional dimension. For him, not being at home with oneself, whether voluntary or enforced, is also the basis for an ethical life. Inhabiting the troublesome zone of discomfort, a split, fragmented self thus also imbues the "you" with a sense of ethico-political agency. This "you" undermines the bubble of snugly enclosed selfhood, about which Rankine reflects that "You said 'I' has so much power; it's insane" (2014, 71). "The eye crashing into you, is this you?" (2014, 75) Rankine asks, playing with the sound of the word "eye" – read out aloud, it becomes indistinguishable from the first person pronoun, "I" – because seeing another being, acknowledging and encountering them as they are is a constant endeavor and not a given.

This transversality re-defines being as porous, to be transgressed and transgressing others. It is easy to underestimate that gesture of an "I" in ruins seeking a "you" because of its tenderness, but in all its precarious searching it still undermines the thought of binary violence, of exclusion itself. Yet because it inhabits the self and the other simultaneously, it does not merely pronounce the Levinasian 'do not kill' in the face of the Other which speaks of its humanity yet remains petrified in the perpetual apprehension of death. Rankine recognizes that the era of bounded individualism is not only over, but might never have begun for those selves not falling into the categories envisaged by the Western, male, and white thought of the Enlightenment. The current rhetoric of narcissistically wounded strongmen gives ample illustration why both human exceptionalism and bounded individualism, "those old saws of Western philosophy and political economics" have become "unthinkable" (Haraway 2016, 30). To re-think the 'I' as a 'you' is one mode of a literary thought that is future-oriented because it is a gesture of participation, an interconnected self blossoming out of nodal points with the other. It is thus akin to Donna Haraway's philosophy of "becoming-with" (2016, 12), which is why Rankine's poetics of the 'you' departs from a diagnosis of racism-induced dissociation and moves towards a poetics of resistance. As an impulse of such becoming-with it defines a new sense of being, thinking, and participating in intertwined worlds.

Literature, in this transversal sense, is not political because it advocates clear visions of alternative worlds. It becomes political when it enquires into the conditions of thought itself. The 'you' also states a refusal to pay credence to the illusions of independence that mark the new nationalism of the 21st century in the Anglophone world. What Haraway, with M. Beth Dempster, calls "sympoiesis" (2016, 35) denotes a practice of thinking collaboratively. Sympoietic knowledge is not mastery, nor does it seek information in the interest of power. Rather it is a process which Haraway describes with the metaphor of string figuring, a thinking-with that requires each being to pass on the strings of thought in the full awareness of being entangled, being precarious, being at risk in the world. The inability (or unwillingness) to imagine one's own entanglement, by contrast, entails what Haraway describes as the "astralization" (2016, 36) of the bounded self beyond the networks of consequence and interconnectedness of the world. The result of this isolationist exultation is not only the impulse of power or mastery. Such boundedness is also the precondition of actively participating in a violent politics of exclusion.

Thinking-with, thus, is not merely a coexistence "with dust in our eyes" (Rankine 2014, 155), a going-along with the violence of the world to survive by adaptation. It is a process of developing what Haraway calls "response-ability" (2016, 12), and thus agency in a wounded and wounding earth. In this sense, this particular literary politics of the 'you' seeks ways beyond the kind of "addressability" which Rankine, recounting a dialogue with philosopher Judith Butler, sees as the basis of why language can be hurtful. If "we suffer from the condition of being addressable" (2014, 49) and thus wound-able, then all forms of the presence she recounts – "your alertness, your openness, and your desire to engage" (2014, 49) – are caught in a doublebind: seeking to respond and talk back, you also become exploitable. Yet the unmappable 'you' that she references is moving, not fixed in a hurtful position; it is transversal, not fixed in an exploitable presence. This transversality can equally be approached from the perspective of a politics of affect. Understood as a series of relations, transmissible patterns and interconnections of feelings in which people participate collectively, affect, as Grattan demonstrates in his 2017 study on contemporary literature, has a utopian potential. The kind of affect that Rankine describes when you sit next to a stranger in a train to fill the conspicuously empty seat beside them – "if anyone asks you to move, you'll tell them we're travelling as a family" (2014, 133) – creates such a shared, unspoken structure. As such, it becomes a precondition for action, one way in which the utopian in texts can "move people, organize affects, and energize action" (Grattan 2017, 2). This is why the ways in which Rankine tunes into currents of both compassion and anger is politically salient, whether it stems from Serena Williams' outbursts at a line judge's biased officiating in the U.S. Open, or Zinedine Zidane's implosion in the 2006 World Cup final in Berlin, head-butting Marco Materazzi two minutes before the end of the match. The currents of anger this creates engulf both those seen as victims and as perpetrators – the speaker herself, Trayvon Martin, those who got killed along with Clementa Pinckney in the Charleston shooting, but also the "Jena Six", a group of black high school kids convicted in the 2006 beating of Justin Barker. Rankine is attuned to anger, not to defend it, but in the hope that this might offer an alternative type of knowledge about individual human beings in particular situations, instead of falling into the narrative of a media-sellable black rage.

Response-ability arises precisely out of such fabrics of interconnection that this 'you-self' can learn to navigate. As the self becomes responseable, language itself changes, too. Rankine's "words like pollen" (2014, 156) have become liberated from the association of language with weaponry which is implicit in the idea of hurtful language, and, as Haraway notices (2016, 39), is woven deeply into the narrative of human history that traces progress, via the emergence of tools, weapons, and words. Considering language as pollen also changes the nature of the word itself. It is not the equivalent of a pre-given concept or reality, but an emergence. Pollen "deterritorializes" (Deleuze and Guattari 1987, 10) the flower when carried by the wasp, and in turn disperses the trace of the wasp when left on other flower stems. The politics of language as ecology, thus, emerges not from truth correspondences but from patterns of dissemination and growth.

The Diatopian, thus, seeks to re-world current realities by making them relational. The dispersal of the relational self emerges from Adornian exile and diaspora into seed-bearing pollen seeking to engender new embeddings and new lives. To speak with Guattari, this dialogue offers "heterogenesis" (2008, 34), a multilinear and multidirectionally diverse narrative in the stead homogenized symmetries of earlier utopias. Its fundamental gesture is that of "opening-out" (2008, 35), not simplified ideological closure, as a way of orientating ourselves towards change and the future. This is why, in the flotsam of silenced voices in *Citizen*, there are the survivors of Hurricane Katrina: "We've never reached out to anyone to tell our story, because there's no ending to our story, he said. Being honest with you, in my opinion, they forgot about us." Rankine's gestural poetics resists by insisting on this dialogue: "Call out to them. I don't see them. Call out anyway. Did you see their faces?" (Rankine 2014, 86).

Ultimately, the Diatopian entails a literary politics which counters violence by refusing clear legibility. The key term of the Diatopian self and the space it inhabits, thus, is not the mappable 'no-where' of the utopian. It is "turbulence" (Rankine 2014, 26). Whereas the historically white space of Rankine's tennis mediations has the effect of throwing Serena Williams' black body into contrast, a stark outline "thrown against a sharp white background" (Rankine 2014, 25) which echoes Zora Neale Hurston, Rankine's turbulence whirls up memories of the Middle Passage within 21st century sports, the vortex of systemic violence to the self, to others, to those long dead unravelling the seemingly clear lines of the tennis court. Readability, in this sense, is byproduct of playing by those clear lines even if, and perhaps especially when, they cover up the deeper tumult within. Rankine had introduced this theme in her 2004 collection *Don't Let me be Lonely*, in which a readable life becomes shorthand for one that is "worthwhile and successful," not one spent in struggle, pain or loneliness (2004, 40). In *Citizen*, the way back into a "legible world" (2014, 27) leads through denial that bad referee calls were stemming from a racist bias – "no, no, no" (2014, 27). Transversal selves complexify, and perform gestures of encounter that motion towards an alternative worlding of a seemingly fractured reality: shaped by encounters between porous selves who are affected by and affecting others, this suggests a politics of tenderness, instead of oppositionality, which acknowledges its own precarious position.

Writing From the Ruins: Politics of Literary Form

Genre is the textual shape we expect our experience to take, yet Rankine's *Citizen* is a border creature of a book, searching for new ways of speaking and thinking politically. Written in lyrical prose it managed the feat of making the New York Times bestseller list by appearing in the non-fiction category. Perhaps it is no coincidence, either, that the search for the Great American novel of our times has recently proved as frantic as it is futile. It seems that the novel, at least when thought of as a singular masterstroke, is not the genre most attuned to our times. The linear storyline cannot respond to crisis. But a broken text can. In times of crisis, those drawers start to rattle and crack in order to give way for a writing that envisages change.

Instead of magisterial narratives, current political literature in Rankine's sense engages writing of ferocious precariousness, in which "the state of emergency" becomes "a state of emergence" (2014, 126). Despite the fact that it is the idea of a 'Great American novel' that continues to capture the public imagination, John William DeForest in his 1868 essay "The Great American Novel" actually singled out poetry as the mode of writing linked to democratic politics: "We may be confident," he asserted, that the "Great American Poem will not be written, no matter what genius attempts it, until democracy, the idea of our day and nation and race, has agonized and conquered through centuries, and made its work secure" (28). Against the obedient language that gives commands, likes and retweets, the disobedient poetic language of our times seeks out the link between poetry and democracy. These, as Derek Mong, the first poet to be included on the Professor Watchlist in Trump's America notes, are "a tandem affair" (2017).

The generic hybridity of Rankine's gestural writing thus points to the politics of textual form in a Diatopian sense. "I'm thinking as if trying to weep" (2004, 89) is how the speaker in Claudia Rankine's *Don't Let me be Lonely* explains her work to a NYC cab driver. More than half a century earlier and seemingly worlds apart, Theodor W. Adorno developed what he called a sad science of damaged life in a post-Holocaust world. "The splinter in your eye is the best magnifying glass" (2005, 50) he writes about his search for a form of thought that grieves, weeps and pierces through the comforting delusions into which we build our lives. This is a common motif: In Luis Buñuel and Salvador Dalí's surrealist 1929 film *Un Chien Andalou*, as I watch cringingly, an eye is sliced. Perception itself is precarious, and the clarity expected from vision might not be the only, or even most reliable, gateway to understanding the realities of the present day.

This sad thought becomes a project shared by two writers who seem to have little in common: Adorno, the Jewish exile from National Socialist Germany and the Kingston-born Rankine certainly never met, nor do their aesthetic projects overlap much – one a theorist of a rather elitist avant-garde art of negativity, the other an acute chronicler of the 21st century colour line. Yet both experiment with the generic hybridity of the fragment in their explorations of the narrative shape that crisis takes in order to "get thought moving," because thought in its traditional conceptual form seems "rigid, conventional, and outmoded" (Adorno 1992, 323).

With the prose fragment, Rankine therefore employs a textual form that is political not merely because it is dialogical. The mid-20th century 'Denkbilder' (thought-images) of Frankfurt School writers such as T.W. Adorno, Ernst Bloch and Walter Benjamin were so called because, like

Rankine's responses to youtube videos and sports coverage, they capture the movement of thought as it arises from perceptions, sensations, and the tangible surroundings of urban life. It also positions the contemporary political imagination in a borderline space.

The Denkbild is liminal in several ways. Published in feuilletons – brief prose pieces with titles such as Walter Benjamin's 1928 "Baustelle" ('building site') or "Frühstücksstube" ('breakfast parlour'), or Adorno's 1951 "Zwergobst" ('dwarf fruit') – it is non-narrative and non-fictional, linking it to the prose poem tradition; especially in Walter Benjamin's case, Baudrillard is, of course, a main influence. These fragments intervene in a specific historical moment: they mark the challenge of developing a practice of thought in the face of the double-bind posed by the critique of instrumental reason on the one hand, and the appropriation by totalitarian fascism (and, in some cases, the complicity) of what Max Horkheimer calls "irrationalism" (1993) on the other hand. Collections such as Adorno's *Minima Moralia*, Benjamin's *Einbahnstraße* and *Kindheit in Berlin*, Ernst Bloch's *Spuren* and *Erbschaft der Zeit,* or Kracauer's *Straßen in Berlin und Anderswo* attempt to define a new and oppositional practice of thought via writing.

Paradigmatic is Walter Benjamin's association of short prose with a building site in *Einbahnstraße*. Understood as a "Neuordnung der Dingwelt" (new order of the world of things), this forges new connections instead of representing a given reality; it realizes the impetus of change via the fragmented textual constellation itself. In celebrating the moment of recognition and the ways in which material reality continues to reconfigure itself, Benjamin's thought-images offer an alternative to the rigid worldview of totalitarian ideologies. Thus, personal relationships enlighten the intimidating urban labyrinth of an unknown neighborhood, as love literally divides space with clusters of light in the fragment "Erste Hilfe" ('first aid'). Of course, the messianic qualities are hard to overlook, as is a certain element of nostalgia when observing the ephemeral nature of human perceptions, which are irretrievably altered by habit and time. Yet these apparently individualized visions carry a deeper political significance. It is no coincidence that they respond immediately to the rise of fascism. Without wanting to overburden the parallels to the 1920s and 1930s that keep cropping up in attempts to analyze the new nationalism of the 21st century, these modernist texts enter our present moment because of a shared ambition: to find a voice that resists the making universal of partial truths (or non-truths), but which also speaks independently and not just reactively.

Interestingly, this same ambition is at the core of one of the pivotal debates about modernism and ideology in the 20th century, between Georg Lukács and Ernst Bloch, during which Lukács charged not only expressionism with fascist complicities. He also tied his argument to one particular text type, the aphorism, which, as Lukács argued in *Die*

Zerstörung der Vernunft ('The Destruction of Reason') (12), by way of its precarious form encapsulated the decadence of modernist art. Hovering between philosophy and literature, social critique and aesthetic production, the Denkbilder are related to the aphorism and, as I would like to argue, prove Lukács to be a little short-sighted.

They offer a poetics that develops not power, but strength of vision, because it is conceived from the wound; Yet even if this poetics is based in a textual precariousness, it is no less forceful for it, aiming, as it does, to wrestle back from fascism the meaning of sensation, intuition, and the irrational. The poetic use of language opens up the possibility of a different kind of thought, focusing on the non-identical, on difference both in the poetics and the politics of these texts. Through their focus on materiality and sensation, the Denkbilder inscribe resistance into a historical reality that has been hijacked by national socialist ideologies (Bloch 1962, 16–18).

This hijacking becomes tangible in particular when Bloch, in his *Erbschaft der Zeit*, radicalizes Benjamin's vision. He transforms the building site into a "Handgemenge" (1962, 18), a physical fight against the intoxicating effect of unifying ideological concepts such as 'soul', 'nation', 'the unconscious', and a battle for a position from which to speak against totality. The ambition of these texts to create a performative thought in motion, therefore, is in many ways a tightrope walk. It looks to material being to retain its critical, forward-driving force; but it also works against the one-sidedness of a purely analytical or instrumental thought. The thought images by these authors refuse to adhere to the threat of complicity with the totalitarian. It is therefore no coincidence that one important topic is that of intoxication, which these texts try to resist. Instead of promising insights into some essential character of the world, the broken, fragmentary, material poetics of the Denkbild refuses complicity by working against the notion of totality as such. The whole is the untrue, as Adorno subverts Hegel (2005, 246).

These short forms, therefore, turn writing into an act of subtle civil disobedience. For Ernst Bloch, writing these fragments is literally an act of punching back (1962, 22). Considering the prevalence of short forms in the digital media, they are precursors to the search for modes of thinking, reading, and writing that can disentangle our speech from the warped public discourse of these times and today.

Rankine's prose poems take the politics of the prose fragment into the 21st century. They give birth to a writing that is on the edge, tipping from fierce vulnerability into strength and back again. The breakdown, thus, is also a *"making plain,"* as Douglas Kearney writes, *"a discontent uncovering content"* (2015, 22). Such stuttered language is set up from within dominant speech but chokes it, challenges it and introduces variation to it from within. Kearney's language cleaves apart the double-binds of Rankine's citizenship as his lines rupture when they respond to the killing of James Byrd by white supremacists in 1998: "the picked-up headlights long the road KRAK buck broke KRAK the white stick" (2016, 44). Yet once these cracks grow from a history of violence onto the surface of contemporary life, it, too, is going to start to bubble and fluctuate, ready – to borrow one of Kearney's favorite phrases – to be messed with. Mess, the process of messing with and being messed with, is his poetic project. A breakdown, it turns the fracture of conventional speech into an opening for new possibilities. Fissures become generative as creativity emanates from friction. Yet like in Rankine's case, this mess poetics, too, insists on immersion and participation. Kearney advocates opening yourself up to the vast confusion of noise and signals from both the present and the past.

One scene from *Don't Let me be Lonely* in particular encapsulates the literary politics of "becoming-with" which the dialogicity of such break-downs engenders. On a day that is "hot, unbearably," a girl climbs up to the roof of her thirty-story apartment building. Unafraid of heights she enjoys the shade of the water tower, letting her legs dangle over the edge of the building. Underneath a sky "drowning in blue with clouds that billow like sails," the girl beings to "shout a Milosz poem to the sky" (Rankine 2016, 35). The title of the poem is "Gift" – something that has no exchange value and poses a counter currency to our free market economies. Above the city weighted down by the heat, this American girl celebrates the lightness of being on the edge. Exposed, she releases the words of a 20th century exiled Polish writer Milosz into the heat in a literary dialogue in which two worlds converge. The poetic clarity of this scene, one of the most beautiful in Claudia Rankine's writing, crystallizes the relationship between imaginative freedom and disobedience as a gesture of transversal readership.

As such this scene evokes a tradition of civic resistance that interconnects readers, writers, speakers and listeners across generations in a dialogue. Wai Chee Dimock (2006, 20) argued that the idea of civil disobedience itself emerged through a network of forward-pushing readers: Henry David Thoreau reading the Hindu Bhagavad Gita, Martin Luther King reading Thoreau, Gandhi reading Thoreau. It is driven by the democratic principle of mutuality and dialogue which generates bottom-up empowerment instead of top-down power. Unlike the utopian, the Diatopian, therefore, is a literary politics that is affective, transversal and hybrid. Yet it is from this very heteroglossia that its resistant impulse emerges. Its fundamental gesture of a participatory "with" – "Anyway, sit down. Sit here alongside" (Rankine 2014, 71) – does not advocate the kind of coexistence that seeks survival through silence. It changes the conditions of how the self is conceived in the world in order to seek change.

The critical impact of such a poetics of fragmentation, be it in Rankine's autofiction or in Kearney's poetic ruptures, is that they work to gain what Eagleton calls an "emancipatory knowledge" (1994, 17) of the spaces which the social system assigns. This exposure in itself is oppositional, and becomes the precondition for a sense of self that, interconnected and participatory, evades entrapment. The political literary self, in this sense, is not a flagbearer, but a wounded trickster who shapeshifts in order to establish connections that are not only beyond the reach of racist ideologies but define an oppositional space in which to become-with. It is a self that is missing and thus to be invented via its lines of connectivity and flight. The politics of such contemporary texts embrace the Deleuzian notion that "the ultimate aim of literature is to set free, in the delirium [. . .] this invention of a people, that is, a possibility of life" (1998, 4) pursuing a politics in the minor key which, instead of imposing power, traces the process of becoming of those who are annulled because they inhabit minority spaces. Yet it is these minor and multiple selves who can promote ways of inhabiting current realities without falling back on dominant ideological formations, having never fully internalized them in the first place.

Rhizomatic Space: De-territorializing the Nation

Transversal gestures require alternative spaces, and this is not purely a 21st century necessity. Against the ideological rigidity that restricted the aesthetics of architecture in the Soviet Union, 'paper architects' – so called because their designs would and could never be built, thus existing only as sketches – drafted visions of spaces infused by movement, metamorphosis, and tenderness. Alexander Brodsky and Ilya Utkin, two of the most well-known representatives of the group, produced highly detailed etchings for futuristic architecture. Their design for the year 2001, for instance, is a "Wandering Turtle in a Maze of a Big City." The turtle is a hybrid assemblage of towers, chutes, curtains, trumpeting figurines and onion roofs on wheels, infusing the rectangular city grid with the joys of movement and playful difference as it passes through. Celebrating "endless play at everything," constantly "renewing and changing," (Brodsky and Utkin 2017) these structures articulate a politics of the imagination expressed as space. They are not rooted, but seek new encounters by circulating through cityscapes, intensifying their environments by shedding traces of creative chaos. They resist the violence of rigidity which threatens to petrify more traditional utopian spaces. These spaces, thus, not only symbolize an anti-ideological politics of resistance but also provide the experimental habitats for it.

Back in the 21st century, the ambition to re-write space remains and is intensified by the need to define the political potential of de-territorialization in ways that resist its neoliberal overcoding. Colson Whitehead's 2016 *Underground Railroad* transfers this project into the slaveholding 19th century, exposing the violence of a politics that revers the borderline – of slave-holding states, of racial divides, of plantation territories – in both a metaphorical and literal sense. Resistance, in this novel, does not operate dogmatically but is continuously in a process of becoming, reaching for connection. Whitehead explores this by rendering literal the titular metaphor. His underground railroad is not a term given to a network of safe houses and escape routes, but an actual, functioning system of tracks, stations and wagons, which under-tunnels state and plantation limits. Cora, a young slave from Georgia, manages to escape her plantation via this system, which to her seems to be "springing from some inconceivable source and shooting toward a miraculous terminus" (Whitehead 2016, 80). This sense of movement without beginning or end is no coincidence, and neither is it a lack: the underground railroad is a system in perpetual motion, "stations are discovered, lines discontinued" (Whitehead 2016, 81), as station master Lumbly explains when he helps the refugees onto their boxcar.

This underground system, through which circulate rickety boxcars as well as well-appointed passenger wagons with lavish fittings, is no utopian space. It does not represent a political philosophy or symbolize the organization of a different, future-orientated society. It exists, solely but crucially, as a practice, a space that performs constant processes of renewal, change, destruction and becoming. Its tunnels include those of which "no one knows where it leads," as Royal, one of the underground agents, describes it; "If we keep the railroad running, and none of us can figure it out, maybe you can," (Whitehead 2016, 319) he continues to explain to Cora, who will indeed find the destination of what seems like a dead end, though only once she decides to run again. This is its key characteristic: the railroad is not a pre-mapped system. It grows as it is discovered by runaways, a performative space, uncovered by the movements of a "stray" (Whitehead 2016, 174) girl with no roots or belonging.

In this sense, it is a rhizomatic space, negating all thought of rootedness as it defines the pernicious politics of slaveholding society – "Know your value and you know your place in the order. To escape the boundary of the plantation was to escape the fundamental principles of your existence: impossible" (Whitehead 2016, 9). The rhizome, if thought with Deleuze and Guattari, not only undoes such "arborescent" notions (Deleuze and Guattari 1987, 15), it also exposes the privileged position of any kind of thought that can be traced back to a unifying idea or 'root cause' in Western philosophy, virulent in discourses of nationhood, genealogy, or racial purity and their politics of frontiers, conquest, and exclusion. Cora's rootedness in the slave plantation, however, steeps such roots in blood, demonstrating how "history," as Deleuze and Guattari suggest, "is always written from the sedentary point of view and in the name of a unitary State apparatus [. . .] even when the topic is nomads" (1987, 23).

As a rhizome, the underground railroad is the opposite of this; it does not seek origins, but is multiple, a map in the process of being formed, fostering connections. As such it de-territorializes the world. Travelling the underground railroad in utter darkness, Cora runs her hands along the walls of the tunnel, her fingers dancing "over valleys, rivers, the peaks of mountains, the contours of a new nation hidden beneath the old" (Whitehead 2016, 363). What she had first feared to be a station master's bitter joke – "look outside as you speed through, and you'll find the true face of America" (Whitehead 2016, 363) she now apprehends not as vision but as touch, from deep within the soil. These "states of possibility" (Whitehead 2016, 82), of course, are not synonymous with opportunity but with risk, leading her to states of violence, too. In the underground railroad, possibility always also includes the possibility of death. Yet the 'new nation' Cora intuits is not a utopian system. It describes the possibility of dismantling the frontiers that defined these United States that she travels under; in this sense it is tempting to read the underground railroad not only as rhizome, but as a 'body without organs,' which Deleuze and Guattari use to describe intensities passing through and beyond organisms, be it that of the human body or the nations state. Yet while her role as a passenger does turn Cora into an energetic particle circulating through and disrupting places where she appears, the underground railroad is too deeply steeped in the cruelty of slavery for such a disembodied reading.

> the tunnel pulled at her. How many hands had it required to make this place? [. . .] she thought of the picking, how it raced down the furrows at harvest [. . .]it was a magnificent operation, from seed to bale, but not one of them could be prideful of their labor. It had been stolen from them. Bled from them.
> (Whitehead 2016, 82)

The tunnels of the railroad allow for that pride, yet like blood, the experience of violence has long seeped into the earth through which it leads.

The politics of this railroad imaginary, thus, emerge from a state of precariousness evocative of Rankine's pollen-like words and the wounded thought of the prose fragment. They do not seek to imitate a grand ideological narrative or utopian project in its spatial formations. Rather they choose the state of the nomad so deeply immersed in the world that space is felt, not seen, the opening of tunnels too close to the torn skin of the traveller to allow for the detaching empowerment of vision. Cora participates in the railroad space, she does not construct it, and neither do the engineers aspire to analyse it into discrete components. As a Diatopian space, the railroad is not gridded but open-ended, participatory, and to be performed. Its off-shoots enable a hurt existence beyond the 'wanted' posters seeking to re-root human beings back in their allotted spaces as somebody else's possession.

From Stratifying Systems to Writ(h)ing Vipers: Literary Politics in Populist Times

> "*What is the difference between poetry and rhetoric?*
> One holds an argument as snake handlers might a diamondback. The rhetorician grips, securely, the scaly collar, ensuring the serpent doesn't bite.
> The poet, however, may find purchase further down the spine, leaving the viper free to writhe, to strike."
>
> (Kearney 2015, 11)

Instead of the distanced, clinical gaze of objectivity, poetry opts for the sting, and again this resonates from our troubled times into the dawn of the 20th century and Franz Kafka's suggestion, in a 1904 letter to Oskar Pollak (27 January 1904) that "we ought to read only the kind of books that wound or stab us." Not precarious, but fiercely tender and willfully imperiled, Douglas Kearney's snake-handling poet teaches the politics of literature in the 21st century. The writhing, risky argument poetry emerges from an encounter between poet and snake, the tactile gesture exposing both to each other, searching for ways to respond with their bodies as well as their metaphors. Simultaneously the snakes' serpentine movements describe a non-griddable space, mapping out new lines of thought from what, in the rhetorician's case, is the straight, linear grasp that aims to entrap. The poetic line of argument, thus, is non-linear, collaborative, and multidirectional. Its force is complexification, whereas populist power is built on simplification. Poetic writing is a very specific "way through," as Kearney further suggests, the cruel normality of "stratifying systems" (2015, 28) and their ideological systematization. Yet this way through is not a shortcut. Quite the opposite, it derives its force from "worrying" such orders, making "a mess of things," not for reasons of escapism, but in order to "map (mis-) understanding as a verb" (2015, 29). Thought through in this sense with Douglas Kearney, as well as Claudia Rankine and Colson Whitehead, literary thought seeks understanding via intentional misunderstanding, infusing the world as it is with doubt.

Literature is an experimental space, de-pragmatized because it insists on its imaginative freedom. Thus it is not political in the sense that it establishes specific arguments or builds up coherent systems of beliefs. Yet it would be equally misleading to assume that it has thus capitulated, retreating into a misunderstood role of a reservoir of 'universal truths' or an aesthetic zone of self-indulgence. To the contrary, its political potency lies in exposing and changing the conditions of thought and experience.

Unlike the language of technocracy that prefers what is literal, to be googled and pinned down, literary language thrives on breaching the norm. Horkheimer and Adorno, with bitter irony, called out the "dutiful child of Civilization" who is possessed by fear of social deviation. Literature calls out this 'dutiful child' along with its thoughtless companions, not only in its existence but also in its habits of thinking, using language, and inhabiting the world.

> the words line up like squads of freed slaves in the snow
> the words line up like a brain trust in a White House photo
> the words line up like a circus in a Duluth intersection
> the words line up like the offense on a December gridiron.
> (Kearney 2006, 82)

Bodies freed, assembling, ganging up on and playing the poem, Kearney's words pulse on the page. They are steeped in history and strain the order of verse to breaking point, celebrating a poetic language which it is impossible to paraphrase or to pin down in a single, unifying interpretation. They re-imagine language as a way of countering dominance. Where power builds walls, texts are force fields which break open constraints and engender new vistas. Poetry can tear language away from complicity, teaching a literacy less saturated with cruelty than the canned speech of mass and social media discourses. Yet it does this from a position of ecology and immanence, with wiring that does not seek the triumph of the sublime but poems that "Lay lines, lay lines (deep // in the earth where the power's at)" (Kearney 2006, 60). This energy writes against the dogmatic petrification of language; "To arrest the meaning of words once and for all, that is what terror wants" (quoted in De Certeau 1984, 165), Jean Francois Lyotard writes in his *Rudiments Païens*. Poetry energizes language to fore-stall such entrapment.

References

Adorno, Theodor W. 1992. *Notes to Literature: Volume Two*, edited by Rolf Tiedemann and Translated by Shierry Weber Nicholsen. New York: Columbia University Press.

Adorno, Theodor W. 2005. *Minima Moralia: Reflections on a Damaged Life*. Translated by E. F. N. Jephcott. London and New York: Verso.

Alaimo, Stacy. 2000. *Undomesticated Ground: Recasting Nature as Feminist Space*. Ithaca and London: Cornell University Press.

Arendt, Hannah. 2016. *Denktagebuch. 1950–1973*, edited by Ursula Ludz and Ingeborg Nordmann. München: Piper Verlag.

Bloch, Ernst. 1962. *Erbschaft dieser Zeit*. Frankfurt am Main: Suhrkamp Verlag.

Brodsky, Alexander, and Ilya Utkin. 2017. *Cancelled 6/21/90*. Paris: L'Esprit de l'Escalier.

Certeau, Michel de. 1984. *The Practice of Everyday Life*. Berkeley: University of California Press.
DeForest, John William. 1868. "The Great American Novel." *The Nation*, January 9.
Deleuze, Gilles. 1998. *Essays Critical and Clinical*. Translated by Daniel W. Smith and Michael A. Greco. London and New York: Verso.
Deleuze, Gilles, and Félix Guattari. 1987. *A Thousand Plateaus: Capitalism and Schizophrenia*, edited and translated by Brian Massumi. Minneapolis: University of Minnesota Press.
Dimock, Wai Chee. 2006. *Through Other Continents: American Literature Across Deep Time*. Princeton, NJ: Princeton University Press.
DuBois, W. E. B. 2017. "The Souls of Black Folk." In *The Norton Anthology of American Literature. Volume II: 1865 to the Present*, edited by Robert S. Levine, 561–77. New York and London: Norton & Company.
Eagleton, Terry, ed. 1994. *Ideology*. London and New York: Longman.
Esposito, Roberto. 2008. "Immunization and Violence." In *BioPolitica*, translated from Italian by Thimothy Campbell. Advance Online Publication. https://aphelis.net/immunization-violence-roberto-esposito-2008/
Grattan, Sean Austin. 2017. *Hope Isn't Stupid: Utopian Affects in Contemporary American Literature*. Iowa City: University of Iowa Press.
Guattari, Félix. 1995. *Chaosmosis. An Ethico-Aesthetic Paradigm*. Translated by Paul Bains and Julian Pefanis. Bloomington and Indianapolis: Indiana University Press.
Guattari, Félix. 2008. *The Three Ecologies*. Translated by Ian Pindar and Paul Sutton. London and New York: Continuum.
Haraway, Donna J. 2016. *Staying with the Trouble: Making Kin in the Chthulucene*. Durham, NC: Duke University Press.
Horkheimer, Max. 1993. "The Rationalism Debate in Contemporary Philosophy." In *Between Philosophy and Social Science: Selected Early Writings*. Translated by G. Frederick Hunter, Matthew S. Kramer, and John Torpey, 217–64. Cambridge, MA: MIT Press.
Huehls, Mitchum. 2016. *After Critique: Twenty-First Century Fiction in a Neoliberal Age*. Oxford: Oxford University Press.
Jameson, Fredric. 2000. "Utopianism and Anti-Utopianism." In *The Jameson Reader*, edited by Michael Hardt and Kathi Weeks, 382–92. Oxford: Blackwell Publishers.
Kearney, Douglas. 2006. *Fear, Some*. Los Angeles: Red Hen Press.
Kearney, Douglas. 2015. *Mess and Mess and*. Las Cruces, NM: Noemi Press.
Kearney, Douglas. 2016. *Buck Studies*. Albany, NY: Fence Books.
Lukács, Georg. 1974. *Die Zerstörung der Vernunft. Band II. Irrationalismus und Imperialismus*. Darmstadt: Hermann Luchterhand Verlag.
Mannheim, Karl. 1995 [1929]. *Ideologie und Utopie*, edited by Jürgen Kaube. Jena: Verlag Vittorio Klostermann.
Mong, Derek. 2017. "An Open Letter from the Only Poet on the Professor Watchlist." *Kenyon Review*, January. Accessed November 23, 2019. https://kenyonreview.org/2017/01/poet-professors-watchlist/
Nixon, Rob. 2011. *Slow Violence and the Environmentalism of the Poor*. Cambridge, MA: Harvard University Press.

Rankine, Claudia. 2004. *Don't Let Me Be Lonely: An American Lyric*. Minneapolis: Graywolf Press.
Rankine, Claudia. 2014. *Citizen: An American Lyric*. London: Penguin.
Rankine, Claudia. 2016. *Don't Let me be Lonely. An American Lyric*. Minneapolis: Graywolf Press.
Ricœur, Paul. 1986. *Lectures on Ideology and Utopia*, edited by George H. Taylor. New York: Columbia University Press.
Whitehead, Colson. 2016. *The Underground Railroad*. London: Fleet.
Wilde, Oscar. 2001. *The Soul of a Man Under Socialism and Selected Critical Prose*, edited by Linda Dowling. London: Penguin.
Žižek, Slavoj, ed. 1994. *Mapping Ideology*. London and New York: Verso.

2 Uncontainable Bodies
Posthuman Biopolitics

Like "bedraggled drones" (Whitehead 2012, 148) the after-work crowd is gathering to sip cocktails and size up each other's misery before the bouncers with their velvet ropes divide the survivors of the neoliberal rat race from those too-far-gone. Yet in this inconspicuous scene from Colson Whitehead's *Zone One*, reality is already trembling, ready to disintegrate. Still wearing their glittery dresses, these office workers will soon roam the town in bands of zombies, infected by a plague that will tempt them to switch drinks and nibbles for the raw flesh and bones of the survivors.

The figure of the zombie exposes the challenges of future-oriented thinking today: Responsive to Ihab Hassan's 1977 caution that "the human form – including human desire and all its external representations – may be changing radically," (Hassan, 212) zombification is not only symptomatic of the challenges involved in this posthuman reconfiguration; as the flip side of neoliberal fantasies of biopolitical perfection, it also slices through the sheen of transhuman ambitions, undermining the idea that death can be kept in check by what Schmeink calls "living 'right' and calculating risk" (2016, 213). Yet while Hassan seems wary of the end of five hundred years of humanism this might spell, his self-diagnosed sense of being "helpless" (212) in designating the new era as one of the posthuman also spells new opportunities. Humanism, after all, cannot escape its entanglements in patriarchal and Western-centric ideas, to the point of Tony Davies' damning statement that "All Humanisms, until now, have been imperial." (1997, 141).

The question what it means to be human, in this sense, has always been a political one, operating on mechanisms of exclusion designed to delineate the boundaries between human, animal, machine, and non-organic nature, but also to violently perpetuate hierarchies within human life. The enlightenment 'human' is infamously white, male and ideally wealthy, making the human a politically deeply problematic and ideologically charged category. It is these humans which zombie fiction targets. "I do not resemble that animal, you tell yourself," an officer engaged on the front of human-zombie warfare tells his charges, "as you squat in the back of the convenience store, pissing in a bucket and cooking up mangy squirrel for dinner" (Whitehead 2012, 158). The zombie indicates that the inadvertent endpoint of such insistently hierarchised bodies, paradoxically, is a descent into the zombie's pure drive to infect others and make them like yourself, the streamlining of normatively defined humanity taken to its violent finale. The zombie signals the bounded, enlightened (hu)man's tipping point. It offers a suitably unsettled position from which to explore the posthuman particularly because it exposes a biopolitical doublebind which hinders human bodies from shaping a less apocalyptic future.

Devoid of personal feelings, the zombie undermines notions of the discrete, bounded self, which is why corporate settings symbolizing phallic mastery lend themselves so obviously to zombie meltdowns. Whitehead locates these questions in a land where bands of predatory skeletons roam and survivors barricade themselves in trees and the lost promised lands of toy stores. Mark Spitz is one of the survivors, or, to be more precise, one of those who remain whilst also retaining their traditional human form, and after years on the road he is dispatched as part of a specialized, though notoriously underequipped, sweeper unit to clean out the tip of Manhattan and boost morale in the young 'phoenix' state. Cleaning here is to be understood as a euphemism, of course: dragging body bags split along the seams, their shifts involve close combat with starving zombies and automatic weapons, a micro-warfare set in the ruins of corporate downtown New York. As such, it is tempting to read the zombie as a marker of failed futurities without hope, offering only "the working through of what it is that makes the present an endless prolepsis of ruin," (Rutherford 2013, 9) which rings true especially when considering its revival in the context of the renewed uncertainties in a post-9/11 Western world. Without a doubt, the zombie personifies the cul-de-sac into which the posthuman can lead when it raises the performance-oriented and competitively streamlined corporeality of late capitalist, Deleuzian societies of control to the telos of humankind.

This is why corporate settings – spaces of uniformity, the office towers more often than not symbolizing phallic mastery – lend themselves so obviously to zombie meltdowns. "The dead came to scrub the Earth of Capitalism" (2012, 124), as Whitehead cynically comments, linking his zombies to a tendency in criticism to read these undead as symptoms of the 'flattening of affect and the quenching of spirit and creativity" (Dendle 2012, 6) that is produced by "overconsumption, media use, or political conformism" (Schmeink 2016, 213). Ironically, Whitehead's protagonist Mark Spitz had worked as an online marketer prior to the zombie breakdown, targeting potential consumers under the guise of social media friendships. Poised like a "binary vulture, ancient pixilated eyes peeled for scraps," it was his job to create "that human touch," a sense of "soul" (Whitehead 2012, 150f) in a simulacrum of human contact skilfully constructed to broaden the customer base. Pouncing on prey, it turns out, is not for online marketers only. In particular, it is no coincidence that Colson Whitehead has his crew chase zombies in Human Resources departments, "the place where human beings were paraphrased into numbers, components of bundled data to be shot out through fibre-optic cable toward meaning" (2012, 17). If zombies have one asset, it is that they are independent, competitive, single-minded and driven- just what makes the ideal employee in a free labor market. But there is an unfreedom to their existence, and it is no coincidence that Steven Shaviro called zombies "a nearly perfect allegory for the inner logic of capitalism" (2017, 8). Such processes regulate the human body by tailoring and honing its life to fit the requirements of a machine, an endeavour which defines current biopolitics. "[I]ts disciplining, the optimization of its capabilities, the extortion of its forces, the parallel increase of its usefulness and its docility" (Foucault 1990, 139) paradoxically dehumanizes its subjects in the quest for ultimate control, a doublebind which the zombie exposes.

On the other hand, though, such a symptomatic reading is not enough, and it would be reductive to read the zombie purely as a critique of the current socio-economic order of the West, the "Capitalocene," to borrow Donna Haraway's succinct phrasing (2016, 47). A focus on economics alone can obscure the political questions that remain virulent, such as the intentional acts and power patterns which create such hierarchies of 'useful' life. I find that reducing the posthuman to the lens of this economic ideology, even when approached as a mode of resistance, ultimately limits its creative potential and restrains the imagination. Mitchum Huehls encounters such a one when he proposes, in his 2016 book *After Critique*, to read contemporary literature like an accountant; however, understanding the process of reading fiction as "being aware of, paying attention to, and bringing order to swarms of information" (Huehls 2016, 167) paradoxically reduces it to the data-driven statistical mode of perception which such literary texts, according to Huehls, supposedly critique. Its more fundamental and more complex force is anchored in its fierce corporeality, which makes the posthuman a biopolitical question, putting the post-human body front and centre when attempting to re-gain any sense of political agency or voice in an ecologically broken world. This is key as the 21st century in the Western world is suffused with the politics of life, though its mechanisms are subtle.

Modern biopower, understood with Foucault, has moved beyond the dictum of "killing or letting live" (1990, 143) and now seeks more subtle means to either foster life, or to disallow it in mechanisms to "qualify, measure, appraise, and hierarchize" (1990, 144) life. Whitehead's zombies satirize such disciplining mechanisms. The zombie is therefore not merely a dystopian foil to the streamlined vitalities of 21st century human life, but – quite the opposite – their inevitable telos. This is due to the ways in which neoliberal biopower has replaced the original mark of sovereignty, the power to decide over life and death, with more subtle but pervasive mechanism of "continuous control," (Deleuze 1992, xxxx), as Deleuze claims in his "Postscript to Societies of Control." The biopolitics of neoliberalism does not rely on strategies of ringfencing as typical of Foucauldian disciplinarian societies, with their hospitals and prisons, instead relying on politicized forms of knowledge such as statistics, demographics, epidemiology, or public health to ensure the regulation of individual bodies. Aiming to "modulate the very vital capacities of human beings as living creatures" (Rose 2007, 3), it targets the modular level of all biological life, manipulating vital mechanisms in order to make life itself "amenable" as Rose continues, to the economic relations of what he terms the "bioeconomy" of "biocapital" (Rose 2007, 7). In this chapter, I will explore posthuman bodies not merely as symptoms of ideological and biopolitical mechanisms, but as potential sources of renewed political agency in their own right. This is therefore also a question of re-politicizing the biopower of the posthuman, reading it against the grain and taking seriously its most fundamental power – to threaten and unsettle – instead of simply negotiating the currents of neoliberal micro-management.

Inscribing the body back into the posthuman is especially significant since the neoliberal fascination with control ultimately leads into entrapment. Transhuman transcendence, as defined by Nick Bostrum in "The Transhumanist FAQ" published on the World Transhumanist Association's website in 2003, promises the maximum attainable capacities by any current human being; like neoliberal biocontrol, it is therefore entranced with visions not far removed from Hans Moravec's image of a posthuman transition. To the sound of the heirs of Frankenstein clapping their hands with glee,

> The robot surgeon delves into your brain, layer by layer, uploading your neural signals onto a hard drive. When the excavation is complete, it leaves only an empty skull shell. Your mind has been successfully transferred from body to machine, leaving your body to die. You open your eyes. You are now inhabiting a new body, carefully tailored to your preferences, which you chose and which had been waiting next to your now discarded tissue. You have metamorphosed into a cyborg, a man-machine hybrid.
>
> (Moravec 1988, 109f)

The perfected, portable mind is also a disembodied mind, offering nothing new conceptually besides tipping a precarious ethical scale irrevocably towards the creation of "manageable subjects" (Jonathan Crary, qutd. in Stapleton and Byers 2015, 2). Yet treating the body as a mere "prosthesis," as Katherine Hayles has argued (1999, 3), not only privileges informational patterns over their material instantiation. It regulates the human body by tailoring and honing its life to fit the requirements of a machine, thus ensuring its Foucauldian docility.

The zombie shifts our focus from the sheen of the newly engineered body to the remains left on the operating table. Both discarded body and cyborg are results of the operation, as the bodily shell remains an inevitable by-product of such disembodiment. This is how the zombie personifies both the telos and garbage of a system that thrives on ultimate calculability. In the zombie, the refuse bites back. When it comes to imagining the future, thus, the idea of the posthuman as 'perfected human' paradoxically entails the zombie apocalypse, and is perhaps an even greater failure as it lacks the zombie's talent for satire.

Unlike Moravec's disembodied mind, the zombie cannot be controlled, a feature of the figure which Whitehead exploits when he satirizes the futility of the survivor's attempts to stem the flow of zombie hordes by building a wall already swarming with the zombie's breakthroughs. As the zombies seek to infect their hunters, nearly succeeding in biting Mark Spitz when he tries to eliminate them in their lawyer's office hideout, the zombies' darkly parodic impact also testifies to a lingering sense of resistance. Significantly, this resistance is inherently linked to the zombie's talent for revealing that humans are made of the same organic, bodily tissue as other animals, exposing connectivities beyond the human that are key for the future-oriented impact of these blood-splattering creatures. The zombie breakdown is therefore also a breakthrough: it spells the end of the utopian if understood as a bounded vision, depending on control as a "means" to the "utopian end" (Stapleton and Byers 2015, 2) of producing cooperative, productive, reproductive and citizens. The zombie seeks out the beastliness within the human at the point when the underside of culture, "blood, torture, death, and terror" (Jameson 1991, 20) surfaced without recall.

The zombie, therefore, is a biopolitical figuration of the posthuman that is geared towards the monstrous rather than the sheen of newly engineered bodies. This is why Whitehead uses the zombie to imagine life "beyond the self" (Braidotti 2013, 13) when the "American checklist" (Whitehead 2012, 9), which lays out your path to success from kindergarten to college, has collapsed. This 'checklist,' after all, has already set humanity at the crest of collapse. Its individualist promise of personalised fulfilment can hardly hide its normative expectations; the bouncers in Whitehead's pre-breakdown Manhattan who divide the crowd are particularly adept at sniffing out the whiff of success or failure in this ratrace. Returning as zombies, the discarded bite back. Originally linked to slave rebellions, the zombie is a figure with a history of such boomerang effects. Returning in the 21st century as waste product, Whitehead uses it to project the flip side of neoliberal fantasies of biopolitical perfection.

This double-sidedness of neoliberal, transhuman body politics, encompassing survival and death in one gesture, is deeply engrained in the notion of biopower per se. Understood in Foucauldian terms, the power which optimizes, controls and monitors life legitimates its reach by positing that the individual's continued existence is at threat (Foucault 1990, 137). Whitehead's skeletal bodies thus still carry remnants of their former selves' attempts to streamline their bodies according to images of perfection. TV-series inspired hairstyles and glossy officewear symbolize their quest to fit the norms of a corporeality suited to the demands of efficiency. The zombie virus, however, reveals the darker side to this biopower. Though epidemics are a core concern of such biopolitics, this one proves impossible to micromanage or control, yet such faultlines are inscribed into the biopolitical project as such. The flip side of survival, thus, is genocide and warfare, or – to reach beyond Foucault's 20th century focus – the death of migrants in the seas of the Mediterranean and at borders erected through the American continents, as some lives are deemed not only less "grievable" (Butler 2009) in a discursive sense, but also assigned to death through the workings of biopower. The violent reality of Foucault's paradox "massacres have become vital" (1990, 137) equates survival with competition and mutual exclusion, as life is either fostered and micromanaged in minute detail, or disallowed to the point of death. "Mustn't humanize them" (Whitehead 2012, 158) is thus the mantra of the lieutenant in charge of the zombie hunt. Only by disavowing that all zombies stem from the darkness within, having metamorphosed and grown from within human communities and families, can the shooter's logic and his unquestionable power of distinction be upheld.

Deep within the violent silence of the zombie, however, lie also the seeds for a notion of the human liberated from the Western, bounded self with its thirst for mastery. As is to be expected, for Whitehead's zombies this path from breakdown to breakthrough is warped and shot through with bloody irony. Yet beneath the deadly spectacle a future-oriented challenge awaits, as the zombie channels human nature away from the illusionary securities of disembodied reason and towards a 'becoming-animal' – or, as Mark Spitz, Whitehead's protagonist puts it with succinct nihilism – "Fuck it. You have to learn how to swim sometime" (Whitehead 2012, 259).

The posthuman, in this zombified sense, spells the end of 'Man' and searches for more humane modes of being human. To be clear: The zombie is not a hallmark of societal renewal, and neither does it embody a participatory bio-ethics. But its nature is more complex than notions of pure apocalyptic breakdown alone would allow. In its genocidal impulses, it re-enacts the history of Western civilization. Yet its corporeal intensities suggest a non-dual mode of being, and ultimately, this is why the zombie eludes the neoliberal mechanisms of biocontrol. It opens up a space beyond the one-way-street of the neoliberal transhuman, a tabula rasa to be re-coded and re-inhabited in order to create more ethically viable posthuman lives. The Bakhtinian grotesque, with its chimeras and upside down worlds, its gaping mouths and walking dead, is a similarly pregnant death: it carries the seeds of a new beginning within. The zombie apocalypse is the step onto the dark plank before taking the plunge, away from the logic of the neoliberal and toward the unknown. The posthuman as I will explore it in this chapter, therefore, is viscerally embodied, but not bounded.

The tragedy of Whitehead's vision, one might say, is not the violence of the zombie, or even the world lost to the virus. It is a failure of the imagination, a sense of being stuck in the Foucauldian doublebind that posits genocide or survival as the only two viable options in a stark vision of a present without a future. After all, even when realizing that the "world wasn't ending: it had ended and now they were in the new place" (Whitehead 2012, 320), no one can think of better plans that have characterised human attempts of control – and their failures – for centuries; they build walls and eliminate the other.

In what remains of this chapter, I develop an understanding of the posthuman which offers ways out of this doublebind. Disinterested in 'transhumanity,' I do not seek perfectibility or biotechnological enhancement. If I seek out the seeds for such a breakthrough also in feminist science fiction in what follows, there is a simple reason for this: what is considered 'mainstream' science fiction – one example of which, *Bladerunner*, will feature in my discussion just below – tends to project the genocidal violence of the human past into the future as star wars. I doubt, though, that perpetuating the patriarchal narrative that reduces history to a cycle of arms races, conquest, demise and renewed weapons proliferation can generate any future-oriented modes of posthuman life on a planet that is already wounded enough. Feminist science fiction is neither docile nor innocent; it is written from the war zone – often, female bodies are the war zone – but it offers a position beyond that of the soldier.

The posthuman as I understand it places the body back into the centre of existence, but in ways that emphasize its connectivities, exchanges and transformative potentials with other human and non-human matter and bodies. This interlinked nature of the posthuman is its Diatopian impulse, opening to the non-human, but without yearning for superhuman or more-than-human augmentation. If one wanted to employ spatial metaphors, such a Diatopian reading of the body and the way in which it appropriates, subverts or evades biopolitical regulation can be described as a ' horizontal' vision of the posthuman: it is interested in how the posthuman body is embedded in ecologies and in dialogue with organic and non-organic matter; this is about envisioning the future, but not in the conventional 'vertical' manner that leads up into space or that relies on teleological notions of the arrow of time. Imagining the future is perhaps the most crucial precondition of any political thought. Yet it requires a fundamental re-think of the agent of political change, the human itself, in order to move towards the future instead of getting stuck in this double-bind between breakdown and perfectibility, two visions which preclude the future.

Cyberpunk Breakdowns

Yet what is this non-docile posthuman body that might be the agent of change and the creative force of a world beyond biopower? Unlike the zombie, the female body in mainstream science fiction, at first sight, seems neither attuned to breakdown nor promising breakthroughs; the posthuman, so it seems, is the ultimate playground fantasy of a misogynist imagination in which women are perfected to satisfy men's pleasures in a genre marked by what Carlen Lavigne describes as its early "complicity with 1980s conservatism" that was "inextricably marked by patriarchal subtext" (2013, 22). When attending to cyberpunk female bodily natures in their often artificially engineered flesh, though, it becomes possible to read against the grain of the narrative of white, male and middle-class dominance in imaginations of the future. The biotechnologically produced body grates and shapeshifts to subvert the smooth encoding that was supposed to ensure its docility.

This only intensifies in dystopian fictional universes that envisage breakdown. "The world is built on a wall, it separates kind" is how Lt Joshi, a high-ranking officer in the fight between humans and non-humans, describes the dystopian world of *Bladerunner 2049* (Villeneuve 2017). For her, walls ensure a desperate survival as the impending apocalypse increases the defensive impulse to fixate life into seemingly controllable categories. On the one side stand the 'replicants,' androids virtually identical to humans were it not for their inability to procreate, to feel emotions, and a drastically shortened lifespan implemented to keep it that way. Created as slaves, they are now banished to live off-world but rebel and return to unsettle the lethal mission of the human 'bladerunners,' specialist executioners whose job it is to hunt down rogue replicants. This futuristic biopower, therefore, is paradoxically of the pre-modern sort, attempting to control non-docile bodies not by regulation but by sheer genocidal force. Yet this wall between humans and non-humans is porous. Not only are the eponymous bladerunners, (Deckard in the original 1982 version and K in the 2017 follow-up) replicants themselves, albeit unawares. Replicants can also develop emotions when living long enough, breaking through the crumbling wall erected on the assumption that interiority is what makes humans singular.

In a universe locked into the seemingly inevitable inter-species war that follows, commodity status is assigned with increasing rigidity to solidify what is actually a fluid species constellation. This affects female figures in particular. When *Bladerunner* protagonist Rachel realizes that she is, in fact, not human but one of the 'replicants' engineered into enslavement, she poignantly summarizes her role in the Tyrell Corporation: "I am the business." This commodification escalates in the figure of Pris, a 'basic pleasure model' Nexus-6 replicant, who has been explicitly designed to satisfy demands for prostitutes. Both are trapped in different dimensions of a power structure that creates and 'retires' life according to its docility, and Pris will in due course pay for her resistance at the hands of Deckard. For Rachel this containment is less viscerally sexual, but no less effective, as she remains trapped in male-centered fantasies of romantic love. This is at no point as apparent as in the alleged love scene between her and Deckard, in which she remains symbolically imprisoned by the bar-like shadows cast on her in the glim light; she initially resists his attempts to kiss her, but succumbs to his requests for romance: his demand "do you love me?" triggers an "I love you," his question "Do you trust me" is echoed by "I trust you." Yet the mechanical natures of these responses signals that she remains commodified, tasked with responding to male desires. Such tropes are taken to the extreme in *Bladerunner 2049*, where disembodied, ethereal hologram girls, who shapeshift from 1950s housewife to sexy modern women at the man's click, are asked to merge with embodied prostitutes for sex, overlaying the prostitutes' female body with their AI shape individually tailored to perfection.

However, the women's apparent docility is deceptive. Female posthumans are, in fact, key breakthrough figures for imagining a posthuman existence that is more future-oriented than the zombies' nihilism. They experiment with modes of subverting the toxicity of patriarchal biopower, offering glimpses of an alternative embodied existence out of the bladerunner's reach. After all, Rachel and Pris both unsettle the order that created them. Pris' resistance operates in the mode of a visceral irony. She employs her masks of helpless homeless girl, or objectifiable gothic doll, to play on various male characters' sentiments and lure them into positions from which she can strike her counterattack, together with her group of escaped replicants. Rachel, on the other hand, subverts the power structures which created her more subtly. She unnerves Deckard's sense of his own humanity (and thus superiority) when he runs the Voight-Kampff test on her, questioning his ability to truly tell the difference besides humans and replicants. A liminal figure between human and non-human life, she exerts an erotic pull on him that leads him to join her in the borderline space she inhabits, as it is increasingly clear that he – the professional killer of replicants – is in fact a replicant himself.

Yet this unsettling effect is not necessarily a product of a willed resistance. It stems from their existence as hybrid bodies, which enable figures like Pris or Rachel to play with their own liminal nature using masks and disguises that are, in the end, nothing less and more than the offshoots of their multiple existences as outcasts, sex objects, and underground agents; yet even more to the point, it is their ability to merge with each other that ultimately makes them uncontainable to the male interests who are hunting and desiring them. The sex scene between K and the merger of female hologram and replicant body is also the point at which he loses control of both. Entwined into one, the embodied replicant hisses to the hologram women "I've been inside you. Not so much there as you think," triggering her desire to become mortal but embodied, too, a wish that will set her free from her console trap. This is no coincidence, as the replicant herself is a resistance fighter in an army of replicants, fighting for their own liberty, and will ultimately rescue K, who is a replicant himself. Merging, thus, engenders resistance.

These interbleeding bodies radicalize the cyborg in a political, not technological, sense. Their visionary force comes from liberating the cyborg from the logic of exclusion – and often slavery – into which it is inscribed. Yet the phrases that K, a bladerunner, compulsively repeats in these texts are symptomatic: "Dreadfully distinct" "in cells interlinked." The women with their hybrid and merged bodies are therefore the pioneering agents of a subversively cross-border reality that is embedded in the depths of the system itself. Entwined in a virtual network of memories and dream figures (albeit engineered), the replicants seduce and ensnare those humans clinging to the slippery certainties of species singularity. Interestingly, the solitude of the neoliberal rat race has no traction for them, as their minds are melded together. The programming originally designed to subjugate them in the most literal form of brainwashing, implanting personal memories that are actually manufactured, has backfired. Looking out into the night, Roy, Pris' lover and both the most violent and most disturbed of them all, bursts out into poetry: "I've seen things people wouldn't believe [. . . all] these moments will be lost in time like tears in the rain time to die." The tests designed to tell replicant from human would implode had they registered this, programmed, as they are, to attribute poetic imagination to humans only.

Ultimately, the replicants' creative force originates in their own illegitimacy. Daughters of the Tyrell corporation's bio-engineering though they may be, they have left behind the kind of loyalty to the humanist myths of original unity and bounded selfhood that leads to the inevitable zombie breakdown. In her 1991 "Cyborg Manifesto," Donna Haraway introduced this notion of the cyborg as the "illegitimate offspring of militarism and patriarchal capitalism" (Haraway 1991, 151), and her work continues to inspire a posthuman lexicon of transformation, hybridity and the imagination to replace the vocabulary of brutality, death and perfection. This notion of illicit descent offers an alternative vision and a bio-ethical view of the posthuman beyond the one -way-street of regulatory neoliberal regimes. Disinterested in their own primordial nature, and instead engaged in constant transformation and reciprocal change, such cyborgs break through the notion that being born into a docile body (or engineered as one) is a destiny to be fulfilled even if this fulfillment means apocalypse. When Haraway suggests that cyborg bodies are "monstrous" in a double sense of combining both organic and non-organic or machine matter, as well as 'de'monstr'ating' (Haraway 2016, 2) and thus signifying alternative biopolitical visions, she changes the register from breakdown to breakthrough.

In the 21st century, encountering reality has become a question of connectivity, and whilst Fredric Jameson diagnosed that the world of late capitalism is not one of deep emotion, it is certainly one of spreading mental states; yet there is actually no reason to assume that depth and dispersal are mutually exclusive. Tellingly, it is not the humans with their walls and bladerunners, but the replicants who are on top of this game of interconnection. Not only do they share memories, but in their android re-incarnation in the 2017 version, they merge bodies and personalities with other beings. There is no innocence to them, but that is besides the point. Needy for connection, they strive for survival, each disillusioned about being themselves the chosen, born one that proves their humanity, but united in the belief that one of them will be. These posthuman female bodies, therefore, offer agencies and modes of existence beyond the male biopower (and male-centered narrative) that seeks to contain them. Circulating, fluid and borderless, they navigate the experience of being digital, animal and human, creating undocile and uncontrollable bodily existences for posthuman times.

Their 'cells interlinked' sow the seeds of resistance even in the apparently docile bodies of hologram prostitutes. When it comes to imagining un-containable bodies, though, there is a limit to this blockbuster imagination, anchored as it remains in heterosexual reproduction and original – often near-biblical – fantasies of 'a child of woman born' as the ultimate marker of being human and thus, by implication, worthy of freedom. In the *Bladerunner* universe, what it means to be human thus remains steeped in heterosexual reproduction. The hybrid replicant existence is here valued only when leads back towards a humanity marked by vague notions of bounded souls and the ability to experience emotions – developed in the replicants already. Ultimately, however, it is a soldier's values, "dying for the right course is the most human there is," that this humanity boils down to in the words of the replicant army. The struggle between cyborgs and humans, therefore, is also a conflict between two different modes of being: the interconnected are subverting the violence of hierarchical order. They do so totally without moral purity, of course. "The cyborg would not recognize the garden of Eden" (Haraway 1991, 151), as Haraway puts it, but the *Bladerunner* replicants cannot quite fulfil the radical promise that inheres in this:

> [I]t is not made of mud and cannot dream of returning to dust. Perhaps that is why I want to see if cyborgs can subvert the apocalypse

of returning to nuclear dust in the manic compulsion to name the enemy.

(Haraway 1991, 151)

These replicants are too rooted in a logic of mutual competition and exclusion, seeking to prove their humanity by military means, to fully work as conceptual metaphor for an imagination beyond the apocalypse. The replicant existence, defined by vertical interbleedings instead of origin myths, suggests a mode of being that is creatively potent and offers a subversive alternative to the zero-sum game of life which defines humanity in this dystopia. It is typical for such a mainstream science fiction imagination, however, to run scared of its own creatures, and to shut down their futuristic potential in the name of a unitary selfhood engaged in constant combat.

Beginning Breakthroughs: Schizo-Analysing the Posthuman

To seek out life that is truly beyond biopower, and not merely resistant to it, further breakthroughs need to occur. The idea of a unified self, whether cyborg, replicant or human, hurtled by its inherent death-wish towards the apocalypse along an arrow of linear time leaves little room for alternative modes of being. Enter the peripheral subject.

> She didn't remember sitting up but then she saw her own hands and they weren't. Hers. [. . .] A mirror. Flynne moved toward it. "Holy shit," she said, staring. "Who is she?"
> "We don't know."
> "This is a . . . machine?" She touched . . . someone. Stomach. Breasts. She looked in the mirror. [. . .] "That's got to be somebody," she said.
>
> (Gibson 2014, 177)

Set in a not-so-distant future in which neoliberalism has gone rampant, William Gibson's protagonist Flynne Fisher inhabits a world of "predatory trading algorithms" (Gibson 2014, 270) in a small town somewhere in the United States where jobs are scarce, unless you count illegal drug manufacture. Yet in what seems to be an inescapably dystopian setting, Flynne is thrown into a nodal point where alternative realities (and time zones) converge. Her present has just been colonized retrospectively, from the future. Being a man of means, Lev Zubov, who lives about 70 years on in a dystopian London, has acquired a suitably expensive hobby. Via the enigmatic workings of an unspecified Chinese server, he has managed to access a 'stub.' This is Flynne's present and part of his past. Like the tail end of a worm which, once separated, wriggles into existence on its own, this stub will now develop its own time continuum (Gibson 2014, 103). Lev has used – or abused – her brother Burton as his "polt," an unsuspecting entrypoint to "dick around" with their world, as Flynne pointedly puts it. Flynne therefore finds herself at a perilous friction point between two different time continua that are not linear, but divergent. With the "jackpot" impending, a climate of catastrophe that preceded the futuristic London of *The Peripheral*, this interruption of linear time is an opening towards agency and change. In Gibson's futuristic London, after all, democracy is dead, and with it the idea that people are decision-makers. Whatever political will remains is dispersed in networks of oligarchs and surveillance machinery, a world that is only seemingly depthless but in fact saturated with the machinations of the powers-that-be, the aptly termed "klepts" (short for kleptocracy, a rule-by-thieves), who perpetuate a world where "terror should remain the sole prerogative of the state" (Gibson 2014, 144). All individuals can do is to keep their heads down, swallow the cognitive therapy modules, and try to keep their defences up otherwise. As the artist Daedra shows, life itself becomes a product. She has developed the habit of removing and replacing her own epidermis once it is fully tattooed, for it to be displayed and sold. The skin-turned-commodity is a key metaphor: this is an existence that is widely distributed across bodies and modules, yet this flatness is strategic, hiding the lurking untold history of the 'jackpot', a climate of catalytic events that killed the about 80% of the population, in an enhanced environment in which all alleged mediocrities, among which counts the past, have been systematically erased.

Yet in this predatory setting, Flynne's body refuses to become prey to the biopower of a government that weaponizes its Marine soldiers' bodies. When her world's colonizers realize that they inadvertently made her the sole witness to a politically motivated murder via drone, they provide her a peripheral body to travel into their future. This tele-presence avatar is infused with Artificial Intelligence and mind-controlled remotely in a future in which embodiment has become "protean" (Gibson 2014, 455). Once she inhabits this body, though, she leaves traces of her own individuality on its expressions, with an effect that is noticeably uncanny. It offers flexibility and, by defamiliarizing herself from herself, enables her to "not be at home in her home" (2005, 39), an Adornian beginning of an ethical position in a brutally unethical world. Gibson here plays the ethical and political impact of different modes of posthuman cyborg *bios* against each other. Whereas her brother and most of his friends had given their bodies in the Marines to be turned into "some kind of drone" (Gibson 2014, 140), she navigates the peripheral body with more agency. Getting "damaged," not injured, as humanoid weapons by an intangible government in an undefined war, these veterans perpetuate the cycle of violence in a replicant-like fixation on seemingly inescapable cycles of violence. Severely disabled, their "violence of action" (Gibson

2014, 140) is not only a symptom of trauma but, in its murderous forms, ensures the persistence of systemic violence. Flynne, on the other hand, uses her own bodily estrangement to prevent the ecological, social and political meltdown of the 'jackpot.' "A schizophrenic out for a walk is a better model than a neurotic lying on the analyst's couch" (Deleuze and Guattari 1983, 2), and Flynne's complete disaffection with depression, trauma or the apocalypse gives her a position from which to re-see her world and its possible future, and envision possibilities of agency and change.

It is the peripheral subject, therefore, that enables the human body to become a site of life instead of an impact zone of biopower. "On the periphery, forever decentered, defined by the states through which it passes" (Deleuze and Guattari 1983, 20), Deleuze and Guattari's schizophrenic subject has long left the oedipal fixations of the replicants, forever hunting their father, behind. A body without organs, this liberates the posthuman from the loop of creation, emancipation, and deathly termination because it is uncontainable to biocontrol. This de-centered body is not a contained system of organs, but a zone of intensity, and thus is the absolute opposite to Moravec's disembodied, portable mind or transhuman desires for perfection. When Deleuze and Guattari figure this as an egg, "crisscrossed with axes and thresholds, with latitudes and longitudes and geodesic lines, traversed by *gradients* marking the transitions and becomings" (Deleuze and Guattari 1983, 19), it becomes apparent that this is the transversal, Diatopian body in its most fundamental form. Despite the abstract language used to conceive it, it is radically embodied to the point of being non-representative; "it is all life and lived experience: the actual, lived emotion of having breasts does not resemble breasts, it does not represent them, any more than a predestined zone in the egg resembles the organ that it is going to be stimulated to produce" (Deleuze and Guattari 1983, 19). Matter, here, becomes passed-through and nomadic, attuned to stimulation and emergence but disinterested in any notion of a creator. It does not resist power, like the replicant rebel against the Tyrell corporation, but rather makes power an irrelevance. This is offers a biopolitics that craves neither servitude nor tranquilization, acknowledging no leader and refusing to shape itself into any image.

In her peripheral embodiment, Flynne becomes the schizophrenic surplus product of capitalism. This surplus quality of a more-than is key to the political impact of such nomadic corporealities. While "the deliberate creation of lack" in a market economy is the "art of a dominant class" (Deleuze and Guattari 1983, 28), the desire that drives Flynne into the future does not originate in an experience of lack, but seeks change. Unlike the traumatic fixation to violence experienced by her weaponized veteran friends, Flynne does not acknowledge the perverted, lack-driven desire of men who "fight for their servitude as stubbornly as men who fight for their salvation" (Deleuze and Guattari 1983, 29). In her dispersed bodies, Flynne scrambles these pre-given codes.

The dispersed corporeality created by the information flow between present and non-linear future thus symbolizes a way out of the tyranny of the past. This schizophrenic state of being radicalizes when shifting the focus from Flynne to some of the novel's other cross-temporal character constellations. Near-future agents Griff Holdsworth and Clovis Raeburn on the one hand, and the distant-future characters Clovis Fearing and Ainsley Lowbeer on the other hand, have the same way of delicately arranging food, the same hands, yet inhabit opposed sides of the jackpot and differently gendered bodies. In *The Peripheral*, it is not just time that forks off. Personhood itself becomes transversal, as Griff and Clovis Raeburn enter into communication with their own future selves who have diverged as the continuum of causality split. "This is no longer their past, so she isn't who I'll become," (Gibson 2014, 422), as Griff puts it, yet their doubled condition gives them doubled agency in counteracting the jackpot at least for the continuum they now inhabit. Their personalities are folded in the Deleuzian sense, as inside and outside, self and other become co-extensive. While Griff deplores that "there is a way in which I lack agency, in all of this" (Gibson 2014, 378), it is precisely this posthuman dialogicity which restores their power to act against the political, ecological and economic corruption of their world. As dispersed selves who do not recognize the myth of a lost wholeness, whether Freudian or in terms of Ash's nostalgic neoprimitivism, they are empowered by the opportunities for dialogue in rhizomatic temporal spaces, navigating the contact points between diverging and converging past, present and future linearities. Against the idea of colonization, they interweave their co-dependencies and patterns of implication. Thus enriched with future thoughts, the cyborg body develops an ethics akin to Donna Haraway's "response-ability" (Haraway 2016, 2) indicating both the ability and duty to respond and be responsive.

Crediting her actions to her "strata of archaic self-determination" (Gibson 2014, 381) alone, however, would mean misunderstanding the conditions of political agency in this novel. Flynne is an implicated subject, and does not experience or seek to be above events as they unfold, manipulating them as a puppetmaster would. Identifying fully with the events as they emerge, her agency is both radically immanent and responsive to the virtual. Both acting and acted upon by the future powers, her acts are a 'counter-actualization' in a Deleuzian sense, a process that is much more expressive and affirmative than the idea of 'resistance' with its connotations of negation. When she immerses herself in her peripheral posthuman body, there is an extent to which she gives herself up to a process in which she is subject and object simultaneously. Her agency, therefore, can only become possible by departing from the idea of the self as master. Yet in doing so, she manages to twist the expected outcome – slow and painful extinction in the 'jackpot' – into a different logic. Ultimately, this is why her capacity to re-see the world is significant, and it is equally consequential that she acquired this in an immersive video game. Going through a loss of control is the key to this posthuman notion of agency, which stems not from a sublimated subject, but from its actualizing power within a Deleuzian plane of immanence in which life is coextensive with itself and thus not un-, but impersonal.

Going forward, however, is only possible when not clinging to the iron ball of the past, yet such a future orientation is paradoxically made impossible in capitalist temporal constellations. On the surface, the capitalist logic seems to affirm a teleological worldview, with time an arrow leading towards greater wealth. "The temporal disposition of economic actors" in capitalism is, as Beckert explains, always orientated "towards the future" (Beckert 2016, 2). Yet this requires imaginaries of the future to work towards. Beckert continues to explore how capitalist actors thus create narratives to sell future states of the world (or your body, or world finance), creating causal links to speculative futures. Capitalism thus is built on the logic of the "as if," with the consequence of a "doubling of reality" (Luhmann 2000, 1). This doubling, though, is not just a doubling of empirically verifiable reality and imaginary states. It also describes how the present overlays the future, as these imagined scenarios are built on present-day conditions. Perhaps this is why any zombie-style capitalist breakdown only leads to further affirmation of the capitalist order – there is a failure to imagine the future as different from the present. The time of science fiction offers and alternative view: constellational instead of linear, and shot through with tropes of time travel, it offers a conceptual metaphor for how the trauma of the apocalypse can become infused with futurity.

In this cross-temporal, dialogic sense the posthuman and its dispersed identities thus offers a mode to infuse the implicated subjecthood of contemporary trauma with agency, precisely because it makes apparent the need to step into what Esposito calls the mode of the "third person" (Esposito 2012). Perhaps trauma studies of the future needs to question what constitutes a 'person' in a more radical manner, beyond negotiating stages of porosity, addressability, or enlightened boundedness. Embracing the posthuman is a mode of introducing the exteriority of the impersonal in order to develop practices that alter current existences by adopting a transversal, transindividual domain. In the philosophy of Deleuze and Guattari, this impersonal force, for instance in the "body without organs," becomes life, making it possible to envisage a more affirmative biopolitics that is not simply defined by the enforcement of power on an individual to be traumatized, but seeks out opportunities to traverse and displace these power structures. In this sense, being human implies not being bounded but being coextensive with other lives and bodies, as Flynne illustrates. As a subject, she does not become inert or passively receptive, but is endowed with the ability to counter-actualize what personhood means. When unchained from the search for singular, bounded and secure personhood, traumatized subjectivity becomes a mode of folding back what it means to be human onto the power patterns of a predatory world.

Gibson's science fiction universe thus re-defines biopower, the power of life itself, by using the enabling forces of a peripherally dispersed, nomadic selfhood, demonstrating that ideas about posthuman trauma do not necessarily lead into a world of disembodied, glib perfectibility. Even the peripheral bodies which Gibson's protagonists inhabit are defined by friction, however much their exterior sheen might be engineered to detract from this. With a focus on agency instead of victimhood, this constellational temporality offers a vision of a less precarious future beyond the seeming inevitability of a neoliberal apocalypse. This emphasis on two-way processes and dialogicity is an alternative to the cycle of violence that turns the traumatized into perpetrators.

Bodies Beyond Control: Transcorporeal Cyborg Feminism

We have now seen how the posthuman body can become a site of resistance to a neoliberal biopolitics that demands docility. This resistance acknowledges vulnerability instead of polishing the sheen of appearances in fantasies of the transhuman, perfect body, seeks connection instead of transcendence, and is nourished by its own multiplicities. Most importantly, though, we have also begun to appreciate that the posthuman body, when its skin ceases to be an enclosing boundary and comes into its own as a transversal friction zone, challenges what it means to be a person per se. In his 2012 book *Third Person*, Roberto Esposito exposes how the idea of personhood continues to rely on differentiating between the subject and its biological being. Subjecthood is not coextensive with the body, but transcends it, be it from a religious perspective which affirms the possibility of an afterlife or from a secular perspective that emphasizes the *res cogitans*, the moral and rational elements of each human. This was the basis, for instance, for the Universal Declaration of 1948, as Jacques Maritain proposed to understand personhood as the "sovereignty" of each human being over their animal being (Esposito 2012, 12).

It is this distinction which enables Flynne to time-travel, but defining the person as that which, although inhabiting a body, is more than the body – through rarely questioned – has deep-seated ramifications. When looking for ways in which the posthuman can become a fully-fledged practice to break biopolitical constraints, two such consequences emerge: firstly it paradoxically implies "being subjected to one's own objectification" (Esposito 2012, 12), as the person becomes the sovereign over their animal body. Neoliberal mechanisms of biopolitical control perpetuate this link between personhood and ownership, as they objectify the body, measuring it in order to tame it; the person, in this sense, owns the body and is expected to groom it according to a pre-given set of ideals. Flynne's schizophrenic existence equally raises such questions, as she inhabits a peripheral body whose 'owner' is absent. Yet the posthuman in Donna Haraway's sense promises to be nomadic and escape the fixity of such calculations as it explores horizons of virtual possibilities, leaving us with a lingering sense that there is more to be explored in the imagination of the posthuman than the figures discussed thus far. Yet objectifying the body also produces a second set of beliefs: the assumption of gradation, or degradation, of various stages of personhood according to their distances to the animal or – in the case of the posthuman – the machine. This is why the violent universe of *Bladerunner* inextricably entwines the posthuman with the slave (a logic not dissimilar to the zombie figures in *Zone One*), as replicants are tools very much in an Aristotelian sense, who have yet to fight for acknowledgement of their own personhood.

The fictions I have discussed so far have suggested that posthuman figures can re-gain agency by establishing subversive connections. These undermine this hierarchical view of personhood to the point of folding it in on a schizophrenic, forked-off simultaneity between two different version of the same person in *The Peripheral*, making the person multiple instead of paying credence to the premise of unitary one-ness and singularity. Yet again, what remains to be seen is how the posthuman can step beyond even such experiments and leave behind the logic of (bio)power per se, to become fully embedded in *bios*, in life.

The 22nd century world which Larissa Lai builds in her 2018 novel *The Tiger Flu* opens a pathway for a posthuman, feminist imagination that escapes such limitations. In her cyberpunk fiction, the 'monstrosity' of posthuman life in Donna Haraway's sense signals biopolitical alternatives to a world in which biopolitics has turned into bioeconomics. Lai's universe lights up and darkens to the cosmic dance of moneyed interests, materialized in the world's two planets – fast-moving Chang and the slower Eng – which have replaced the natural cycles of the moon. The tangible pull of gravity which the "bloated, angry and sick" (Lai 2018, 56) Chang exudes on the denizens of Saltwater Flats, like Kora Ko, when he leans on the earth "way too intimately" (Lai 2018, 56) is of a corporate nature. Both Eng and Chang have been artificially launched into their circuits as sites of evacuation for humanity, in a project of colonization which, as one of the key initiators puts it, "was meant to be a humanitarian one" (Lai 2018, 55).

On the rooftop terrace of her high-rise home, Kora Ko observes the movements of Eng and Chang above and the streets 40 stories below, in which women go about their daily business but which are empty of men, who remain shut up in their houses, coughing and dying from the tiger flu. This is a world in the last thrashes of the economy and ecology as we still know it; however, and intriguingly, this is also a breakdown of the patriarchal heterosexual reproductive order. While Kora is chatting to her pet goat – an indication of the entwinements between women and animals to come – a flu-stricken friend of her brother's, who has been preying on her, attempts to rape, infect and kill her in a last rash flare-up of misogynist violence. This scene is symptomatic not merely as a last outbreak of the patriarchal themes of cyberpunk, which Lai swiftly leaves behind. It also indicates that if posthumans are to truly seek out a new sense of agency, it is not enough to break through the bio-economic commodification of the body; beneath the encoded sheen awaits the deeper layer of the habitual oppression of female bodies. We have already seen that this is the marker of limitation for cyborg bodies in mainstream science fiction; for feminist cyberpunk authors like Lai, it is the departure point towards feminist posthuman figurations.

This corporate vision of posthuman life as escape route from a planet in which nearly all men are dying of the 'tiger flu' operates on the logic of verisimilitude and disembodiment. Yet not only are these uploads botched, offering survival but not a life of any depth of experience; the 'LiFT' uploads again, and paradoxically, make disembodiment the precondition of ultimate biocontrol. The clones and flu-ridden men who are the preferred test subjects to increase the verisimilitude to be experienced on those planets "have left their bodies and are held captive" (Lai 2018, 216), leaving their former opposition to the upload behind along with their bodies, even if – and particularly when – the upload is forced. "Alive of mind but heavy of body" (Lai 2018, 294) on the interface to Eng, Doctor Kirilow's mother, a woman who had preached against the lure of disembodiment to her community, comes back "changed, ever so slightly" (294).

This change, however, is significant; she has become manipulated to, in turn, manipulate her remaining daughter to join her in an existence she knows has drained her being when being stunted in the digital transfer. The gap between embodied and uploaded being, therefore, is the space the corporations inhabit to perpetuate their own interests. Made exploitable by disembodiment, this is the space that is politically potent; within an economically constituted loop that generates addictions to 'tiger wine,' which, in turn, fuels the feared tiger flu, thus providing a steady supply of humans desperate enough to choose upload or weak enough to be coerced, the political has thus effectively been shut down, creating an encompassing system in which life is not only cloneable, but in which becoming a docile corporate subject is the only chance of survival for most.

How to find any position of resistance in and to a world so cosmically defined by bioeconomic moneyed interests? In this radicalized allegory of neoliberal biocontrol, Lai explores how the smoothly encoded operation of disembodied uploads conflates the promise of survival with the creation of docile subjects; this suggests a need for friction against the logic of the code, which seeks complete translatability. Resistant posthuman bodies will need to "insist on noise and advocate pollution" (Haraway 1991, 176) to imagine a future that is free from teleological time and history, seeking connection rather than supremacy. Ultimately, this is a question of how to re-politicize the bodies that have become bioeconomic objects, infusing them with voice, agency, and a sense of shared value to seek a world of cohabitation in the ashes of corporate breakdown.

This feminist posthuman emerges from Lai's 'Grist' sisterhood. Originally created by a clone company linked to the upload operations, "bust [us] from their greasy bottles like so many cheap genies" (Lai 2018, 20), all women in this community share the DNA of their original mother. Nevertheless, their voices in the novel are grittily distinct, with personalities clashing, so that one key baseline of their biopolitical impact becomes immediately apparent: not only have they escaped the 'sister factories' and successfully established their own communities, adopting the knowledge of artificial reproduction to use for their own purpose and against the cloning corporations who continue to hunt them down as a perceived threat to be contained in the upload operations. In their bodies, a strong post-human interiority has become detached from DNA; although they are rooted in their original mother's genetic makeup, their own reproductive procedures transform this into a rhizomatic and horizontal mutational regrowth, instead of a line of ancestry that goes back in time.

Living in the forests and deeply immersed in the ecosystem they inhabit, the Grist sisters reproduce in a "long, lizardy love" (Lai 2018, 20) in which "one becomes two" (Lai 2018, 21). Living in triangulated communities of grooms, doublers and starfish, each sister offers her own body to be merged and shared with the others. While the grooms are doctors, caring for their starfish or doubler lovers, it is the doublers who can become pregnant with litters of several baby sisters to be breastfed and raised by all in the community. The groom's task, however, does not only encompass healing in the traditional sense. Because their DNA are limited, the Grist sisters mutate, for better or worse; in order to create more resilient and vital mutations and to counteract the ones detrimental to life, the grooms cut the starfish's bodies for transplants in an erotic, "sexy suture" (Lai 2018, 21). These transplants are a gift by the starfish to their sisters, which they are able to offer because of their ability to regrow any organs, salamander-like. Reproduction, therefore, operates by mutation and regrowth, creating bodies shared along multiple lines and which continue to be regrown, infused with other starfishes' offerings, throughout their lives. This lizard theme is a typical trope of feminist posthuman theory; Donna Haraway's cyborgs equally emerge from the generative re-growth of salamander limbs. This is no coincidence; such creative "bestiality" (Haraway 1991, 152) frees the posthuman from the chains of the myth of a male creator, whether heterosexually reproductive, biblically divine or biotech engineer. They are figurations of what Stacy Alaimo terms the "transcorporeal" (2010, 12) in which the environment becomes the basis of humane existence, thus suggesting and existence beyond Foucauldian regulatory regimes. Technologically enabled but animal-inspired, these Grist sisters transform the cyborg from a human-machine fusion to a triad of animal, human and engineered life, a posthuman vision that breaks through the dual nature of conventional human life.

In a universe of even more radical ecological collapse and corporate biotechnological control than *Bladerunner*, Lai's 'starfish' humans and cloned 'Grist' sisters offer a vision of posthuman existence that replaces heterosexual reproduction with various procedures of embodied sharing to generate new life. Their bodies – hybrids of biotechnological engineering, animal life, and human shape – offer a viable alternative to corporate attempts to 'upload' human life from a flu-infested planet, which would disembody life to make it manipulable and easier to control. This posthuman life is deeply bodily, but as genes and body parts are shared in a network of sisters instead of passed down in a line of ancestry, it remains dynamically changing and cannot be contained. Life evolved beyond the reach of biocontrol thus knows interiority and individuality, but no bounded selfhood. Operating rhizomatically instead of along unidirectional roots, such sisterhoods are uninterested in mythical origins or endings, and would not understand interspecies war. They therefore offer modes of being posthuman beyond the pull of the apocalypse.

This shift from notions of ancestral lineage to horizontal sisterhood mesh is central to the ways in which the posthuman imagination can escape the clutches of corporate control. Organised in communities tightly knit around their shared bodies and shared value systems of communal and ecological enmeshment, the Grist sisters' bodily natures give rise to the only politically consequential agency in Lai's fictional universe. Significantly, this is an existence that, though able to defend itself, has no place for the logic of two-way interspecies warfare that still defines the Bladerunner movies. As in Haraway's question "[W]hy should our bodies end at the skin?" (Haraway 1991, 178), these enmeshed bodies tap into the idea of interconnection that was much more widely spread in the earlier posthumanist discourses of the 1980s. Paul Churchland, for instance, speculated in 1981 about converting neural activity into a joint symphony between people, which would render unnecessary some aspects of what we consider literacy. It would also eliminate war.

But just because there is no sense of warfare does not mean there is no politics. The Grist community is lived resistance, a performance of alternatives to disembodied docility that relies not on ideology but on bodily matters. Responding and re-activating resistance to the prior discursive and regulatory assignments of bodies in a neoliberal biopolitical regime, the Grist sisters re-introduce the idea of an ethico-political agency that works from within inhabited bodies up. The embodied posthuman, therefore, does not negate the discursive construction of biopolitical power but seeks ways in which to empower matter to (as Stacy Alaimo proposes) "*act* in ways that jostle or jolt that very construction" (Alaimo 2000, 12). Diatopian posthumanism, thus, addresses the very basis for any change: the ability to imagine the future instead of merely managing its potential risks. This requires a posthumanism that seeks to overcome not the human body per se, but its dual and mutually exclusive nature.

If the imagination of an embodied posthumanism is therefore to take on biopolitical challenges, this requires an "ethics of mattering," as Karen Barad advocates, that "is not about right response to a radically exterior/ized other, but about responsibility and accountability for the lively relationalities of becoming of which we are part" (Barad 2007, 393). Such a body politics, however, is not distinct from or opposed to discursive and symbolic figurations; indeed, quite the reverse is the case, as the Grist sister's language is as heteroglossic as their bodies are multiple. Kirilow, a groom in the Grist community, thinks in bursts of rhythm and phrase that are shot through with the Saltwater City human's culture, entwining her own language with the culture that created, but also oppressed and exploited her own. In utmost concentration when cutting her starfish, who is relaxing in erotic pleasure, her voice begins to pulse with pop-culture tunes, "the first cut is the sleekest" (Lai 2018, 22).

Posthuman body politics, therefore, remain intrinsically entwined with language in the quest to replace the docilely operations of coding in both bodily and language-based matters. Lai's figures display a playful version of Haraway's "powerful infidel heteroglossia" of a "feminist speaking in tongues to strike fear into the circuits of the supersavers of the new right" (Haraway 1991, 181), but this playfulness is of a serious nature, as it taps into the energies of what Jean-François Lyotard defined as the "Inhuman" (1991). The alienating and commodifying effect of advanced capitalism on the human, to Lyotard, is of course primarily discursive, yet this language-based focus needs to be entwined with affective and bodily energies to generate a sense of political resistance. Lyotard thus explores a non-discursive, inner core of inhumanity which is non-rational and non-volitional; according to Lyotard, this is what makes us quintessentially human, but the humanity of this 'inhuman' is akin to what Deleuze describes as the becoming-animal of the human, acknowledging life as a process of becoming driven by desire. It is this doubling of the human into discourse and embodiment that makes it possible to tap into broader, more-than-human life forces as a site of resistance by humanity itself against the dehumanizing effects of technology-driven capitalism.

Like Donna Haraway's doubled cyborgs or Lai's Grist sisters, who simultaneously inhabit a coded matrix and sprout salamander- like limbs, it is the immanence of the posthuman subject which sustains friction. Disinterested in seeking to transcend the human body in the transhuman, self-glorifying narcissistic consciousness, Donna Haraway's cyborgs, Stacy Alaimo's transcorporeal bodies or Rosi Braidotti's posthuman subjects acknowledge that the life that sustains them does not, as Braidotti puts it, "bear your name" (Braidotti 2013, 138). It remains critical of housing the posthuman in extraterritorial (and extra-terrestrial) spaces. The posthuman subject is the post-humanist subject, in that it is nomadic and multiple instead of unitary, and relational instead of striving towards supremacy. In this sense, posthuman subjectivity becomes the basis of a new ethics; embodied and embedded, its perspective is always situated, thus expressing a "partial form of accountability, based on a strong sense of collectivity, relationality and hence community building" (Braidotti 2013, 49).

Bladerunner's Ridley Scott once said that he refuses to think in straight lines. This tumbled thinking offers an apt metaphor for the political significance of the sci-fi imagination: It is not about the end of man, or the progress of humanity. It is about reconfiguring connections to find alternative ways of being embodied in a post-capitalist world. Instead of craving wholeness, cyborg imaginations celebrate their own monstrosity, revelling in their own perversion of the capitalist logic whose illegitimate offspring they are. They are tricksters, chimeras. This is why they embody the reality we need to re-imagine towards a future of survival. It is a mixed, monstrous, mingling one. And despite the power-hungry craving for perfection that glimmered in the replicants' creator's eye, as all illegitimate offspring, the cyborgs are disloyal to their fathers. They are not interested in perfection, nor in totality, nor lured by the sheen of ultimate control, but this is precisely why "we can learn from our fusions with animals and machines how not to be Man, the embodiment of Western logos" (Haraway 1991, 173). To dance with the cyborgs means creating visions of shaping the future that do not inevitably end in apocalypse. Their monstrosity, their embodied matter and irony might be the way to go.

Feminist science fiction can thus open up possibilities for collective human agency beyond the tyranny of gradation, exclusion, and competition which give biopower its current ideological frame.

> I cut open my arm with the ceremonial obsidian knife I carried with me, and watched my blood drip into the channel carved into the stone for that purpose. Blood. The old people say it is the carrier of ancestral memories, and our future's promise. I am a child from the stars – a refugee, driven from my true home. My blood is red, an alien colour on this world. But I am lucky because this planet knows my name.
>
> (Amberstone 2015, 161f)

Celu Amberstone's refugees are displaced humans on a planet which, though foreign, harbours them as they feel the agonizing pain of Earth's complete implosion. Yet like most of the postcolonial science fiction collected in Nalo Hopkinson and Uppinder Mehan's anthology *So Long been Dreaming*, or imagined by writers such as Octavia Butler, she creates a posthumanism in which star wars or android rebellions have no place. The posthuman, here, is an imagination responsive to pain, yet it imagines healing not as a process of regaining any lost wholeness of the self. To the contrary, the blood which flows through the planet and the protagonist herself establishes a deep connection that is both physical and spiritual, thus describing healing as a pathway through symbiosis. This child from the stars is posthuman not because she is a space-traveller, in dialogue with aliens and is herself a cyborg, reliant on implants making cross-species communication possible; she is posthuman because she practices a human existence beyond the premises of ownership and hierarchy implied by personhood. An active member of her community, with deep emotional connections to her family and non-human surroundings, her life is impersonal in a sense that Esposito develops in dialogue with Deleuze: not de-individualized or anti-personal, but united with forces of life, *bios*, and uninterested in either power or sovereignty (Esposito 2012, 19). Exploring lives that are migratory, embodied and embedded at once, this is a common trope particularly – and perhaps unsurprisingly – in science fiction written by women.

Octavia Butler's novel *Dawn*, originally published in 1987 and republished as part of *Lilith's Brood*, already explored another such nomad's journey with a different species, learning to inhabit a spaceship that is coextensive with the aliens' themselves. Bodies shaped by tufts of sensors, these aliens teach the humans how to live nomadically and in symbiotically: "We serve the ship's needs and it serves ours. It would die without us and we would be planet-bound without it. For us, that would eventually mean death" (Butler 2007, 35). This link between being a nomad and being in symbiosis is key from a biopolitical point of view, because it envisions intelligent life without paying credence to any notion of hierarchy, which Butler's alien explicitly compares to a cancerous growth which entrenches human intelligence, leading it on a path to self-destruction. Both these instances of the posthuman, thus, are sensitive to the pitfalls of understanding personhood in terms of body ownership, and seek to explore instead forms of existence which do not seek power over life, but are embedded in *bios* and move with its forces. This is imagined even more radically, perhaps, in Devorah Major's "Trade Winds." "We are always home," (Major 2015, 183) is the phrase with which Enrishi, inhabitant of a space ship, introduces herself to a slightly perplexed human translator, and like Octovia Butler's aliens, her species are travellers. As Donna Haraway's cyborgs who relish in the end of Edenic origins, Enrishi requires neither homeland nor ancestry. Life, for her, flows in crossing streams, joining "the waves and eddies that link the stars" (Major 2015, 191), a rhizome of encounters liberated from roots. Her communication as well is open, and the metaphor of rocks, so often used to evoke a sense of stability, for her equals entrapment. "Our words are trapped in rocks" (Major 2015, 188), she explains once she realizes that her cross-species communication with the human Jonah is imploding. The moment of this breakdown is important, too. Jonah has been instructed to trade for water, yet his efforts to negotiate a price are foreign and incomprehensible to Enrishi, for whom all life is reciprocal trade – "As we give so we are given" (Major 2015, 188) – yet based on symbiotic exchange, not exchange value. This crucial difference not only makes this tale, like the other science fiction texts just mentioned, an implicit critique of neoliberalism. It also reveals the full extent of impersonal life in this imagined world, as the exchange of water not only involves droplets absorbed through Enrishi's skin, but ultimately Jonah, whose body is to a large extent made of water, is himself exchanged and moves to Enrishi's space ship, though not entirely voluntarily. As in all these texts, Major explores how such impersonal, symbiotic existences jar with the idea of individual free will. This is not a painless process, yet all these science fiction texts assume that such a change is necessitated by the destructive impact which conventional ideas of personhood have on human and planetary existence itself. Refugees from a world they themselves burnt, the return to *bios* marks the end of the sublimated individual and its entry into the posthuman.

In these texts, the posthuman has morphed from visions of perfection, so easily exploited by mechanisms of control, to a fluid life that knows forcefields, energies and encounters, but on which hierarchical power has lost its grip. These posthuman bodies know not the boundaries of skin, the nature of which Enrishi struggles to even grasp until she describes it as "bark" (Major 2015, 191). Thus they allow us to think the posthuman as a "body without organs," though tenderly and without the recourse to the sadomasochist intensities of pain which Deleuze and Guattari rely on to introduce what initially seems like one of their more elusive concepts (Deleuze and Guattari 1987, 153). Like these alien species, the body without organs is a practice of circulation, movement, and coming to pass, "nothing more than a set of valves, locks, floodgates, bowls, or communication vessels," (Deleuze and Guattari 1987, 153), unformed and unstratified. Re-imagining he human body as a field of waves, vibrations, migrations and thresholds – a "zone of intensity" (Deleuze and Guattari 1987, 156) is the absolute opposite to Moravec's disembodied, portable mind or transhuman desires for perfection. Though the body without organs screams out "They've wrongfully folded me!" (Deleuze and Guattari 1987, 159) at the idea of being a unitary organism, it does so not because it disdains corporeal being. What it fears, like Major's Enrishi or Octavia Butler's be-tentacled beings, is being a subject, "nailed down" (Deleuze and Guattari 1987, 159). Imagining the future without repeating the past, therefore, means re-imaging human life per se, shifting the focus from bio-power to participation in *bios*. From an ethical point of view, these transversal posthuman bodies become sites of addressability and response-ability beyond the clear-cut distinction between self and other. The posthuman self as intensity suggests a non-dual mode of being, and ultimately, this is why it eludes the neoliberal mechanisms of biopower. As in the encounter between Enrishi and Jonah, the embedded posthuman body lives on a different plane from the unitary subjecthood of current Western thought, liberating it from the need to articulate either opposition or adherence to the notions of perfectibility. The posthuman in this sense is neither resistance nor apocalypse, but a true alternative.

Conclusion: Cells Interlinked

At the beginning of the 20th century, Mina Loy suggested to think of "life as a Deific Electricity" (Loy 2011, 240), open to erotic, light, electric vibrations. This thought experiment entwines *eros* and electricity as the base currents of existence and pitches them against man's "Domination over all things" (Loy 2011, 237). Her work demonstrates how long of a tradition this kind of posthumanism has, smoothly interlinking organic life and electro-magnetic currents, yet it also highlights even more starkly how dangerously any posthumanism continues to be marginalized if it does not pay credence to the premises of a competitive race for ultimate optimization. Despite a century of feminist deviation from the 'cogito ergo sum,' the mainstream imagination continues to reduce itself to cyborgs polished into docility. Yet this is precisely where the political impact of the posthuman, with its potential to re-imagine human existence as something that is not bent on performing its own destruction, is at its most provocative and powerful. These futuristic human species make visible a different version of being human: not one that has lost all depth, as Jameson diagnosed for late capitalism. The terror of development and progress, after all, is also inhuman in another sense, in its violent dismissal of anything that does not fit its sleek narrative. But one that turns its back to the tyranny of flattened-out living and shows no interest in establishing ever more complex systems of differentiation in a desperate attempt to uphold the embattled narcissism of human exclusivity. The reason why Donna Haraway offers the cyborg to the oppressed, the disenfranchised, and the silenced to code, is that in a world glorifying strength and health, vulnerability has become the site from which to see things differently. In the end, it is no coincidence that all these texts have an element of trauma in them. In the anguish underneath, the inexplicable desires disrupting our thoughts, the minds haunted, agitated, delirious with unknown senses, is where this posthumanism begins.

These texts also offer an alternative to the "neoliberal circle" (Huehls 2016, 4), which critics like Huehls deplore, and which describes the grasp of neoliberalism on representation to be so totalizing as to make it impossible to represent things otherwise. Against such a surrender of both critique and the imagination, searching for the impersonal as a marker of the posthuman opens our perspective to the transformative power of literature. Roberto Esposito describes how impersonal modes – be it as the neuter or the third person – are at the heart of literary writing. The writer, he argues, delegates the power to say "I" to the characters, relinquishing the authorial hold in favour of a multiplicity of third persons (Esposito 2012, 130).

The texts explored in this chapter, and particularly in its last section, thus not only explore the posthuman as a conceptual idea and object of interest. They also perform it, not only thinking about the posthuman, but thinking as if posthuman and thus impersonal, multiple, and flowing. "But literature takes the opposite path," as Gilles Deleuze argues, existing "only when it discovers beneath apparent persons the power of an impersonal" (Deleuze 1998, 3). This impersonal might be symbolized in the joint bloodstream between refugee and host planet, or in the inter-linked cells of replicant artifice; whichever form it takes, it embeds the human into the multiplicity of life, rescuing it from the need to immunize until life becomes mere survival. The posthuman in this sense is thus not only a more ecologically sustainable version of human existence; it also makes it possible to imagine life in a way that does not inscribe all human existence into the trauma of separation and lack. The politics symbolized by the wall which the humans in *Bladerunner* feel it necessary to erect, mirrored by the nation-state borders from within which many are content to watch others on the outside die, can thus be countered by a politics that acknowledges the implicated and interconnected nature of human life. The posthuman, in this sense, spells the end of 'Man.' Considering the latter's talent for self-destruction, this imagination of the future spells out opportunities that we cannot afford to ignore.

References

Alaimo, Stacy. 2000. *Undomesticated Ground: Recasting Nature as Feminist Space*. Ithaca and London: Cornell University Press.
Alaimo, Stacy. 2010. *Bodily Natures. Science, Environment, and the Material Self*. Bloomington, IN: Indiana University Press.
Amberstone, Celu. 2015. "Refugees." In *So Long Been Dreaming: Postcolonial Science Fiction and Fantasy*, edited by Nalo Hopkinson and Uppinder Mehan, 161–82. Vancouver: Arsenal Pulp Press.
Barad, Karen. 2007. *Meeting the Universe Halfway: Quantum Physics and the Entanglement of Matter and Meaning*. Durham, NC: Duke University Press.
Beckert, Jens. 2016. *Imagined Futures: Fictional Expectations and Capitalist Dynamics*. Cambridge, MA: Harvard University Press.
Braidotti, Rosi. 2013. *The Posthuman*. Cambridge: Polity Press.
Butler, Judith. 2009. *Frames of War: When Is Life Grievable?* London and New York: Verso.

Butler, Octavia. 2007. *Lilith's Brood*. New York and Boston: Grand Central Publishing.
Churchland, Paul M. 1981. "Eliminative Materialism and the Propositional Attitudes." *Journal of Philosophy* 78 (February): 67–90.
Davies, Tony. 1997. *Humanism*. London: Routledge.
Deleuze, Gilles. 1992. "Postscript on the Societies of Control." *October* 59: 3–7.
Deleuze, Gilles. 1998. *Essays Critical and Clinical*. Translated by Daniel W. Smith and Michael A. Greco. London and New York: Verso.
Deleuze, Gilles, and Félix Guattari. 1983. *Anti-Oedipus: Capitalism and Schizophrenia*. Translated by Robert Hurley, Mark Seem, and Helen R. Lane. Minneapolis: University of Minnesota Press.
Deleuze, Gilles, and Félix Guattari. 1987. *A Thousand Plateaus: Capitalism and Schizophrenia*, edited and translated by Brian Massumi. Minneapolis: University of Minnesota Press.
Dendle, Peter, ed. 2012. *The Zombie Movie Encyclopedia, Volume 2: 2000–2010*. Jefferson, NC and London: McFarland & Company.
Esposito, Roberto. 2012. *Third Person: Politics of Life and Philosophy of the Impersonal*. Translated by Zakiya Hanafi. Cambridge: Polity Press.
Foucault, Michael. 1990. *The History of Sexuality. Volume 1: An Introduction*. New York: Random House.
Gibson, William. 2014. *The Peripheral*. London: Penguin Books.
Haraway, Donna J. 1991. *Simians, Cyborgs, and Women: The Reinvention of Nature*. London: Free Association Books.
Haraway, Donna J. 2016. *Staying with the Trouble: Making Kin in the Chthulucene*. Durham, NC: Duke University Press.
Hassan, Ihab. 1977. "Prometheus as Performer: Towards a Posthumanist Culture?" In *Performance in Postmodern Culture*, edited by Michael Benamou and Charles Caramella, 201–17. Madison, WI: Coda.
Hayles, N. Katherine. 1999. *How We Became Posthuman: Virtual Bodies in Cybernetics, Literature, and Informatics*. Chicago and London: The University of Chicago Press.
Huehls, Mitchum. 2016. *After Critique: Twenty-First Century Fiction in a Neoliberal Age*. Oxford: Oxford University Press.
Jameson, Fredric. 1991. *Postmodernism, or the Cultural Logic of Late Capitalism*. Durham, NC: Duke University Press.
Lai, Larissa. 2018. *The Tiger Flu*. Vancouver: Arsenal Pulp Press.
Lavigne, Carlen. 2013. *Cyberpunk Women, Feminism and Science Fiction: A Critical Study*. Jefferson, NC and London: McFarland & Company.
Loy, Mina. 2011. *Stories and Essays of Mina Loy*, edited by Sara Crangle. Champaign and Dublin: Dalkey Archive Press,
Luhmann, Niklas. 2000. *The Reality of the Mass Media*. Cambridge: Polity Press.
Lyotard, Jean-François. 1991. *The Inhuman: Reflections on Time*. Translated by Geoffrey Bennington and Rachel Bowlby. Cambridge: Polity Press.
Major, Devorah. 2015. "Trade Winds." In *So Long Been Dreaming: Postcolonial Science Fiction and Fantasy*, edited by Nalo Hopkinson and Mehan Uppinder, 183–200. Vancouver: Arsenal Pulp Press.
Moravec, Hans. 1988. *Mind Children: The Future of Robot and Human Intelligence*. Cambridge, MA: Harvard University Press.

Rose, Nikolas. 2007. *The Politics of Life Itself: Biomedicine, Power, and Subjectivity in the Twenty-First Century*. Princeton, NJ: Princeton University Press.
Rutherford, Jennifer. 2013. *Zombies*. London and New York: Routledge.
Schmeink, Lars. 2016. *Biopunk Dystopias: Genetic Engineering, Society and Science Fiction*. Liverpool: Liverpool University Press.
Scott, Ridley. 1982. *Bladerunner*. Film. Distributed by Warner Bros Pictures.
Shaviro, Steven. 2017. "Contagious Allegories. George Romero." In *Zombie Theory: A Reader*, edited by Sarah Juliet Lauro, 7–19. Minneapolis: University of Minnesota Press.
Stapleton, Patricia, and Andrew Byers, eds. 2015. *Biopolitics and Utopia: An Interdisciplinary Reader*. New York: Palgrave Macmillan.
Villeneuve, Denis. 2017. *Bladerunner 2049*. Film. Distributed by Warner Bros Pictures.
Whitehead, Colson. 2012. *Zone One*. London: Vintage.

3 Transversing the Event
Beyond the Trauma of Terrorism

In one of Frank Bowling's 'map paintings,' the South American continent gleams bright from the core of the canvas, de- and re-centering Eurocentric cartographic conventions. To its right, almost melting into the colorful continental margins which radiate and run into each other, is the African continent. Its rims blood-red against Latin America's oceanic blues and greens, Bowling's map inscribes the passages of slavery into the heart of the earth. This blood-red tone reappears dotted across the Northern American continent, as the whirling colors in between wash up the lines of the Middle Passage. This 1971 painting, however, is titled "Polish Rebecca." If Bowling remaps the world according to histories of geographical displacement, then this title indicates that what is at stake here is not the memory of slavery alone. The centrally placed continents, Africa and South America, also make visible the experience of diaspora and genocide that occurred in the dark patch that is Europe. Bowling shows that the trauma of systemic violence is, as Michael Rothberg would phrase it, "multidirectional" (Rothberg 2009). This painting not only subverts Eurocentrism; it also makes a deeper and more fundamental point about the link between memory and identity. Memories are not closed entities to be owned by a group, claimable as authentic and pure foundations of identity; they emerge in dialogue, a back-and-forth movement which acknowledges that no simple 'we' or 'you' exists. The lines between different communities' histories of suffering cross and traverse each other, precisely because the patterns of power and violence inflicting this suffering overlap, too. The European Totalitarianism which caused the most genocidally violent phase of the Polish diaspora here referenced by Bowling is inscribed, too, into the history of the British Empire and its slave trade. Re-mapping the world to expose this is not a simple backlash, but a complex project of unearthing the patterns of implication and complicity which would otherwise remain hidden underneath the deceptive clarity of a history as seen through the lens of singular nation state entities. Bowling's map is gestural, and testifies not only to the precariousness of human lives but also the porosity of any construct of cultural identity reliant on notions of exclusive memory ownership.

Let's contrast this with another instance of memory culture in response to a large-scale act of terrorism which struck in 2001. At the dawn of the 21st century, heroism and unity emerged as "narratives of redemption" (LaCapra 2001, 155) as a new era of global terrorism began with the attacks in New York, Washington, and Pennsylvania. In J. Michael Straczynski's *The Amazing Spiderman* 9/11 special (2002), Spiderman is aghast and speechless at the sight of Ground Zero; his initial reaction – "Some things are beyond words. Beyond Comprehension" (Straczynski 2002) – replicates the discourse of traumatic unspeakability and singles 9/11 out as an event too large for words. The superhero bows to the allegedly even greater heroic powers of the humans living through this catastrophe, standing "blinded by the light of your [*the human heroes'*] unbroken will. Before that light, no darkness can prevail. [. . .] and stand tall" (Straczynski 2002). Straczynski prefaces this with a gesture of inclusion, when he describes how "we as a people have been tribalized and factionalized by a thousand casual unkindnesses," but have now "become one in our grief. [. . .] We are now one in our determination. [. . .] One as we recover!" (2002). This gesture of respect, however, also serves to sublimate the attacks in their immediate aftermath, echoing the exceptionalism which soon came to mark the politics of counter-terrorism. Even if when ignoring the irony of Spiderman's shock, forgetting for a moment that scenes like Ground Zero are a common superhero comic staple, the agenda behind this is therefore revealed fairly swiftly: An emotionally paradoxical gesture which prescribes strength as much as it postulates grief, this runs counter to Bowling's mapped encounters of vulnerability. While the vibrant colors in Bowling's maps equally testify to both visceral wounding as well as to resurgent vitality, there is no need for heroism here, as this map privileges gestures of encounter over any superficially inclusive collective 'we,' and remains disinterested in presumed sameness.

Nevertheless, the superhero remains emblematic of a memory culture complicit with nationalist discourses, in which such notions of triumphant strength abound: Jeffrey Melnick interprets the role of Flight 93 as an allegory for the heroism of the ordinary (American) man and woman facing deadly struggles (2009, 77). The second volume of the popular *9/11 Artists Respond* editions, too, dedicates a whole section to the heroism of first responders. The 9/11 'hero' might include a fireman who exemplifies the "human spirit" (Kahn and Levitz 2002, 68), or be charged with troublingly martial undertones (Kahn and Levitz 2002, 89–93). Imbued with notions of sanctity, the narrative of a "hallowed ground" (Rudolph W. Giuliani in his 'Farewell Address', December 27, 2001), of a "space full of horror but also of heroism" (Kaplan 2005, 12) cannot be overestimated in its impact on the politics of remembering at the dawn of the 21st century. Indeed, it has become the official narrative of national trauma. Allison Blais and Lynn Rasic, writing in the *Official Book of the September 11 Memorial*, echo Spiderman's sentiments almost word by word when they comment that the "attacks of September 11, 2001, changed our world forever," but also revealed "stories of heroism and sacrifice that inspired us all" (2011) amidst the loss and grief. This is politically driven, and was indeed elevated to official policy when medals assigned by the 'True American Heroes Act' in 2005 were awarded to representatives of each victim.

Such redemption, however, privileges the politically charged emotions of excessive and national grief, loss, or heroism over critical thought and affective complexity. This is not unusual, as Robert Jay Lifton has demonstrated that the narrative of a struck but resilient community can provide a vital framework to re-establish collective and national identity after the impact of the planes (2003, 137). Such post-traumatic solidarity, however, typically comes at the cost of the identification of a "hated out-group" (Smelser 2004, 269) to be excluded in the name of unity. As Bertolt Brecht said, pity the land that needs heroes.

In contrast to Bowling's map painting, which gestures towards a seemingly unconnected history of violence to expose hidden links and global relations, the be-flagged nationalism that followed the 9/11 attacks posited unity not as an invitation, but as a normative injunction. The very notion that 9/11 was singular, echoed by leading intellectuals such as Don DeLillo who argued that "In its desertion of every basis for comparison, the event asserts its singularity" (2001, 39), is therefore inherently problematic. Its exceptionalism prepares the ground for a response equally detached from legal or political frameworks, as the ensuing 'war on terror' amply demonstrated.

Trauma, therefore, is a visceral term when it refers to a collective phenomenon; it seems innocent enough to extrapolate to the collective level of a "wounded New York" (Kaplan 2005, 136) or a stricken "Homeland" (Däwes 2011, 204) from an individual pathology of shock, which Cathy Caruth defines soberly as "a response, sometimes delayed, to an overwhelming event or set of events, which takes the form of repeated, intrusive hallucinations, dreams, thoughts or behaviours" (Caruth 1995, 4f). Yet the public sphere is not an individual psyche, and memory cultures are spheres of ferocious politicization and confrontation, as the debates about the 9/11 memorial (and about a mosque close to the site) demonstrated only too clearly. Such paralyzing symptoms as "psychic numbing" (Meek 2010, 5) and singular suffering are only too easily embedded into a politics of nationalism which, as Marc Redfield points out, seems to some to provide an easy remedy to "make sense of the shock" (2009, 4) but works as "garlic one might put on a door to ward off vampires" (Spiegelman 2004) to others.

If states survive by scripting traumatic events, as Edkins provocatively suggests (2003, 7), then this nationalist weaponization of 'national trauma' not only precludes gestures towards another's suffering as offered in Frank Bowling's maps. Once notions of 'patriotic' behavior and an 'axis of evil' were established, any multidirectional remembering was swept off the table as the personal perspective was, as Judith Butler argued, "misused to displace broader, historical frames of reference" (2004, 4). For trauma studies to move towards the future, therefore, this indicates that a change of focus is in order, away from the individualized vision of Freudian psychoanalysis. After all, concentrating on individual injury alone can, as Pieter Vermeulen argued, effectively contribute to a politics of vengefulness (2014, 141).

This chapter thinks with transnational fictionalizations of 9/11 and the ensuing war on terror to explore a transversal politics of remembering violence. On the one hand, this is an urgent matter as it counteracts the identity politics which continue to deform remembrance cultures, and which have spiraled from the militarist pre-emptions and illegal black sites of the Bush administration into the overt racism of the Trump government. The erection of a border wall to Mexico, after all, is only a physical manifestation of the division of the world into spheres of good and evil as proposed by George W. Bush. Incidentally, Donald Trump draws lines from the 9/11 heroism discourse to his own presidency, falsely claiming he had been with the first responders. His virulent and neo-fascist nostalgia for an alleged greatness lost in trials including 9/11 exposes the urgent need for an alternative memory culture to counteract such weaponization in the hands of the alt-right, as is occurring, too, in the British Brexit debate, which is legitimized on the basis of white-washed and historically misleading dreams of imperial independence.

Trauma, therefore, exposes how memory, affectivity and time are politicized. If it can be defined with psychoanalyst Dori Laub as the "tyranny of the past" (Laub 1992, 79), because its flashbacks and nightmares return to haunt the patient, then trauma breaks through the linear progression of time and engulfs the future. Such an engulfing past, therefore, implies a future that cannot arrive, making trauma a breakdown phenomenon of a psychoanalytical kind. Trauma becomes a testcase scenario for the posthuman and its potentialities, raising the question whether trauma is not, in fact, a pathology of history or crisis of remembering the past, but instead a crisis of imagining the future. "Those who cannot remember the past are condemned to repeat it," as George Santayana put it in 1905. A dark century of cyclically returning violence later, though, it is time to re-phrase that question: what if those who cannot imagine the future are condemned to repeat the past? The literary responses to terrorism in this chapter are interested in precisely such a future-oriented approach to trauma, exploring new modes of developing agency and voice in a world of violence.

On the other hand, though, such a literary politics in response to trauma revolves around questions of the borderline, both on an individual and on a collective level. Can we exist precariously without the reflexive impulse of re-erecting boundaries, and if yes, what would such an open mode of survival entail? Freudian trauma theory certainly relies on the notion of the boundary, which trauma pierces and renders porous; yet the reliance on the constitutive force of the borderline remains. The Freudian self is bounded, and suffering puncture, it seeks to heal the breach. This offers stark alternatives: If we think of trauma as rupture, as breakage of a unified self, then this leaves only a non-choice between being whole or being shattered, which – in the early times of trauma studies – also constituted the divide between voyeur and dehumanized object. In Charcot's Salpêtrière, hysterical women were exhibited to the interested public; those counting as allegedly 'whole' and 'sane,' therefore, were perpetrators in their own right, using their own position of power when abusing those more vulnerable as a spectacle. This chapter explores the option of a third way, searching for ways to inhabit a vulnerable and wounding world with a view towards the future.

Underlying any such issues concerning trauma's time in general and its futurity in particular, however, is the question whether violence equates rupture. Is trauma necessarily an 'event,' a singular core which might make itself known in flashbacks or which can be unearthed in psychoanalytical therapies? Such 'eventness,' after all, is the foundation for the narrative of national trauma as introduced above, as any notion of epochal rupture necessitates the thought of a sudden intrusion. Arguably, as notions of slow violence have shown, this is not a given, and a trauma theory attuned to the demands of the 21st century accordingly needs to take into account that the traumatized self has changed over time. In the globalized sphere of contemporary socioeconomic, ecological, and terrorist violence, trauma exposes an "implicated subject position" (Rothberg 2014, xvii), as Michael Rothberg argues, in which the self can be both perpetrator and victim simultaneously. The situation, therefore, is not any more a Levinasian one, in which inmate and concentration camp guard look at each other across the wire fence; but one which resembles the complex network of violence and vulnerability in which Salman Rushdie entangles his protagonist in in his 2005 novel *Shalimar the Clown*. Culminating in the assassination of a victim who – as counter terrorism chief and metaphoric seducer of Kashmir as a colonizable region – is himself a perpetrator, this stabbing is the tip of an iceberg under which simmer and fester decades of unequal global power patterns, regional conflict, and personal injury. Rushdie's terrorized is also the terrorist, and vice versa, in a biting comment on the short-sightedness of the idea that a 'singular' event can even be possible.

As such, it is the freedom and responsibility of literature to experiment in a de-pragmatized sphere in order to unsettle the hotly politicized notions of innocence or 'evil,' and to explore what ethically viable positions remain if neither of these dual descriptors fully applies. Politically, this moves trauma beyond the borderlines of the nation state. Such a de-territorialized memory responds to Judith Butler's call for an alternative framing of global terror to replace "a sphere in which the trace of the cry has become hyperbolically inflated to rationalize a gluttonous nationalism, or fully obliterated, where both alternatives turn out to be the same" (Butler 2004, 147). The trace of this cry, however, cuts across a multiplicity of skins and territories, and can never be traced back to one unitary source. To acknowledge this is the task of a literary politics of memory oriented towards the future instead of succumbing to the tyranny of a violent past.

Where the literature of the immediate aftermath traced the cry of the wound, be it Jonathan Safran Foer's *Extremely Loud & Incredibly Close* or Don DeLillo's *Falling Man*, more recent literary interventions are more acutely aware that such a focus on the wound, "speaking wordlessly in the dark" (Gibson 2005, 316) might also efface critical engagement with the historical, economic and political structures from which such violence emerges. Whilst it might be true that the ethics of trauma literature resides in "the power to be affected" (Onega and Ganteau 2014, 11) by the vulnerability of the Other, Ruth Ozeki and Kamila Shamsie are among the writers reminding us that such affectivity is always also politically conditioned.

This chapter, therefore, explores the literature of terrorism beyond trauma. Interested in what Sam Durrant has termed "critical mourning" (2014, 94), I argue that the politics of trauma literature reflects on our own position within a history of violence, betraying structures of power, reciprocity or implication. In other words, what does it mean to render trauma transversal? To ground a multidirectional politics of memory and trauma in the human body thus requires not only surviving implicated subjecthood, but inhabiting it in a more agentic and more ethical manner. In opening the traumatized body using ideas of transversality, affect and de-territorialization, I re-frame it as an agent created by its own porosity. This post-human self's vulnerability differs from that of the Freudian self which, though pierced by trauma, remains self-sufficient and autopoietic in its conception, a bodily and psychic organism creating its own memory patterns and unconscious realm of dream imagery. Yet trauma, in such a non-Freudian sense, is not a phenomenon of breaching a borderline, as it is set in a world that shaped by porous selves that are infiltratable, and subject positions that are implicated in violence as much as they are subjected to it. It therefore does not seek to re-establish its boundaries and cover its wounds with re-grown skin to go 'back' to being 'whole.' Beyond trauma, vulnerability remains a matter of negotiating ways of coexisting, sustainably and in empathy, with each other's lives as they are rendered precarious by shared histories of violence; yet it also demands new visions for the kind of agency that can originate in such breached bodies, and to develop more future-oriented modes of response to our implicated being. Breaking through the repetition compulsion, with its cycles of injury, pre-emption and renewed violence, is therefore a deeply political project as it creates structures of time, horizons of possibility and currents of affectivity beyond the reach of the nation-state that seeks to instrumentalize trauma.

The three texts which I think these ideas with are not focused on the terrorist spectacle of the 9/11 attacks, but immersed in the networked histories of violence which the sheer force of the planes' impact momentarily distracted from. The historical and textual connections which can radiate out from literary language constitute political interventions; Ruth Ozeki, Thomas Pynchon and Kamila Shamsi offer three distinct examples of how literature can expose such hidden networks and use them to counteract, in their alternative worldings, what Baudrillard has described as "terrorism's true victory" (2002, 31): the unpredictable spiral from 'crime' to 'crackdown' in which the very idea of freedom and the possibility of change begin to fade. As Georgiana Banita pointed out, the aim of literature when responding to terrorism cannot be merely to "cease judging the Other," but to "show how we are judging even when we think we are not, how we have judged wrongly and how to make amends for it, how simply ceasing to judge is not the solution to a political crisis where judgment continues on" (2012, 26). I agree that such engagement is key to a literary criticism in this context that is not just ethical, but political, too. However, I am not sure if a focus on otherness and judgement alone can lead away from this spiral. It is, perhaps more fundamentally, the 'judging' self in its perceived position in time and space, with its agency and voice, that the wound inflicted by terrorists calls on us to re-define in order to escape the double-binds of terror.

Transnational Scars: Uncontainable Bodies

> She had stepped out of the shadow of the roof's overhang and into the harsh sunlight so there could be no mistaking the three charcoal-coloured bird-shaped burns on her back, the first below her shoulder blade, the second halfway down her spine, intersected by her bra, the third just above the waist. [. . .] he touched the grotesque darkness below her should blade – tentatively, fearfully – as though it were a relic of hell, clamping his teeth together at the outrage of the lumps his fingers encountered. [. . .] Birdback,' he said.
>
> (Shamsie 2009, 91)

"The body keeps the score," Bessel van der Kolk wrote in 1995 (215). The bird-shaped burns on Hiroko's back – protagonist of Kamila Shamsie's 2009 novel *Burnt Shadows* – tell of a pain that seems to elude comprehension or words. A survivor of the atomic bomb in Nagasaki in 1945, Hiroko had felt her whole neighborhood burn itself into her skin in a flash of light. She saw her father die covered in the scales to which his immolated skin had shrunk, and left first for Tokyo, and then to Delhi, carrying the bird-shaped patterns of her mother's wedding kimono inscribed into her back. These burns, too, carry the shadows of other literary figures such as Toni Morrions' Sethe, a runaway slave whose 'tree' of scars on her back is such a bodily outgrowth of inhumane violence. They will accompany Hiroko throughout her life and well into the 21st century, setting her apart more and more from the post-9/11 New York where she lives in old age.

Witnessing bodies are at the core of traumatic memory. An experience so overwhelming it seems to defy networks of remembering, Freud defined trauma as a 'foreign body' ([1908] 1952, 85) within the mind, to which only the body with its scars, re-enactments or symptomatic pains can retain what DiPrete called a "privileged relation" which, "not accessible to cognition, cannot find verbal expression" (2006, 10). The scar thus speaks what the mind cannot tell, as experiences of shock are so profound they dissociate the mind and render memory in two, into traumatically embodied and narrative dimensions. The body, therefore, is at the heart of the unspeakability thesis which assumes trauma to be "the enigma of the otherness of a human voice that cries out from the wound" (Caruth 1996, 3), unspeakable and inaccessible to memory and words (see Donn 2016 for a detailed discussion of this). Hiroko's burnt scars testify to this bodily memory. When I therefore ask what constitutes the body politics of trauma in the 21st century, I do so in order to explore how the wounded body can become a site not of numbing inscription but also of transversal affectivity, opening to transgression, resilience and mutual survival, instead of closing in on hurt. Yet before I expand on the complex, transversal patterns hidden underneath the only seemingly dead skin, let me briefly reflect on the political significance of such corporeal dimensions.

I have already begun to sketch how such notions of incomprehensibility were emphasized in 9/11 memory culture, with problematic political implications; this left the human body hanging in ambivalence, vulnerable and ephemeral as it is. Some bodies were deemed containable in narratives of patriotism and redemption, whilst others remained uncontainable. This is not a new phenomenon as sch, as Kamila Shamsie makes clear when she references the Japanese stigmatization of atomic bomb survivors as hibakusha, leading Hiroko to hide her burnt body from the eyes of her fellow Japanese citizens even in exile. Judith Butler has described such hierarchies in memory politics in terms of a life's "grievability," a term she uses to denounce the undeniable "fantasy of mastery" (Butler 2004, 29) that served to marginalize bodies that did not 'fit' – racially different, unheroic, disabled, or falling bodies. In using the term 'containable,' though, I want to draw attention to the limits of such memory politics of the traumatized body. Uncontainable bodies strive against the silencing of the ungrievable body, and are mourned for, though not, perhaps, by adherents to the patriotic master narrative.

In the face of an event perceived so shattering as to herald a new era of world history, traumatized bodies, paradoxically, remained whole. Gestures of shock featured in the genre of 'onlooker photographs,' a recurrent feature of, for instance, the *Here is New York* photographic exhibition. Though driven by a democratic impulse to collect infinite and unfiltered perspectives of all New Yorkers alike, the bodily stances of these onlookers where surprisingly uniform. Faces turned upward, hands held up in shock, these groups of witnesses stunned into silence embody the traumatized nation, effectively suggesting the body in a moment of stillness, a silent center within the whirl of the city coming down, as the appropriate response. What Susan Lurie describes as a "trauma of spectatorship" (2006, 46) knows no scars, no burns, as the actual injury remains beyond the frame. The unspeakability of trauma thus turns into a spectacle, which simultaneously foregrounds and represses the human body. Its "negative sublimity or displaced sacralization" (LaCapra 2001, 23) stuns the observer into bodily paralysis; however, the horror of the sublime, if understood with Kant, ultimately confirms the shocked observer's being. The sense of annihilation is thus reassuringly confined in the moment of the event, which the onlooker's being – their bodies still standing, still strong and unripped – will survive. These onlookers have an emphatically collective dimension. Gone through the trial of strength, the wounded nation, too, they suggest, will regain strength in unity and coherence. As trauma punctures the skin and shatters defenses, the collective spectacle of trauma ultimately re-affirms the boundaries of skin and country. The contrast to Hiroko's wounds could not be starker, whose injured body is literally foreign in its suffering and in its nationality to the Delhi in which the scene I quoted initially takes place.

This collective dimension, steeped in the nation-state, is often inadvertent, but none the less impactful; it surfaced, too, in the New York Times' "Portraits of Grief" series, which – despite originating in the wrenching sorrow of the posters put up to search for the missing- presented not scars but everyday heroism, not wounding but a loose assemblage of 'American' values. The prescriptive quality of these sketches of men and women adhering to family values, volunteering in their communities, or known for quirky music tastes projected an image of the US as a truly "moral community" (Neal 1998, 21) based on the values of family, ambition, and solidarity. Such normative framing of grief in terms of a nation-state imaginary has since become a staple of mass responses to terrorist attacks, commodified on facebook, where users can design their profile pictures in the colours of the country where an attack occurred, overlaying their own photographic bodies with national symbols – especially if that country is located in what counts as the global West.

The national flag thus seems to open the wounded national body to others, but this move is always also exclusive and seeks symbols of strength instead of actual dialogue. This is even more apparent when seen in contrast with other forms of bodily memory, which refuse to wrap wounds in flags. Jenny Holzer's LUSTMORD (1993–94) series, for example, made the female human body the site of memory for the war crimes committed against women in Bosnia. Holzer inscribed her texts, written from either the viewpoint of the perpetrator of the rape, the victim or the observer, onto bones or the skin of female volunteers. Photographed and cropped into a square image, skin inscribed with memories of violence is both intimately individual and gestures towards shared conditions of humanity. There is no inherent difference about the skin on which the different roles are inscribed, forcing the reader to acknowledge her or his own ways of being implicated in the symbolic and material structures of power, gender and ethnicity that enabled these systematic crimes. Holzer's embodied memory traces unsettle because they are visceral, and subvert any notion of easy identification into the universal victimhood of the Western world. The nation-state based redemption, in contrast, as Dominick LaCapra warns, entails the danger of taking trauma to legitimize any action which cannot be justified otherwise (LaCapra 2001, 163), and relies on the spectacle. Only what is controllable as singular event, forcefully unforeseen yet also clearly locatable in time, can fit into such redemption. The bodily stances of shock testify to this.

Post-9/11 body politics, therefore, are selective, privileging precisely those bodies easily containable in redemptive narratives of a collective trial of strength, which paradoxically lack what DiPrete called the body's direct relation to the traumatic core, having pushed it beyond the photograph's frame. Repressed are the uncontainable bodies, among which Hiroko's would surely count. After 9/11, such transgressive bodies were the falling ones, whose unhaltable motion immediately sets them apart from the stillness of the spectacle's onlookers. "Sometimes the message of artists is a downer", is how developer Larry Silverstein summarized Jenny Holzer's installation in the new 7 World Trade Centre, "Down here, after 9/11, we need positive stuff. Good stuff, as opposed to the miseries of 9/11" (Glen Collins, *The New York Times*, March 6, 2006). The core of the conflict was the inclusion in the installation of the poem *Photograph from September 11* by Wislawa Szymborska, a lyrical response to Richard Drew's photograph 'Falling Man' which shows a man in headfirst fall from the burning World Trade Centre. Its precariousness seen as "too graphic" (Klara Silverstein, quoted in Collins 2006), it was eventually excluded from the installation, a fate shared by Eric Fischl's sculpture *Tumbling Woman* in the Rockefeller Center or Sharon Paz's installation of cut-out silhouettes of falling people in the windows of the Jamaica Centre for Arts and Learning. In a memory politics predicated on 'rising' (Melnick 2009), bodies in fall seemed offensive, transgressive, because, as Tom Junod criticized in his 2009 *Esquire* article, "we have somehow deemed the act of witness, in this one regard, unworthy of us" (Junod 2009).

Images of tortured bodies in the war on terror shattered these body politics of the immediate aftermath. The images of the torture Abu Ghraib made the abused human body a marker of how quickly such simple notions of victim and perpetrator can become unsettled, and these, as Roger Luckhurst, noticed, "were not diluted or disrespected," so that their "meanings were continually de- and re-contextualized" (2010, 15). Instead of pushing violence beyond the frame, this centrality of the scarred body encouraged networks of association and response, an opening that was part of their explosive power. They questioned, rather than simply affirmed, a politics that sought to respond to an allegedly containable spectacle with a military retaliation equally – so the intention was – containable in space and time. That this proved to be an illusion testifies to the failures of a memory politics that seeks to de-limit and reduce the complexity of the global lines of power which engendered the attacks. The hooded figure linked to electricity cables embodies these networks, as his violent exposure to currents of electricity also symbolizes his implication in broader global forcefields. The human body is therefore a key site for memory politics, but it is not an unproblematic one. As these 9/11 examples show, it is not prior to discourse but deeply embedded in it.

It is time, now, to explore the uncontainability of Hiroko's 'birdback' more deeply. Stigmatized and marked as foreign though her body is, this does not make her life 'ungrievable' in Judith Butler's sense. "At home in the idea of foreignness" (Shamsie 2009, 141), Hiroko creates encounters with others who mourn with her, sharing the fairy tales she made up to communicate the horror of the bomb to her son – about "monsters who spread their wings and land on human skin" (Shamsie 2009, 177) – with those she trusts. When she tells Kim these tales, her friend's granddaughter in New York who is shaken to the core of her being after the 9/11 attacks, there is no sense that Hiroko's life, marked by an American bomb and spent, for the most part, in Pakistan, is deemed less grievable in the personal networks of the novel. It is, however, not containable, and this is ultimately what the surreal mode of the fairy tales communicates. Her body is characteristically disobedient.

The birds on her back are shadows of multiple losses, cast not in a unilinear fashion but transversally, one memory transecting shadows of another, cast by a global history of violence that sought, unsuccessfully, to territorialize her body as Japanese target for American bombs. Most literally, the bird-shaped burns are traces of her mother's wedding kimono. In anticipation of her own wedding she put on that garment mere moments before the atomic bomb incinerated her neighborhood, father and her fiancée, and is since tattooed by this moment of hope burnt to ash. "Urakami Valley has become her flesh. Her flesh has become Urakami Valley" (Shamsie 2009, 27), yet this ash also carries within it the remnants of a cherry blossom tree her father, 'traitor' to the war cause, had planted in memory of a neighborhood boy who lost his life as a kamikaze pilot. The local community's chairman set fire to this alleged insult to the exaltation of the boy's sacrifice, arresting her father in the aftermath. The birds thus carry the seeds of resistance to the weaponization and dehumanization of bodies in warfare, but also cast their shadows forwards in time to another set of suicide pilots. When working as a school teacher in Pakistan, Hiroko dismisses the Islamic zeal of her students, "with their strange fervor for a world of rigidity" as mere "posturing youths" (Shamsie 2009, 142) in comparison to the boys she taught in 1940s Japan, dreaming of kamikaze missions. The birds, thus, are also planes, creatures of flight turned deadly.

Suffusing these transhistorical patterns is a yearning for a world in which such deadly rigidity has no traction. Another flock of birds had been reduced to ashes by the bomb. Her fiancé Konrad had documented his search for the pre-war cosmopolitan Nagasaki, in which nationalities mixed and intermarried uncomplicatedly, in purple notebooks. War had "fractured" (Shamsie 2009, 6) this view, so Konrad hides his "birds," as Hiroko had called these light papery dreams, as a mobile in a tree. Underneath the foliage they remain invisible to those searching for evidence of anti-state activity, as Konrad rightly assumes that those officers "can always be deceived by a simple act of imagination" (Shamsie 2009, 9). His writing a search for "a pattern of people moving towards each other" (Shamsie 2009, 68), this notebook mobile is attuned to a world in movement and fluidity, which any and all of the war-related ideologies included in the novel, including World War II, Partition, and 9/11, seek to paralyze in fixity.

Hiroko's scars are therefore multivalent and infused with the "multidirectionality" (Rothberg 2009) with which memories of violence can transgress the arbitrariness of national boundaries. Her body, therefore, does not merely 'keep the score' but transgresses any notion of a bounded 'record' of trauma to be unearthed, identified, and contained. It strains against all attempts to pin it down, be it in national borders, in languages, or in specific instances of historical violence. In the New York of the 9/11 aftermath, Hiroko's scars therefore infuse the rigidity of patriotic gestures, which seek bodies "hewn into solidity" (Shamsie 2009, 18), with an excess of meaning. Her body, thus, is more akin to Martha Graham's dancing body in 'Lamentation.' In this choreography the grieving body is bound by swathes of elastic fabric, both contained and straining against the restraints in swaying motions that move away from any ideas of trauma as a rupture which shatters relations. Such dancing bodies in motion gesture towards encounters, seeking expression even if what they lament can surface only through the openings of metaphoric or gestural language, not a record but a desire, a want that does not spring from lack but from a passion to relate, communicate, and transgress the boundaries of the bands rendered elastic by the dancer's own movements. It is a body that performs the transgression of its own skin, making the moment of lamentation a momentum for adaptation and transformation.

Trauma, in such a lamenting body, does not mark skin off with death, but strains through pain towards motion. Such dancing bodies, as Erin Manning argues, are "involved in a reciprocal reaching-toward that ingathers the world even as it worlds" (Manning 2009, 6), shaping their own reality even whilst reaching out. Hiroko, too, is a being driven by desire, a want for the world she lost but also a drive to "find something different to want" (Shamsie 2009, 100) in order not to be reduced to the bomb. Yet what she wants is not the boundedness of a singular being with an exceptional history. When Kim suggests that Hiroko should put "all the weight in the world" in her own suffering, the older women sears with fury; "Is that why Nagasaki was such a monstrous crime? Because it happened to me?" (Shamsie 2009, 294). The affects that drive her, which run through her body into a history of violence, are driven by the desire for relation.

The body politics of Hiroko's burnt skin figures, thus, is a politics of affect. Defined by Massumi as the "principle of unrest of a world in becoming" (Massumi 2011, 2), affectivity in the 9/11 aftermath was consciously limited to a climate of fear in which the media instrumentalized the normative patriotism of the memory culture I sketched above, predicated on uplifting narratives instead of the fall, in order to modulate the public's affects to a redemptive satisfaction: the climate of fear and collective precariousness was addressed by the president's military intervention, with the aim, amongst others, of making the public feel better about their own country but also with the effect of cutting down any critical enquiry. To question the feelings of patriotic redemption when the American flag was briefly raised in Iraq was, in this logic, an act of affective sabotage. Affect modulation, in this sense, is a tool of power, and increases in valence in the narratives of a nation at threat constructed by the Trump administration to secure public support for otherwise irrational projects.

Hiroko's affectivity counteracts such restrictions. Her body, from whose scars connections to histories of pain and others' loss radiate, performs its way out of the grid of ascribed roles in the complex national and personal power patterns she transverses. Understanding that the world is in ongoing transformation, her anger at being asked to sublimate her own pain is a current of affect that cuts through the categories of objectivity and subjectivity, as her scars link her being irretrievably to her fiancé's lost writing as well as to the boy soldiers she had taught. Straining against the requirements of collective trauma that immobilize her by asking her to pick a side, this affective velocity which propels her into survival also leads her to work as a translator for the Americans, a job she accepts almost inadvertently because of the American officer's aura of gentleness, against "her birds displeasure" (Shamsie 2009, 287). She leaves this job, driven by a similarly affective response after that same officer had mentioned his take on the bomb; it had, as he reasons, been a necessity to save American lives. The currents of affect which flow through Hiroko's body thus lead her to seek relation, yet resist any attempt to rank lives in hierarchies of grievability of national worth. Her affects lead her to create a life in which no dehumanization is possible.

She thus performs not displacement but transformation, inserting herself into the languages and spaces of Delhi, Karachi, and New York. This appears in its most radical form when she holds her son responsible for the life of a boy he had convinced to join the mujahedeen in Afghanistan in a moment of teenage thoughtlessness; he will later attempt to redeem himself by helping this boy, now a grown man, escape the FBI, accepting his own internment in Guantanamo Bay as a prize for his earlier recklessness. Trauma, in this sense, becomes impersonal, but not de-personalized. The way Hiroko inhabits a vortex of history – in which nation-states are bloodily born almost overnight in the Partition she experiences as a refugee, as power balances shift in the threat of nuclear war between India and Pakistan, or conflicts become de-territorialized as in the American intervention supporting the Taliban against the Soviets – creates what Deleuze terms a "plane of immanence on which all bodies, all minds, and all individuals are situated" (1989, 122)." Bodies, in this plane, are affected by others and affect others themselves; in this affective plane inspired by Spinoza, bodies are not fixed as substances but defined by dynamic motion and interrelations, coming into being "in the relations of motion and rest, of speeds and slownesses between particles" (Deleuze 1989, 123). Hiroko's scars move her body into such being, making her relational to the core. This relationality is lived resistance to the instrumentalization and weaponization of trauma in the interests of militarist politics.

Yet her body suggests also a micropolitics that performs the possibility of being uncontainable to any the attempts to assign her a fixed position in grids of nationhood, class, or – as she disgustedly puts it – "vengeance or justice" (Shamsie 2009, 49). Offering an alternative to the restriction of public affect to narcissistic hurt, fear and vengeance, Hiroko's scarred body makes her an "aggregate" of human and non-human energies (Blackman 2012, xii), as the affects she responds too are often carried by non-organic matter, violence pulsing in the monsoon rain or anger spreading in droplet of ink thrown through the air. She performs what a climate of fear seeks to make impossible, namely the possibility of being "as much outside itself as in itself" (2010, 3), as Seigworth and Gregg define an affective body webbed in its relations, until ultimately these distinctions might cease to matter. Her body, thus, is the opposite to a life made grievable by its entry into a patriotically constructed moral community. Subverting the impulse of exclusion that always underlies such inclusion, her scars compose her being through the forces of encounter. Her traumatised body thus does away with the notion of a bounded organism that might be punctured, and should seek to heal. She instead enacts bodily and psychological elasticity, in the mode of Martha Graham's lamentation dance, in order to remain open to a world that can only survive, instead of reverting into spirals of violence, if the impulse of fearful foreclosure is rendered porous from the start. Her fiancé Konrad had told her that "barriers made of metal could turn fluid when touched simultaneously by people on either side" (Shamsie 2009, 82). This fluidity is what she seeks to live.

Hiroko not only transverses histories of violence; her life is also shaped by shifts in global power patterns that implicate her. Her body, thus, is a micro-site of memory disobedient to the demands of clearly cut lines in time or space. Her perpetual nomadism, too, traces lines of flight through the idea that nation-states are solid entities and the sole agents of history. Where does such a desire-driven, scarred body in perpetual motion leave us in a politics of memory of the aftermath that is marked by patriotic rigidity, petrifying the globe, in Bush's words, into new axes of good and evil that remain significant to this day? What is the political valence of such a body in a world definitely not at home with the idea of foreignness?

Hiroko's burnt body becomes politically potent when its counteracts what Robert Jay Lifton has diagnosed as the 'superpower syndrome,' a "mindset assuming omnipotence, of unique standing in the world that grants it the right to hold sway over all other nations" (2003, 3), which can refer to both the American and Islamist sides in this war. With the fear of vulnerability at its core, this syndrome is at the heart of the cycle between aggrievement and vengeance which has engendered a "worldwide epidemic of violence" (2003, 1) since the 9/11 attacks. This is precisely the mechanism Jacques Baudrillard described as "terroristic situational transfer," in which one superpower seizes the cards of the game for themselves to regain the upper hand (2002, 15), ultimately inciting all 'losers' to take revenge. Yet such a transfer is only possible when politics is envisaged to be composed of intentions, which make it possible to link causes to effects in a linear manner. This is the precondition of treating 9/11 as an exceptional spectacle, the very singularity of which makes it actable-upon, as an embedded step in the logic of this 'game.'

Yet the spectacle conceals as much as it reveals. The strength of Hiroko's way of inhabiting such a world is that she gives no credence to these rules, and instead exposes how the nation-state, with its "rock-bottom comfort in one's language and one's home", as Gayatri Spivak remarks, "is not a positive affect" (2010, 15). Her affect-based, transformational velocity is infused with intentionality, but disgusted with the kind of agency that seeks mastery. She modulates her own being to the power patterns of colonisation, terrorist and nuclear threat, but this is not merely an adaptive move; it requires utmost willpower, as it propels her to go against the flows to which her son, for one, has ceded his being when becoming implicated as contractor with the CIA. Without transformation, there is only breakdown. "Why have the English remained so English?" (Shamsie 2009, 82) her future husband Sajjad asks of the representatives of Empire in Delhi in 1947. It is not only the refusal to hybridize and mix which makes this remark seem such a poignant observation at the moment of imperial dissolution. It is also the need to position oneself in the national grid as such that Hiroko, migrating several such national boundaries in her life with her birds as constant companions, questions. The traumatised body, thus, is not just an object to become immobilized or inscribed; it is also an agent creating acts of micro-resistance by simultaneously becoming affected and the source of affects in a relational world.

From Traumatic Certainties to Virtual Possibilities

The vulnerable body in the 21st century, however, is broken open by dynamics other than affect, too. After all, no image evokes the impact of 9/11 like that of the 'Falling Man,' a person in headfirst fall from the World Trade Center captured by Richard Drew. This body momentarily suspended in freefall seemed emblematic of the deadly contrast between human vulnerability and a seemingly impenetrable architecture of glass and steel. Precariously caught on the threshold between life and death, it became a global icon for the impact of terrorism, despite being pulled from media publications soon after its first appearance for ethical reasons. However, where is this body to be located? After all, this picture was both intimately corporeal and viral; as such it is steeped deeply within what is perhaps the key paradoxon of 21st century experiences of terror: trauma has been digitized. The live television coverage of the towers falling, broadcast globally in real time, has caused critics like Marc Redfield to wonder whether "the event disappears into its own mediation" (2009, 14), exerting an impact that is both immediate and strangely unreal. Trauma in this sense does not just return in nightmarish dreams or ghostly hallucinations; it has itself turned "spectral" (Redfield 2009, 15), enmeshing injured bodies in flows of reproduced global coverage until the body itself becomes intangible, an iconic presence rather than a sensory and sensing, affecting and affected agent. This is what Slavoj Žižek has described as the "thrill of the Real as the ultimate 'effect'" (2002, 12); for did the 9/11 attacks not seem like shots taken from a catastrophe movie, making the "Real Thing" (Žižek 2002, 12) seem like a semblance of itself?

In Thomas Pynchon's 2013 novel *Bleeding Edge*, Manhattan-based protagonist Maxine is struggling with what she calls a "what is reality issue" in the aftermath of the attacks. She sees the dead, sees kids in the streets ageing into adulthood in the blink of an eye, and feels stranded at "the barroom floor of history [...] the bleak feeling, some mornings, that the country itself may not be there anymore, but being silently replaced screen by screen with something else" (Pynchon 2013, 339). This is not a psychological question; it expresses a visceral sense that as reality itself recedes, the individual is left behind, affected but unable to affect changes herself. Yet if this is the case, then which forces are at work in such realities turned digitally spectral? And what form would a critical agency need to take that can work against such forces?

Pynchon's post-9/11 Manhattan is a convoluted palimpsest of dusky cityspaces, dreams, and the risky experiments of the Deep Web. In this imaginative universe, the impact of the planes has turned sonic. The terrorists' voices echo through the white noise of a cab radio, while conspirators network between Middle Eastern oil, the Mossad and the Manhattan IT nerdspace. Pynchon takes a satirical bite out of the desire for truth after the attacks, when Roger Rosenberg proclaimed the death of irony. His protagonist Maxine Tarnow is a counterfeit fraud examiner and the leading detective through this maze, turning this novel into a version of Pynchon's quest narrative in which the 'truth' is in regress and thus can only be exposed and critiqued in equally innovative ways. Maxine and March Kelleher, a blogger, former left-wing activist and conspiracy theorist, are in search for a way to tackle the global yet hidden networks which shape their world. Both are motivated by a desire to find a way out of what Maxine calls the "possibility of some stupefied consensus about what life is to be, taking over this whole city without mercy, a tightening Noose of Horror, multiplexes and malls and big-box stores" (Pynchon 2013, 51). Yet both are also aware that the modes and preconditions of judging and critiquing have changed along with the nature of the object of their critique, "dwarfed by deep time and fractal space" (Huehls 2016, 159f).

"After the 11 September attack," March editorializes, "amid all that chaos and confusion, a hole quietly opened up in American history, a vacuum of accountability, into which assets human and financial begin to vanish." This "new enemy" is "unnamable, locatable on no organization chart or budget line" (Pynchon 2013, 399). Such a hole might be filled with the inaccessible suffering of those in the towers, Pynchon suggests, but it is shaped in a world on the edge between veils of conspiracy, obscure financial patterns and layers upon layers of code.

As the experience of terror turns virtual, Pynchon therefore raises the question if critical agency is possible at all in such a context. This is not merely a question of the 9/11 aftermath; indeed, as Huehls has argued, it is a challenge of the neoliberal system per se;

> In a world in which neoliberalism touches everything but the barest of life, you can certainly make critiques, challenge norms, and offer

competing representations of the world, but given neoliberalism's omnipresence, the position you hold will be just as neoliberal as the position you're against.

(Huehls 2016, 5)

Such paralysis is an inadvertent consequence of the condition of being implicated in the world: implicated subject positions make the very idea of detached critique impossible, as there seemingly is no outside space to step beyond this reality which is continuously regressing into a series of screens. Pynchon's protagonists, too, despite their passionate left-wing politics, are suitably entangled. Maxine's main nemesis is Gabriel Ice, who ironically is March's son-in-law, is a neocapitalist robber baron who has visions of colonizing the Arctic for his IT operations, making this neoliberal context – unsurprisingly for Pynchon – particularly strong here. It is, however, immediately entwined with a complex history of international security and surveillance operations; Maxine has an affair with Lester Windust, who had acquired "a portfolio of pain and damage" (Pynchon 2013, 109) long before the 2001 attacks in his role in US security operations in South America which had taken a turn for the "sinister" and began to stretch to duties including euphemistically named "noncompliant-subject relocations" (Pynchon 2013, 108). When Maxine thus falls into the trap of complicity via their erotic relationship, this highlights how Pynchon emphasizes the position of the subject to be one that is torn between attraction to, or desire of, ideological certainty and the responsibility to resist this.

However, trauma touches the barest life, the only dimension which even Huehls acknowledges to be beyond the reach of such ideological engulfment (Huehls 2016, 5). Interestingly, though, Pynchon offers a vision for how critical agency can form anew precisely at the point where such visceral corporeality aligns with virtual horizons. Unlike the digital, which operates via binary encoding, the virtual also describes an opening. This is why so far I have avoided the term 'virtual trauma,' as employed by Marc Redfield, as I want to uphold this differentiation (2009, 29). Whilst the digitized terror of 9/11, with its television loops and returning images, closes down any possibility of envisioning realities other than this screened universe, the virtual is more attuned to horizons of change.

The Bleeding Edge has four planes of reality which intersect and entwine, opening each other into unforeseen relations; the New York City urban space, the Deep Web, Corporate Surveillance, and the human mind (especially Maxine's). On the one side looms the urban "meatspace" (Pynchon 2013, 168) symbolized by the 'Deseret', a building and microcosm, with a criminal twilight for a pool and residents who transform, grotesquely and neon-coloured, in raucous Halloween parties. Deeparcher, at the other end of the spectrum, is a virtual space navigable via avatar. It is not in opposition to reality but a formative dimension of reality, and as such a potentiality in Deleuze's sense (1988, 97). Built to provide an encoded refuge, it transforms into a desert of invisible links after 9/11. "A darkness pulsing with whatever light was before light was invented" (Pynchon 2013, 75), the Archer aims towards the "immeasurable uncreated," and reveals its trajectories only when a random click hits a hidden link. "It's all about losing, not finding' (Pynchon 2013, 404), as Maxine articulates it, making the DeepArcher the space of the virtual as such.

This multidimensional reality, therefore, is not merely a constellation of singular and isolated entities. Pynchon's fictional universe is shaped by virtual openings and affective currents in between. Such relational coming-into-existence is the point from which new critical agency emerges. Interbleeding, this subverts the rigidity of a post-terrorist reality in which, as March notices, "everything has to be literal now" (Pynchon 2013, 335). This impulse to narrow down reality to the supposed core of what was considered the truthfulness of the event, after all, constitutes a foreclosure of critical thought, especially as the reality to which such loyalty was demanded was never fully exposed. Critical agency, Pynchon suggests in contrast, can only emerge when re-positioning ourselves in a reality that is complex.

This becomes apparent as the planes of reality permeate each other more and more, overlapping and reflecting each other's dimensions. The Deep Web, initially an autonomous space, is gradually subjected to the kind of urban development which the novel criticizes throughout, with its digital streets and spaces turning into sites of marketing and gentrification. The crack between the virtual and the material becomes visible in moments of intuition, which, ultimately, is the prime form of cognition in the novel. Thus, the financial patterns of embezzlement and money laundering cause "convection currents in Maxine's coffee keep bringing something to the surface just long enough for her to muster "Hey, wait . . ." before submerging again too quickly to ID it" (Pynchon 2013, 82); this sense of interconnectedness, though not defineable, opens up material reality towards the virtual patterns of potential links and vectors, or, to quote Deleuze once more, "Intuition leads us to go beyond the state of experience into the conditions of experience" (1988, 27). Such intuition is always also bodily. Conckling is a prime example here, a professional 'nose' who can smell the chronology of events as they happened, for instance in a murder scene, thus re-instigating a sense of linear time in the patterned spaces of the text. Maxine herself, not without irony, use her bladder as a sensor to steer her towards clues she needs in her examinations.

These intuitive openings into difference and change highlight the fact that all of these – even the more intrinsically material ones, such as the urban space – are actualizations of a vast horizon of possibilities of what might have been in history, or of the to-come in the future, and hold these potentials present. This intuition, therefore, is not the fear of the paranoids who, as Elias succinctly phrases it, "strive to unmask the logic of history in which they move" (2012, 126). It is certainly responsive to the totalitarian control of secretive global tycoons, multinational corporations and military-industrial conglomerates, but not fully caught up in it. Instead, the interbleeding and overlapping of realities which Maxine intuits lead her into moments of more resistant connections; Elias explains this using the concept of the subjunctive, a state of openness in which multiple possibilities of interpretation can exist simultaneously. Opposed to the rigidity of the literal, such simultaneity disrupts normative, rational thinking and can open up "possibilities for alternative ways of being, thinking, and acting" (Elias 129); these, however, are not targeted at a utopian future, which is the fundamental reason for March's realization that the old conspiracy theories of the left do not hold any more; they require re-positionings in a present that is thick with the past but also with future potentials.

In the experience of their difference, which is not additive but constitutive, a process of discovery for Maxine unfolds. This operates as speculative thought which negotiates between ideological belonging and critical distanciation, remaining a doubled movement between being implicated and effecting change in moments of encounter, when realities and entities come into contact to move away again, becoming changed and interbled in the process.

Bleeding Edge, ultimately, is a novel about developing a new compass to deal with a new world by getting "constructively lost" (Pynchon 2013, 76) in it. The human body is not merely falling. It disperses into avatar and material dimensions and thus re-introduces the possibility of an outside space that is so crucial to any form of critical agency. By allowing herself to become doubled in the 'meatspace' and the Deep Web, Maxine carves a subject position that takes her beyond the series of screens which she initially finds her reality to have become. This re-positioning is an alternative to the stark non-choice which Žižek diagnoses in a post-9/11 world, which, as he feels, offers only the options of democracy or fundamentalism. But it also negotiates the other binary which 9/11 foregrounded, that between the real and the digital, by inhabiting the tangent spaces between both. This is the actual outcome of what has makings of a detective novel, but ultimately, of course, isn't. The novel ends in few resolutions. But it does offer a way to get the individual off the 'barroom floor' of history, by simultaneously inhabiting the digital, virtual and material spaces which all imploded into each other after the 9/11 attacks. Pynchon's interbleeding body is therefore a starting point for counteracting the paralysis of shock that emanates from the body, suspended in fall yet virally alive, that opened this reading.

Gyres of Time: Subverting the Logic of Pre-emption

> But something's gone wrong with the words in time – syllables linger, refusing to dissipate or fall into silence – so that now there's a pileup of sounds, like cars colliding on a highway, turning meaning into cacophony, she knows it, she is adding to the din, wordlessly, soundlessly, with a cry that rises from her throat and goes on and on forever. Time swells, overwhelming her. [. . .] there is no up. No down. No in. No out. No forward or backward. Just this cold, crushing wave, this unnameable continuum of merging and dissolving.
>
> (Ozeki 2013, 347f)

Ruth, one of the protagonists in Ruth Ozeki's 2013 *A Tale for the Time Being*, is engulfed in the dissolution of linear time. Though shot through with a cry, this is not trauma's time as conventionally conceived. If Ozeki imagines time not as an arrow but as a gyre, this is no coincidence in a novel that is oceanic in its figuration. A writer living on the Canadian Pacific Coast, Ruth has become obsessed with a piece of jetsam she found, refracting sunlight, on the shore. Sealed up in the neon-colored 'Hello Kitty' box along with the lingering smell of a girl's fruity shampoo is the diary of a Tokyo teenager. This girlishness, however, is deceptive. Nao is offering her thoughts on the trauma of bullying and attempted rape, her family's history of mental illness and suicide in the pages skillfully inserted into a copy of Marcel Proust's *A La Recherche du Temps Perdu*. The novel, thus, is immersed in transhistorical and transnational networks of trauma and violence, and as responsive to 9/11 as it is to the Tsunami and nuclear disaster in Fukushima or the Jewish diaspora. This immersion is not purely metaphoric. "We're by-products of the mid-20th century" (Ozeki 2013, 32), as Ruth's husband Oliver observes, but there is no sense of competing memories constructing rigid group identities here. Memory, rather, is offered by the Pacific Ocean and the flotsam it carries on its gyres, which draws moments in time "like plastic confetti," into "the gyre's becalmed center, the garbage patch of history and time. The gyre's memory is all the stuff that we've forgotten" (Ozeki 2013, 114).

Inspired by her great-grandmother's Zen Buddhist philosophy of time, Nao has added older artifacts, creating such gyre memory in miniature in the bundled time capsule. Ruth slowly realizes that the added stack of French letters and a carefully inscribed watch belonged to the girl's great-uncle, a student forced to serve as Kamikaze pilot in World War II. When it comes to figurations of time, the gyre symbolically counteracts the watch. Suffering from what can more aptly be called trauma's time, the soldier Haruki had wished to

> Smash the clock and stop time from advancing! Crush the infernal machine! Shatter its bland face and rip those cursed hands from their

torturous axis of circumscription! [. . .] But no, there is no use, no way of stopping time, and so I lie here, paralyzed, listening to the las moments of my life tick by.

(Ozeki 2013, 322)

His paralysis by the 'infernal machine' of unforgivingly linear time is fundamentally different from Ruth's whirl in time's gyre. Submerging the human micro-being, gyre time not only "deepens" (Dimock 2006), but shapes being into co-existence, with all the possibilities of change this entails. Turning memory into "virtual coexistence" (Deleuze 1988, 60), this evokes a Bergsonian conception of time more interested in simultaneity than in succession. Nevertheless, the key word here is 'virtual;' the whirls which submerge Ruth entail not inchoate obscurity but lead into a horizon of emergent possibility, of encounters with letters jumbled and sounds unfolding. After all, if formerly sequential patterns turn into noise they also become open to new ways of merging and dissolving. The gyre thus infuses time and its allegedly uncompromising forward march from past to traumatic future with the possibility of alternative moments, to be actualized from the noise. This is particularly interesting when considering the inclusion of the kamikaze soldier – a suicide bomber – as a transhistorical and transnational gesture in a novel containing both protagonists' narratives about their personal experience of 9/11.

Interestingly, linear time not only announces the trauma of a death-to-come in a moment of individual realization, to be read psychologically. Ozeki's time figurations are part of a broader pattern in 9/11 fiction, which politicizes linearity when it associates it with the terrorist plot. "The plot shapes every breath he takes," (DeLillo 2007, 176) is how the terrorist Hammad experiences the run-up to his suicide mission on September 11, 2001, in Don DeLillo's *Falling Man*. This reference to the terrorist trajectory as linear plot shot through with inevitability demonstrates how complex the entanglements of trauma, time and politics are. In consequence, even such a brief snapshot of the temporal metaphors – time as gyre or ticking clock – indicates the link between time and agency. While the former opens up not-yet-actualized potentials, the latter forecloses the future and engulfs the present in the threat of the to-come. Temporal figurations thus, can describe the difference between incapacity and the emergent agency to affect change.

In this section, I propose that imagining time and memory as gyre is a key political intervention in the context of collectively experienced trauma. In the face of experiences that are visceral at the most extreme level, and situated in a political context that enacts global power with force, questions of time might seem frivolously abstract. However, notions of time which emphasize rupture and inevitability are a core precondition of the politics of pre-emption and military intervention that characterized the 9/11 aftermath. Re-imagining time, therefore, can offer ways to step out of this delusion of stark necessity, and open up alternative modes of response. The first question this raises, however, is a link I have already made implicitly: that between traumatic time and the politics of pre-emption, and before moving on, this deserves some clarification.

9/11 marked the beginning of pre-emptive time. Operating in the name of security and an alleged state of exception, the pre-emptive logic of the war on terror defied hitherto accepted norms. Its legitimacy increasingly in question once the focus shifted from Afghanistan to Iran, the pre-emptive rationale served to vindicate 'black sites' beyond the rule of law, such as the infamous institutionalized human rights abuses in Guantanamo Bay. It is also partly led virtually, via drones, exposing a tendency towards legal and emotional detachment from the de-humanized collateral damage on the ground. Yet pre-emption is also a temporal phenomenon. Based on a sense of epochal rupture, as "time stood still" (Spiegelman 2004, 3), the legal unhinging of the 'aftermath' is framed by a time out of joint. The trauma of the 9/11 attacks thus led to the sense that time was "skewed" (Huehls 2008, 44), precluding the future because the present itself seemed ungraspable in the "moment of witness before eventness takes hold" (Glejzer 2008, 101). Trauma, in this sense, is caught between the 'tyranny' (Laub 1992, 79) of the past and a future that fails to materialize. The temporal dimension it overwhelms, therefore, is the present, and that is a crucial point, as it is in the present that actions initiate their effects. To describe trauma as a "super-present" (McGlothlin 2008, 105) is therefore misleading. The traumatic flashback, even when the event is past, will ensure its immediacy and swallow the present moment. The eternal televised re-runs of the collapse of the Twin Towers exposed this traumatic time paradox; the linear progression of time, which Ozeki's doomed kamikaze soldier rightly feared, ensures the inevitability of the fall and thus forecloses the future. Trauma thus paralyses agency as the very temporal dimension that is supposed to be transitory, affected by and affecting change – the present – grinds to a stand-still.

Pre-emption, at first sight, appears to offer a way out of this double-bind because it foregrounds action, which was part of its political attraction after the attacks. It is, as Brian Massumi has argued, a "time concept" denoting "acting on the time before: the time of threat, before it has emerged as a clear and present danger" (Massumi 2015, vii). Massumi's time before is the immobilized present I have just described, yet once pre-emption operates, this "intensive contraction" (Massumi 2015, 208) becomes even more drastically foreshortened. A pre-emptive logic predicts the future and takes action to then impede its own prophecy, thus paradoxically fulfilling it. What Massumi calls the "self-completing" (2015, 208) effects of pre-emption thus describes a bent temporal field. Pre-emption, with its actionist focus, impedes futurity from unfolding, a move that is only viable because it occurs in a context in which everyone is already primed to fear-producing cues, a condition which trauma, with its emotional upheaval, throws us in. Paradoxically, just as the logic of pre-emption prescribes perpetual readiness in the name of fear and security – ready for the next strike, the next attack – this readiness is precisely what hinders being and acting in the present. This "perpetual condition of futurity in the present" which "not only never sets but never rests" (Massumi 2015, 242) is thus the politicized equivalent to the time of trauma.

Yet the politicization of trauma in the logic of pre-emption is both ethically problematic and built on a reductive understanding of the processes of memory actually occurring in trauma. Regardless of how prevalent and metaphorically suggestive notions of a 'tyrannical' past might be, whose repetition compulsion renders both memory and present life impossible, traumatic temporality is actually a dynamic phenomenon. Traumatic memories do not just impose themselves on the present, but also offer cross-temporal, dialogical potential in what Laplanche calls a "seesaw effect" (2002, 102). When discussed on a social macrolevel, this is a crucial point that tends to go missing in debates which foreground rupture alone, as it gestures towards other histories of violence, other traumata, which the public discourse might repress. In a Freudian sense, memories activate each other, and Gilles Deleuze points out that Freudian flashbacks of trauma are also much more dynamic that meets the eye. Dreams or re-enactments of trauma, after all, do not repeat with photographic fidelity, but obey a logic of mask-like variation in which trauma is certainly repeated, but also opened to fragments of other memories that are part of such fragmented dream-scapes, too. Literature exposes such trans-historical and transnational patterns to subvert the territorialization of trauma by nationalist politics in which states, as Edkins, too, argues, "take control of trauma time, to operate through or in a permanent state of exception" (2014, 127).

The notions of singularity and epochal rupture on which the politics of pre-emption are built therefore already appropriate trauma to the narrow frame of military intervention. Most importantly, though, this politically instrumentalized link between the time of trauma and pre-emption raises the question which I have already touched upon when discussing the difference between time as gyre, and time as infernal machine: "How do you act politically under such conditioning, in the absence of any reasonable assurance that the quantum of causal force you apply will bring expected results in any linear fashion?" (Massumi 2015, 242).

Ozeki responds to this question by immersing her characters into what Wai Chee Dimock calls "deep time" (2006). The connection which opens up between Nao and Ruth is not just one between reader and writer, engaging in a dialogic creation of a traumatic "record to be made" in Dori Laub's psychoanalytic sense (1992, 57). It is also the undoing of what Dimock criticizes as the "short chronology of a young nation" (Dimock 2006, 1) which renders its citizens insensitive to other and older cultures, as demonstrated in the burning down of the Iraqi National Library and Islamic Library by American Marines in 2003. Deep time cannot be measured "with fixed segments, fixed unit lengths, each assignable to a number" (Dimock 2006, 2); it instead resists the abstraction of the clock, which delimits time like the border marks off the nation state, and is instead embedded in material irregularities and contexts. In deep time, different nations' chronologies begin to burden each other. Time, thus, becomes a complex network of "projective and recessional" frames, along which currents move both ways "into many loops of relation, a densely interactive fabric" (Dimock 2006, 4). Where pre-emptive time is framed by the nation-state, deep time is immersed in multitudinous life. Both temporally and politically, this is the fabric of Ozeki's novel. Her narrative focalizers, Nao and Ruth, co-create each other's presents in order to survive, although these present moments differ as the time of reading is years after the time of writing. Their time is not only deep but reciprocally folded.

In Ruth's present, a time that is post-9/11, post-Fukushima but already sensing the imminent urgency of climate breakdown, a Japanese crow appears in their Canadian forest. Oliver, Ruth's ecological artist husband, guesses that the crow must have ridden the Pacific gyre along with the plastic waste dispersed there, making its improbable way over to their shore. In a novel so decidedly dialogical between cultures, languages and nations, this crow is initially treated with a touch of irony, as it scares the native birds but supports Oliver's idea about building ecologies better equipped to survive climate breakdown. His plan to re-forest Canada using extinct, paleontological species that might be better attuned to the challenges to come had been blocked by local concerns about (21st century) native species, in a poignant aside on Ozeki's part about the politics of climate change. In this novel, all beings, including the crow, are part of an ecology of migration.

For Ruth, however, the crow becomes a hinge through folds of time. Crow imagery infuses her dreams, one of which I quoted at the beginning of this section. Her dreams take her to Nao's world, or her great-grandmother's Buddhist temple more specifically, where the nuns wear wide garments with sleeves like "wide black wings" (Ozeki 2013, 122). "Feather-like touches" (Ozeki 2013, 123) accompany Ruth's repeated immersions into an unformed condition, which she initially experiences with horror as "a feeling, of nonbeing, sudden, dark and prehumen" (Ozeki 2013, 122), a "vast and empty ruthlessness" (Ozeki 2013, 122). The feathery touches, however, calm her until she feels "cradled in the arms of time itself" (Ozeki 2013, 123). This insertion of difference into a prior vastness suggests a similarity to Deleuze's diagrams, or "biograms" as Manning terms these abstract cartographies of material being (Manning 2009, 124). A biogram, after all, is a state of preformed life that can be revived to orient further lived experience. The obscure darkness thus becomes infused with the creative promise of futurity. As a state of emergence, it opens Ruth's horrified first reaction to an affective sense of emergence, as her subject position disperses and gestures towards a newly entwined body, about to be actualized. As a state of "exfoliation" (Manning 2009, 124), the dream begins to provoke the alleged fixity of things, suffusing reality with the promise of change.

As chaotic diffusion gives way to a horizon of possibilities, Ruth begins to perceive a sense of agency as she – if she learns from the crow's feathery touches – might also be able to affect change in this ocean of time. Virtual possibility thus describes the precondition for Ruth's agency. "Thick with past activity" (Massumi 2014, 61) and directed towards the future, Ruth's immersion into the virtual indeed emphasizes the embodied dimension of such non-linear being, as the virtual becomes a hinge between the non-sensuous past and actual, material effects. Ozeki herself offers glimpses of how she conceives such a time by referencing Zen Master Dōgen's ideas about granular time, in which each moment is both ephemeral and tangible like a grain of sand. In a political light this is evocative, as it suggests a mode of being that is fundamentally non-dual. Immersing humans into the deep conditions of the world in which they, like waves on the ocean, are "[n]ot same. [. . .] [N]ot different either" (Ozeki 2013, 194), the old nun Jiko uses these ideas to teach her abused granddaughter to overcome her anger and vengefulness, showing her "how not to kill anything" (Ozeki 2013, 204). Against the idea that trauma and injury necessitate revenge, being a 'time being' thus opposes the logic of pre-emption, which relies on a vengeful affectivity charged with fear.

Yet the crow is not just a guide from Western to Eastern Buddhist philosophy. I mentioned earlier that it guides Ruth through time folds, and this is meant literally. The novel, after all, and typically for trauma literature, warps reality. Ghost figures travel through time, such as Haruki, the kamikaze pilot, who returns to talk to Nao when she is seeking out his story. The dividing lines between spheres of space and time are therefore as porous and shifting as the tectonic plates after the tsunami, which, as Oliver reminds Ruth, moved Japan closer to Canada in the earthquake.

The temporal constellations in *A Tale for the Time Being*, therefore, are distinctly different from linear time, so clearly associated in post-9/11 literature with the terrorist plot. Time, here, is akin not to the line, but to the fold. In his 1991 essay "The Fold," Deleuze describes the baroque fold thus:

> Matter thus offers a texture that is infinitely porous, that is spongy or cavernous without empty parts, since there is always a cavern in the cavern: each body, however small it may be, contains a world insofar as it is perforated by uneven passageways, and the world,

surrounded and penetrated by an increasingly subtle fluid, was like a "pond of matter in which there are different currents and waves."
(Deleuze 1991, 230)

It is easy to see how the time spheres in Ozeki's novel correspond to this texture: shot through by perforations and access points, they spatialize time as a convoluted and kaleidoscopic space to be traversed by nomadic, and often schizophrenically hybrid bodies. This elasticity is fundamentally different from the static inevitability of causal linearity. Interestingly, the fold is thought here as an operation, a folding and unfolding, which puts the individual into contact with a sense of agency that does not stem from an individual 'inside,' but from their implication in a process of becoming which is impersonal. Individuals are not suffocated by the folds, just as Ruth remains only temporarily submerged, but are nourished by difference and the agentic forces that come with that. The fold twists, diversifies, moves continuously, and puts inside and outside into communication. It thus offers an affirmative model of time that enables the process of becoming into the future, instead of collapsing into the zombie apocalypse. The fold also offers an interesting thought experiment where trauma is concerned: the darkest and most inaccessible part of the fold within the depths of matter can be read as a metaphor for trauma. Yet in the unfolding, this is the part to be exposed most radically, transforming it and everything around it. Instead of entailing a repetition compulsion, understanding trauma as a twist in the movement of folding, spatialized and material time not only liberates the wounded into a new possibility of agency; it also acknowledges the necessity, and possibility, of radical change as trauma is exposed. As Ruth gradually uncovers Nao's family history, her dreams begin to have such an unfolding impact on her world.

"What does separation look like," Ruth wonders. "A Wall? A Wave? A body of water? [. . .] What does it feel like to push through?" (Ozeki 2013, 346). Ruth's dream renders the separating walls fluid, as she swims along the ocean in the wake of the crow and the debris that fills the sea. She had earlier noticed that Nao's diary, which she still hasn't read up to the end, seems to have lost its words. She knows that it was initially filled up to the very last page with Nao's handwriting, but the letters seem to now have slipped from the page. This enigma still unsolved, she travels through a mirror in which her reflection unhinges its jaw, "its mouth gapes, bloodred, dripping with saliva – a terrible orifice" (Ozeki 2013, 349). This mouth of a hanged person is Ruth's but also projects Nao's father, whose suicide plans the girl had just written about. Her bodily being thus rendered dual, Ruth feels the earth shuddering and then follows the crow to a park. There, she meets Nao's father, and convinces him to stay alive. As gravity once more fails, "the world releases her from its embrace" (Ozeki 2013, 353) and catapults her back into her Canadian home. The surreal images here are typical dream figures in a Freudian sense, yet more apt considering the transformative force of these dreams is Gregory Bateson's observation that "dreams and percepts and stories are perhaps cracks and irregularities in the uniform and timeless matrix" (Bateson 1980, 23). After all, Ruth's dream has striking consequences: the next day, Nao's diary is filled again. Both she and her father have survived and are now engaged in the burial rites for Jiko, who passed away peacefully. Bateson's ecology of the mind seeks to re-think thought's interaction, moving away from the notion that there is a grid or pattern that pre-shapes ideas. This interactional quality is key here, and is, after, Ruth's initiating impulse. The separating walls she is trying to break are not just those of nation-states, or indeed of time. She is seeking a way of being that is not predicated on pre-given grids.

This is all the more important is it is directly responsive to the patterns of power, cause and effect in which these histories of violence originate. Folded deep time is a counter-figuration to the tyranny of both pre-emptive time and traumatic repetition compulsion precisely because it endows with agency those caught up in the "tangled world of cause and effect" (Ozeki 2013, 321). This affects Haruki, who, in offering himself up as a willing object to the violence of his officers, inadvertently causes the death of the very friend he had intended to save. What I initially characterized with Michael Rothberg as implicated subject positions are, after all, visceral realities for those affected. Nao's father, too, exemplifies this. A helpless bystander to his own daughter' abuse, he quit his job after 9/11 because he could foresee that the software he was building would be weaponized in the war against terror, thus causing his own depression and his family's bankruptcy.

By reading and dreaming Nao's life, Ruth has therefore succeeded in co-creating a better future. In contrast to the operations of pre-emption which sacrifice the present for the threat of the to-come, the end, for Ruth, is continuously "receding" (Ozeki 2013, 375) and reappearing in Nao's letters. Her intervention set up conditions for a "new now" (Ozeki 2013, 376) by travelling the crow's link between multiple worlds, setting up "two moons, talking" (Ozeki 2013, 40) in an encounter between seemingly distinct temporal and geographic planes. In a radicalization of William Gibson's forked-off time, Ozeki thus immerses her protagonist into gyre time in order for her to regain agency. Ruth's actions take effect on a micro-level, of course, with significance for Nao and herself but not directly for the world at large. As an experimental figuration, however, this provides a forceful interposition as regards the seeming inevitability of terrorist acts or the necessity of pre-emptive war to preclude them. This intervention is only possible as a co-creation. It is not unilaterally authored but co-initiated by Ruth and Nao, who address each other across time to shape the present into a better 'now.'

The smooth teleological progression of linear time might engender heroes. Ozeki's folded time, in contrast, suggests that being immersed in a deep present, offering relationality and co-creation, is a more future-oriented alternative. Such temporality opposes the preconditions of the nation-state which, in the aftermath of 9/11, was conceived as the prime unilateral agent of pre-emptive action. It offers the temporal conditions for a relational present to take shape, one that might counteract the seeming inevitability of warfare and suicide soldiers in which it originated. More pragmatically, such politics of deep time on a nation-state level might signal a deliberate pause for dialogue and reflection, a latency period as Freud would call it, before launching into the pre-emptive foreclosure of both present and future. This could open crow-like, uncharted channels for real thought, action and communication in which both bodies, like Ruth's and Nao's, can mutually adjust themselves to become responsive to each other and co-create a present that is more sustainable for the future.

Conclusion: A Politics of Wounded Relation

"What, politically, might be made of grief besides a cry for war?" (2004, xii) Judith Butler asked in a 9/11 aftermath defined by nationalist discourse, surveillance mechanisms, and suspended constitutional rights. The transgressed and transgressive bodies of a terrorism literature beyond trauma give an answer that refuses the kind of narrative which begins the history of terrorism with September 11, 2001, a simplicity that has proven as alluring as it is weaponizable. Instead, these writers experiment with subject positions that emerge from globally implicated realities. Viscerally embodied and virtually opened, they seek to co-create a future beyond the violent loops of ever-returning forcefulness. It is this centrality of the body in a digitized present, both shot through with the traces of violence and radiating with affective currents, that is most politically poignant. While the scar inscribes seemingly everlasting marks in rigidity, the openness of these literary protagonists to virtual dimensions of the real, to affect and gyres of time dynamizes trauma so that envisioning the future becomes possible again. These bodies are simultaneously intimate and outside of themselves, a doubling that is particularly poignant in a context in which the valence of life and death has become commodified in a media-based wound culture. These bodies' steps beyond themselves makes them uncontainable. They are, thus, both scarred and resistant, and become primary sites of a relationally created present because they offer a narrative that is de-centered from the absoluteness of the injured 'I,' be it individual or that of a nation state, which reduced emotional horizons to victimization and vengeance in the war on terror.

References

Banita, Georgiana. 2012. *Plotting Justice: Narrative Ethics & Literary Culture After 9/11*. Lincoln and London: University of Nebraska Press.
Bateson, Gregory. 1980. *Mind and Nature: A Necessary Unity*. London: Fontana Press.
Baudrillard, Jean. 2002. *The Spirit of Terrorism and Other Essays*. Translated by Chris Turner. London and New York: Verso.
Blackman, Lisa. 2012. *Immaterial Bodies: Affect, Embodiment, Mediation*. London: Sage.
Blais, Allison, and Lynn Rasic. 2011. *A Place of Remembrance: Official Book of the September 11 Memorial*. Washington, DC: National Geographic.
Butler, Judith. 2004. *Precarious Life: The Powers of Mourning and Violence*. London and New York: Verso.
Caruth, Cathy. 1995. *Introduction to Trauma: Explorations in Memory*, edited by Cathy Caruth, 3–12. Baltimore: The Johns Hopkins University Press.
Caruth, Cathy. 1996. *Unclaimed Experience. Trauma, Narrative and History*. Baltimore and London: The Johns Hopkins University Press.
Däwes, Birgit. 2011. *Ground Zero Fiction: History, Memory and Representation in the American 9/11 Novel*. Heidelberg: Universitätsverlag Winter.
Deleuze, Gilles. 1988. *Bergsonism*. New York: Zone Books.
Deleuze, Gilles. 1989. *Spinoza: Practical Philosophy*. Translated by Robert Hurley. San Francisco: City Lights Books.
Deleuze, Gilles, and Jonathan Strauss. 1991. "The Fold." *Yale French Studies* 80: 227–47.
DeLillo, Don. 2001. "In the Ruins of the Future: Reflections on Terror and Loss in the Shadow of September." *Harper's Magazine* (December): 33–40.
DeLillo, Don. 2007. *Falling Man*. London: Picador.
Dimock, Wai Chee. 2006. *Through Other Continents: American Literature Across Deep Time*. Princeton, NJ: Princeton University Press.
DiPrete, Laura. 2006. *'Foreign Bodies': Trauma, Corporeality, and Textuality in Contemporary American Culture*. New York and London: Routledge.
Donn, Katharina. 2016. *A Poetics of Trauma After 9/11. Representing Vulnerability in a Digitized Present*. London and New York: Routledge.
Durrant, Sam. 2014. "Undoing Sovereignty: Towards a Theory of Critical Mourning." In *The Future of Trauma Theory: Contemporary Literary and Cultural Criticism*, edited by Gert Buelens, Sam Durrant, and Robert Eaglestone, 91–109. London: Routledge.
Edkins, Jenny. 2003. *Trauma and the Memory of Politics*. Cambridge: Cambridge University Press.
Edkins, Jenny. 2014. "Time, Personhood., Politics." In *The Future of Trauma Theory: Contemporary Literary and Cultural Criticism*, edited by Gert Buelens, Sam Durrant, and Robert Eaglestone, 127–40. London: Routledge.
Elias, Amy J. 2012. "History." In *The Cambridge Companion to Thomas Pynchon*, edited by Inger H. Dalsgaard, Luc Herman, and Brian McHale, 123–35. Cambridge: Cambridge University Press.
Freud, Sigmund. (1908) 1952. "Studien über Hysterie." In *Sigmund Freud, Gesammelte Werke. Chronologisch Geordnet. Bd. I. Werke aus den Jahren*

1892–1899, edited by Anna Freud, E. Bibring, W. Hoffer, E. Kris, and O. Isakower, 75–312. London: Imago.

Gibson, William. 2005. *Pattern Recognition*. New York: Berkley Books.

Glejzer, Richard. 2008. "Witnessing 9/11: Art Spiegelman and the Persistence of Trauma." In *Literature After 9/11*, edited by Ann Keniston and Jeanne F. Quinn, 99–122. New York: Routledge.

Gregg, Melissa, and Gregory J. Seigworth, eds. 2010. *The Affect Theory Reader*. Durham, NC: Duke University Press.

Huehls, Mitchum. 2008. "Foer, Spiegelman, and 9/11's Timely Traumas." In *Literature After 9/11*, edited by Ann Keniston and Jeanne F. Quinn, 42–59. New York: Routledge.

Huehls, Mitchum. 2016. *After Critique: Twenty-First Century Fiction in a Neoliberal Age*. Oxford: Oxford University Press.

Junod, Tom. 2009. "The Falling Man." *Esquire*. September 8, 2009. http://classic.esquire.com/the-falling-man/.

Kahn, Jeanette, and Paul Levitz, eds. 2002. *9–11. September 11th 2001*. Vol. II. New York: DC Comics.

Kaplan, Ann. 2005. *Trauma Culture: The Politics of Terror and Loss in Media and Literature*. New Brunswick, NJ: Rutgers University Press.

LaCapra, Dominick. 2001. *Writing History, Writing Trauma*. Baltimore and London: The Johns Hopkins University Press.

Laplanche, Jean. 2002. "An Interview with Jean Laplanche." In *Topologies of Trauma: Essays on the Limit of Knowledge and Memory*, edited by Linda Belau and Petar Ramadanovic, 101–26. New York: Other Press.

Laub, Dori. 1992. "An Event Without a Witness: Truth, Testimony, and Survival." In *Testimony: Crises of Witnessing in Literature, Psychoanalysis, and History*, edited by Shoshona Felman and Dori Laub, 75–92. New York and London: Routledge.

Lifton, Robert Jay. 2003. *Superpower Syndrome: America's Apocalyptic Confrontation with the World*. New York: Thunder's Mouth Press, Nations Books.

Luckhurst, Roger. 2010. "Beyond Trauma: Torturous Times." *European Journal of English Studies* 14 (1): 11–21.

Lurie, Susan. 2006. "Falling Persons and National Embodiment: The Reconstruction of Safe Spectatorship in the Photographic Record of 9/11." In *Terror, Culture, Politics: Rethinking 9/11*, edited by Daniel J. Sherman and Terry Nardin, 44–68. Bloomington: Indiana University Press.

Manning, Erin. 2009. *Relationscapes: Movement, Art, Philosophy*. Cambridge, MA and London: MIT Press.

Massumi, Brian. 2011. *Semblance and Event: Activist Philosophy and the Occurrent Arts*. Cambridge, MA and London: MIT Press.

Massumi, Brian. 2014. "Envisioning the Virtual." In *The Oxford Handbook of Virtuality*, edited by Mark Grimshaw, 55–70. Oxford: Oxford University Press.

Massumi, Brian. 2015. *Ontopower: War, Powers, and the State of Perception*. Durham, NC and London: Duke University Press.

McGlothlin, Erin. 2008. "'When Time Stands Still': Traumatic Immediacy and Narrative Organization in Art Spiegelman's *Maus* and *In the Shadow of No Towers*." In *The Jewish Graphic Novel: Critical Approaches*, edited by Samantha Baskind and Ranen Omer-Sherman, 94–110. New Brunswick, NJ and London: Rutgers University Press.

Meek, Allen. 2010. *Trauma and Media: Theories, Histories, and Images.* London and New York: Routledge.
Melnick, Jeffrey. 2009. *9/11 Culture: America Under Construction.* Malden, MA: Wiley-Blackwell.
Neal, Arthur G. 1998. *National Trauma & Collective Memory: Major Events in the American Century.* New York: M.E. Sharpe.
Onega, Susana, and Jean-Michel Ganteau. 2014. "Introduction: Performing the Void." In *Contemporary Trauma Narratives: Liminality and the Ethics of Form*, edited by Susana Onega and Jean-Michel Ganteau, 1–20. New York and London: Routledge.
Ozeki, Ruth. 2013. *A Tale for the Time Being.* Edinburgh and London: Canongate Books.
Pynchon, Thomas. 2013. *Bleeding Edge.* London: Jonathan Cape.
Redfield, Marc. 2009. *The Rhetoric of Terror: Reflections on 9/11 and the War on Terror.* New York: Fordham University Press.
Rothberg, Michael. 2009. *Multidirectional Memory: Remembering the Holocaust in the Age of Decolonization.* Stanford, CA: Stanford University Press.
Rothberg, Michael. 2014. "Preface. Beyond Tancred and Clorinda – Trauma Studies for Implicated Subjects." In *The Future of Trauma Theory: Contemporary Literary and Cultural Criticism*, edited by Gert Buelens, Sam Durrant, and Robert Eaglestone, xi–xviii. New York and London: Routledge.
Rushdie, Salman. 2005. *Shalimar the Clown.* London: Vintage.
Shamsie, Kamila. 2009. *Burnt Shadows.* London: Bloomsbury.
Smelser, Neil J. 2004. "Epilogue: September 11, 2001, as Cultural Trauma." In *Cultural Trauma and Collective Identity*, edited by Jeffrey C. Alexander and Ron Eyerman, 264–82. Berkeley: University of California Press.
Spiegelman, Art. 2004. *In the Shadow of no Towers.* New York: Random House.
Spivak, Gayatri Chakravorty. 2010. *Nationalism and the Imagination.* London: Seagull Books.
Straczynski, Michael J. 2002. *The Amazing Spiderman: Revelations.* New York: Marvel Comics.
Van der Kolk, Bessel A., and Onno Van der Hart. 1995. "The Intrusive Past." In *Trauma: Explorations in Memory*, edited by Cathy Caruth, 158–82. Baltimore: The Johns Hopkins University Press.
Vermeulen, Pieter. 2014. "The Biopolitics of Trauma." In *The Future of Trauma Theory: Contemporary Literary and Cultural Criticism*, edited by Gert Buelens, Sam Durrant, and Robert Eaglestone, 141–55. London: Routledge.
Žižek, Slavoj. 2002. *Welcome to the Desert of the Real! Five Essays on 11 September and Related Dates.* London: Verso.

4 Emergence, Submergence, Insurgence
Politics on Liquid Ground

As on a sunken ship, chairs float through the refracted light of a space made for human habitation, though deeply submerged in water. Peacefully suspended, a young woman enveloped by the waves is sleeping, before her alarm brings her back to dry reality. Her dreaminess develops into doubt, when the voiceover begins its narrative with a questioning gesture: "If I spoke about it, if I did, what would I tell you? I wonder." The double meaning of 'wonder' appears particularly suited to this surreal scene, which opens Guillermo del Toro's 2017 movie *The Shape of Water*, introducing both the miraculous and the uncertain in equal measures. The centre, in this scene, does not hold. As the waves develop their own agency, the human being, afloat, is herself absorbed, moving with non-human objects through space as our lines of vision refract and turn into kaleidoscopic patterns in light shimmering, diffracted, throughout this watery world.

Taking the scene out of context, a human being sleeping through a flood provides an apt metaphor for current environmental politics, which Bruno Latour diagnoses as a case of deadly "stoicism" as humanity is "sleepwalking" through its own destruction – though not without commenting that such a sense of an altered relation to the world is also the "scholarly term for madness" (Latour 2017, 10). Whilst we like to present ourselves as singled-out, Aristotelean political animals, I will argue that core precepts of our politics, including notions of voice, agency, territory, and the Other, need to undergo a fundamental re-think if we are to inhabit a wounded and wounding planet more sustainably. Donna Haraway's poignant question what might happen if "human exceptionalism and bounded individualism, those old saws of Western philosophy and political economics, become unthinkable?" (Haraway 2016, 30) is thus at the centre of my interest in fluid being. How can water, which is among the least cooperative things when it comes to being contained in words and deeds" (Linton 2010, 4), help shape a more ecologically diverse and dispersed notion of politics? Just because nature is uncontainable to our language and unavailable to unilinear, uni-causal actions, after all, does not mean it is unpolitical. Ultimately, the impact of climate change not only unhinges the ecologies in which all human and non-human life participates, it also changes the very conditions which we base our political practices on. This is reflected in a resurgence of grass-roots activism challenging the inactivity of the political players, as school strikes and Extinction Rebellion roadblocks revive civic unrest and disobedience as regular and necessary features of contemporary politics.

On a deeper level, climate change is not only a challenge for politics, but to politics as such. A concept and practice that is exclusively anthropocentric, our current politics struggles with the potency of non-human actors, such as the sea washing up against the beach, inviting sunbathers but potentially also flooding vast strips of land and human inhabitation in uncontrollable tsunamis. As Timothy Morton reminds us, it is an often un-discussed side of the Anthropocene that "we can no longer think history as exclusively human" (Morton 2013, 5); this requires a conception of politics which does not exclude non-humans, but acknowledges humankind as "an ecological being that can be found in the symbiotic real" (Morton 2017, 3). A more sustainable politics would thus require us to let go of the tendency to "hyperseparate" (Plumwood 2002, 9) ourselves from nature; the ecological breakdown, in this sense, has exposed the failure of a self-entitled human identity as the singular reason-endowed political animal. Nature calls into question the assumption that it is human agency alone that shapes life, an assumption that is central to our self-perception as sole political actors within terrestrial life. In this chapter, I propose to take politics onto "liquid ground" (Irigaray 1991, 37) to shape new responses to this question.

However, one may rightly ask what is political about the scene I just opened this chapter with. The protagonist Eliza, a young woman whose inability to speak is mysteriously linked to long scars on her neck, leads a nocturnal existence, constantly drawn to the erotic pull of water. Upon waking up from watery dreams she takes nightly baths and masturbates within and with the water, yet the cleaners' attendance clock at her workplace, a secret government laboratory in Baltimore, jars her sensuality and throws her into a harsh and isolated existence. It is the time of the Cold War arms race, a politics of division, marked by the iron curtain cutting through Europe as much as by the toxicity of chemical warfare in Vietnam. The watery refractions in the opening scene are thus an immediate counterpoint to the territorialisation of the world and the weaponization of human and non-human bodies. In contrast to the watery beginning of this movie, the iron curtain's death strip does not countenance doubt.

This emergent political dimension takes bodily shape as a hybrid being imprisoned in a tank of murky water in the secret government lab which it is Eliza's job to clean. Mythological and future-oriented at once, this creature from the U.S' cultural periphery (having been kidnapped in the Amazon river) appears nevertheless vital and powerful when electric currents begin to run across his skin, lighting it up in coloured semiotic patterns whose meaning is utterly unavailable to the officers in charge. These currents also heal any wounds inflicted by the army men, transforming the energies of the electric shocks to which he is subjected into sustenance for the body they had been intended to damage. If the merman's body, thus, is a site on which military power attempts to inscribe its traces, its very unavailability to such power – a quality that simple notions of resistance cannot quite capture – is apparent from the start.

The military men's desired arms race 'asset,' therefore, is already and literally 'too much' for them, holding a surplus of meaning which their violence cannot contain. Del Toro further develops the amphibian man into a nodal point for politically institutionalised de-humanisation. Exclaiming "it's not even human" and threatening vivisection, General Frank Hoyt and Colonel Strickland inadvertently raise broader questions about the nature of humanity in this 1960s reality. The merman becomes entwined both symbolically and emotionally with other dehumanized creatures and dehumanizing politics. Key dimensions include misogynist violence, as Hoyt threatens Eliza with rape and pushes his bloody hand into his wife's mouth during sex, as well as the rampant racism which Eliza's colleague Zelda is subjected to. Yet the merman not only embodies, but also energises the marginalised. As he communicates with Eliza through erotic touch, gesture and his skin's currents of light, their encounter lays the foundation for a moment civil disobedience to the powers that be when the marginalised collaborate to free the merman from the lab. More significantly, though, this encounter is transformational on a deeper level, as Eliza's scars are activated into gills. What Eliza's and the merman's amphibian being demonstrates, therefore, is the political potency of watery bodies which operate not in the mode of resistance, but offer the alternative of uncontainable being. Their potency inheres in the utter unavailability of the merman when he is imprisoned, as those in power prove powerless against his modes of expression and signification as well as his bodily energies. This is subversion by political illegibility, and it is potent.

Thus, when Luce Irigaray calls for the birth of a "new human being" (2017), she bases this on the recognition that a human being cannot grow from roots like a tree does, but engages vertically and horizontally in currents of water and air. This un-rootedness places those who appear peripheral – hybrid creatures like the amphibian merman – at the very center of an ecological politics. With it, though, comes the responsibility to gauge the human role in the ecosystem without reverting to a politics that operates on the principles of power and exploitation.

In this chapter I will explore how such ecologically framed political spaces and agencies can be understood. Water is a key matter for such a literary ecological politics, precisely because of its apparent resistance to the programmatic nature of institutionalised politics: attuned to diffraction, refraction, erosion, porosity, dispersion and liquefication, water seems to materialize all that runs counter to a purpose-oriented political activism. Such a view is deeply ingrained in Western culture; yet it is short-sighted, and not only when it pertains to a literary politics that is always a proto-politics, more interested in core precepts that ideological conflict. Teeming with ecological ambivalence, water is associated as much with "fecundity or potentiality" as it is with "scarcity, pollution, war, and crisis" (Linton 2010, 6), and thus at the forefront of an ecological breakdown. Unbound from the rootedness of the earth, it is a trickster element that can permeate and change all. On the one hand, of course, water exposes breakdown; the toxicity of lakes and rivers, plastic pollution at the ocean floor and the invisible threat of nuclear fallout in rainwater all demonstrate the failure of current climate politics. On the other hand, though, water remains a horizon of possibility and change. Its potentiality is undeniable in stormfloods indifferent to human inhabitation, but also in river floodings which, at the heart of the ancient civilizations that grew in deltas of the Euphrates or the Nile, render the earth fertile. Linton's key intervention, though, is a different one: he suggests considering water "as a process rather than a thing" (2010, 4), hence its 'uncooperativeness' when it comes to pinning things down. What language would seek to contain it, though? Linton's focus is on water's resistance to a language of formulae. Yet water, surely, has been at the heart of the literary imagination since the beginning of the written word; Homer's *Odyssey* grapples with the force of the oceans, whilst flood narratives feature prominently in the Christian Old Testament as well as the Sumerian *Epic of Gilgamesh*. Darren Aronofsky's 2014 remake of Noah into a blockbuster movie which links the wrath of an Old Testament God to postapocalyptic imagery of ecological breakdown is only one example of how water narratives shape the ecological imagination.

Even more striking is the (repressed) centrality of water to the beginning of politics in the Western sense. "To shield politics from the perils that are immanent to it, it has to be hauled on dry land, set down on *terra firma*" (Rancière 1995, 1) is how Jacques Rancière describes this process when evaluating Plato's *Republic*. And indeed, before Plato takes us into the cave, his dialogues are aswim with references to "life-giving children of Inachus, river of Argos" or visceral descriptions of hero figures such as Achilles, "tossing" and "pacing in frenzy the shore of the vast untameable ocean" – however, these watery metaphors are selected only to be purged from Plato's ideal city. Rancière, however, also notices the proximity of the harbour to the political centre in Athens, "making the whole project of foundation a hopeless one [. . .] The sea smells bad. [. . .] it smells of democracy" (1995, 2). However much repressed, the protean oceanic impulses thus remain a hidden but virulent centre in politics, injecting it with transformative potentials. This undercurrent beneath our feet becomes significant as it challenges us to reconsider our own nature and position within an ecology in which we claim to be politically both active and of consequence. When making the case for oceanic studies, Hester Blum makes a provocative suggestion:

> [w]e might take the bobbing, surging, unfixed shadows on the cave wall as an encouragement to understand political and planetary questions as similarly composed of a matter whose substance owes more to the ductility of the watery world than has been heretofore measured. Democracy requires an accord with the "fatal and seductive" aspects of the imaginative and material oceans.
> (Blum 2015, 28)

In taking up this project, I do not think that the 'fatal and seductive' dimensions of the ocean are sufficient to grasp this potential; water, after all, is never neutral. Despite its elemental force, it is deeply entwined with politics. Perhaps more than the flows of air and breath which Luce Irigaray suggests to be at the heart of her new ecological human (2016, 20), water can show us what it means to be literally submerged within non-human ecologies. Our bodies are made of water, yet at the same time, Astrida Neimanis reminds us that these waters' flows "are directed by intensities of power and empowerment;" Currents of water, in this sense, are also "currents of toxicity, queerness, coloniality, sexual difference, global capitalism, imagination, desire, and multispecies community" (2017, 15). This breathless list can serve to illustrate how water, though omnipresent, is not universal; it infuses all, yet it is never the same, as it changes with contact when passing through boundaries of skin or into dumping sites. It is not de-territorial, but runs across territories, remaining Diatopian when it pervades specific topoi.

Water, therefore, has complex political potencies: Firstly, this "swirling landscape of uncertainty" (Neimanis 2017, 17, quoting Stacy Alaimo 2010) not only changes ideas of how we are embodied; we simultaneously comprise water and are transversed by it, "made mostly of wet matter, but also aswim in the discursive flocculations of embodiment as an idea" (Neimanis 2017, 1). Imagining ourselves as "bodies of water", as Astrida Neimanis suggests, thus emphasizes the urgency to respond to ecological breakdown as it makes any notions of being discrete or distinct from nature utterly untenable. Secondly, though, water is an interesting figure politically as it challenges us to think difference and confluence together. Each body of water, be it human or non-human, pools its own distinct qualities; yet always a hybrid, it is also porous and open to uncontrollable incursions from other bodies of water, whether unwelcome or life-giving. Bodies of water thus differ, but their "differing from one another, their differentiation, is a collective worlding" (Neimanis 2017, 29). Water, after all, is not universal but localised, as toxic pollution shows in particular. Neimanis describes Katsi Cooke's "Mother's Milk Project" which revealed that women on the reservation and eating fish from the polluted St. Lawrence River had a 200% greater concentration of the toxic PCBs in their breast milk (Neimanis 2017, 35). Whilst water differentiates, it infuses other bodies of water, human and non-human, with the by-products of capitalist production. An ecological politics conceived in these terms inevitably draws attention to difference in connectivity. This is a notion which a politics conceived purely as a stage for conflict cannot quite capture.

Seen as a "potential for diffractive relationality" (Neimanis 2017, 122), it is not merely the human figure but the light reflected in the waves in del Toro's opening scene which introduces this most clearly. Multilinearity replaces the time-based and linear logic of nostalgia, seeking water instead as a site to explore what an immersive politics based on movements of relationality, differentiation, and transformation might look like. Inherently opposed as a structure of thought to the politics of the border wall, diffraction and refraction are core dimensions of an ecological politics of water. A "material practice for making a difference, for topologically reconfiguring connections" (Barad 2007, 381), this opens new ways of reading and responding to human material immersion. Water, thus, is not just an origin, be it chaotic or motherly, but an element in which the hierarchies and certainties which shape earth-bound life do not hold.

A literary politics of watery insurgence, seeking out the political side of Amitav Gosh's observation that climate change is also a "crisis [...] of the imagination" (Gosh 2017, 9), positions itself at the nodal point where literary form and non-human voice collide. This becomes clear when cross-referencing the work of two critics deeply invested in the links between literature and climate change: Amitav Gosh and Rob Nixon. The former focuses on cataclysmic events such as storms, which seemingly overwhelm the regularity of what he calls the "modern novel," thus accounting for their alleged resistance to literary form. Yet it is notable that Rob Nixon, in his seminal study of climate change and activism, ascribes the inaction of politics when responding to "slow violence" to a failure of representation, too. This seeming cross-purpose of two arguments, tracing the apparent literary intangibility of climate change back to either slow or sudden eventhood, is partly due to differences in focus; while Gosh is interested in the vague idea of "serious" fiction, Nixon contrasts the ease with which media outlets incorporate narratives of catastrophic climate events into global news coverage, such as hurricane Katrina or the 2011 Fukushima tsunami, to the more widespread yet gradual violence of toxic drift or reforestation which remains largely "out of sight" (Nixon 2011, 2). Both, however, share the impression that such watery events require innovative conceptions of literary representation, figurative bodies and voices.

"[H]ow to device arresting stories, images, and symbols adequate to the pervasive but elusive violence of delayed effects" (Nixon 2011, 3) is a challenge that Nixon responds to by focusing on activist writers, who are deeply committed to confronting what Edward Said called the "normalized quiet of unseen power" (Nixon 2011, 6). Interestingly, he proposes 'apprehension' (2011, 14) as a critical term in this context; in linking perception, emotion and action, apprehension challenges the primacy of vision in contemporary culture and, as Nixon hopes, can help seek out different ways of making legible initially imperceptible threats. As a mode of perception to be honed and developed in ecological political literature, apprehension particularly lends itself to the genre of the testimonial, which, indeed, is Nixon's main focus. Despite a lingering sense of disconnect between the passion of these writers engaging in "testimonial protest, rhetorical inventiveness, and counterhistories in the face of formidable odds" (Nixon 2011, 6), and the stillness which the stance of apprehension encompasses, his advocacy of new writing as core precept of changed ecological politics is vital. It is striking, too, that this project of apprehension seems surprisingly reminiscent of what Amitav Gosh describes as the tendency in the modern novel to "behold" a scene, along with the connotations of controllability, regularity, and rationalisation that this entails (2017, 19) – a tendency which he denounces as counterproductive when trying to respond to the "centrality of the improbable" in a world shaped by climate change (2017, 23). Gosh and Nixon might thus seem to be at loggerheads in both their literary projects and ecological focus, yet such a dismissal out of hand would overlook the crucial fact: both acknowledge that the "grid of literary forms and conventions" (Gosh 2017, 7), be it related to activist testimonials, realist or fantasy fiction, is strung too tightly.

Water's potential of osmosis disperses agency across human and non-human beings. The political poetics of water, thus, offer a symbolic sounding board for what dispersed, relational and enmeshed narrative and political potentiality might entail; it exposes the vulnerability of all beings to each other whilst flooding the injured ecology with creative renewal; this is not a dialectic or dual, but a triangulated movement of destruction, seeding and transformation, negating the notion of a politics staged as conflict of the either-or, between the self and adversaries. Submerging in watery whirls the rooted human who seeks security in thickened skin thus does away with the notion that an ecological politics needs to be earthbound. It offers a 21st century alternative to the idea of emplacement, perhaps precisely because it resists the kind of containment which ideas of the word as weapon or formula aspire to.

The challenge inherent in recognizing human beings as participants in, rather than masters of, terrestrial ecologies is thus a matter of voice and narrative; yet it becomes self-limiting when based on the ultimately anthropocentric perception of the apprehender alone. My hypothesis, therefore, is that literature becomes political in an ecological sense when it helps us acknowledge how agency and signification are more-than-human.

Contrasting the idea of a human 'beholder,' contemporary literature presents us with a human participant in forcefields generating a broad array of agential potentials and diverse patters of semiotic-symbolic expression. This is why this chapter seeks out the insurgency of fluid bodies and watery matters. Nature, in contemporary fiction, is not just there as an object to be apprehended. It assumes metaphoric potentiality of its own, symbolically exploring how to de-centre and de-anthropize the earth.

Processes of emergence, submergence and insurgence describe the literary politics I seek here. The semantics of this are intentional: instead of the reactive impulses of resistance, emergence, submergence and insurgence all reflect fluid energies. Neither is the triangulation of these processes coincidental: it is responsive to the triadic patterns of Hubert Zapf's literary ecology, which explores the role of literature within culture as an ecology in its own right. In replacing his categories of a culturally critical meta-discourse, an imaginative subversive discourse and a reintegrative discourse with this watery triad, I emphasize the non-anthropocentric processes involved in this literary ecology but also aim to expose the political undercurrents inherent in such a view of literature. In 'emergence,' ecological breakdown and the slow violence this engenders come to the surface. "Writing can help make the unapparent appear," can "challenge perceptual habits" and "focus apprehensions" of the catastrophe of climate change unfolding, as Rob Nixon argues (2011, 15). This is the most immediately tangible dimension of a literary ecological politics. When the merman triggers a moment of civil disobedience, such emergence happens as the apparently peripheral voices and agencies of the de-humanized – be it because they are disabled, amphibian, or black – take over the center of the narrative. Yet such an ecological literary politics is not about witnessing alone. Processes of 'submergence' transform ideas of a disconnect between human and posthuman nature into a sense of enmeshment; the human being becomes porous to other natures filtering inwards and outwards. In *The Shape of Water*, this occurs when Eliza turns into an amphibian being herself, posing fundamental questions about the de-limitation of the human species. Finally, 'insurgence' describes the upheaval thus caused. Encompassing both a sense of 'urgency' and the 'surge' of a flood, nature not only writes back but inundates outmoded ideas of human untouchability and natural exploitation, deluging them in the forcefields of the oceanic imagination.

This chapter focuses on 4 key precepts of politics, exploring how water-based ecological figures and voices can change notions of voice, agency, border, and the Other. I have consciously chosen texts that do not neatly fall into the genre of climate dystopia. While decidedly political, apocalyptic narratives have a tendency for being politically cynical, and their "resignation to calamity" (Cohen 2014, x) is paradoxically also easier to embrace than the complex ethical and political demands of relational being. Before moving into these areas, though, I offer a more in-depth theoretical exploration of the fraught relation between literature politics and ecology. More apt than soil to flood and submerge rigid borderlines, water has a singularly subversive potential to turn ecological politics into a future-oriented discipline free from earth-bound nostalgia.

Literature – Ecology – Politics: Unravelling the Knot

What is this 'ecological politics' which literary texts might engage in? Politics, after all, even in its progressive and democratic forms, is ultimately an anthropocentric undertaking, assigning agency to humans (and not even necessarily all humans) only. If one focuses on ecology as the object of politics, an issue to be tackled, this seems an easier question to answer. Rob Nixon's concept of slow violence is only one of many examples of how a literary ecocriticism can be politicized; Nixon showcases ecocriticism's link to activism by addressing the "often fraught and frictional" (Nixon 2011, 6) relations between activists and writers as a creative and generative challenge between pragmatized grassroots politics and de-pragmatized, symbolic provocations. Nevertheless, the question whether a critical movement as diverse has a unified political purpose – or whether it even needs of one – is more difficult to answer. Whilst there is a broad consensus that "technofix solutions" (Plumwood 2002, 8) are ultimately ineffective as they try to accommodate sustainability into an inherently unsustainable capitalist culture of profit, this still leaves more basic issues of political organization open for debate. Are ecological issues entwined with democratic legitimacy, or does the urgency of a climate catastrophe propel ethical imperatives above such questions? Can and should ecological issues be implemented in an eco-friendly autocracy or by eco-guerillas, or even by eco-terrorists?

As this chapter will make clear, the ethical challenges of re-thinking the role of human actors in the world are based on dialogue, relation and implication, and thus root ecological politics firmly in the spectrum of democratic values. It is a matter of becoming alert to the "the thousand responsive songs" of both human and non-human voices, which Walt Whitman calls to on the "liquid rims and wet sands" of Paumanok beach in "Out of the Cradle Endlessly Rocking," a polyphony of voices not conceivable in an autocratic framework even of an ecological kind. "Democratic cultural change strategies are our best hope" (2002, 3), as Plumwood also argues, not because they are the only solution available but because they present the framework most responsive to the interconnected and interdependent (which does not mean harmonious) workings of ecologies.

Along with thus dismissing eco-authoritarianism, ideas of restoring a "supposed pre-modern nature-culture coexistence" in a project of "uncivilization" (Zapf 2016, 55f) are equally to be repudiated. There is no future in nostalgia, and certainly none in reactionary politics. This pertains, too, to the lexicon of wonder that shines through definitions of the field as a "story-laden mode of re-enchantment," (Cohen 2014, x). Despite being spiritually attractive, this is evocative yet perhaps not sufficient for a re-think of literary ecological politics. It is ethically charged with relation and entanglement, assumes non-human interiorities, but remains politically passive.

When attempting to answer these questions, the reactionary ideas mentioned above seem to be particularly adept at creeping back into the project of political ecology. Bruno Latour's *Facing Gaia* lectures are a case in point. Despite the future thrust of his premise that "[f]rom a conceptual standpoint, political ecology *has not yet begun to exist*" (2004, 2) – or perhaps because of this striking dismissal of long-existent intersections between politics and ecology – Latour remains caught within the difficulties involved in re-thinking politics as ecological. He traces the apparent opposition between ecology and politics back to the history of the Western concept of nature, invented, as he claims, as a strategy of immunizing nature from contestation, disagreement, or, to rephrase, from politics (2017, 224). Equally thought-provoking is his subsequent strategy to replace 'nature with 'Gaia,' a life-force borrowed from Hesiod. "Prolific, dangerous, and savvy" (2017, 81), nature as Gaia is not a figure of harmony but challenges the nature-culture dualism when she intrudes into the "universality of laws, the robustness of facts, the solidity of results, the quality of models," previously used to unite minds and nation-states (2017, 226). Interconnected but resistant to totality and too dynamic for any conception of the whole, Latour's Gaia is not an organism but challenges us to re-think order without hierarchy. So far, the idea of Nature as Gaia, a coordinating agent that is disobedient to anthropocentric authority and seeks other connections between agents of elemental or human matter, seems powerful enough for what a democratic ecological politics might look like. The path of grassroots dissemination, dispersed voices or bodily enmeshment, however, is not what Latour chooses.

Jarringly, Latour immediately channels Gaia into questions of sovereignty and supreme authority. This is connected to his search for an "earthbound" (2017, 4) modesty in religion, the sciences and politics. While it is not immediately obvious why an unprecedented ecological emergency should be encountered by a 'back-to-basics' approach rather than unmatched ambition, this nostalgia for the pre-modern is deeply engrained in Latour's ecological politics. "The whole paradox of modernization," he argues, is that it has lost touch with the "down-to-earth," as its materiality only relates to capital but not to being with and in terrestrial ecologies (2017, 200). The reactionary connotations of a 'down-to-earth' approach in this project of "reterrestrialization" unfortunately increase with the introduction of Carl Schmitt, an overtly Nationalist Socialist lawyer, into the equation. Latour uses Schmitt's differentiation between the adversary (*inimicus*) and the enemy (*hostis*), defined as "the other, the stranger," who is the only entity with whom political conflicts are possible; clashes with an adversary, after all, can be resolved by police action. Latour takes this as metaphor for criticizing that ecological problems seem to be solvable by interventions or arbitrations (2017, 237), and instead suggests using the figure of the *hostis* to conceptualize nature's role in an ecological politics, in order to re-politicize it. It is striking that even if attempting to differentiate his earthbound approach from the National Socialist *Blut and Boden* (blood and earth) ideology, he still chooses Schmitt as his first point or reference. While this might re-politicise nature, it is not fully clear how future-orientated this approach truly can be, seeing as both Schmitt's enemy and adversary call for annihilation. Latour's pathway through Gaia thus comes full circle back to concepts of soil soaked with blood, and is clearly not the way forward, perhaps because it re-thinks nature rather than our role in it. After all, it is not nature, whether as Gaia or ecology, that is the problem, but precisely the anthropocentric language of trials of strength which Latour imposes on it.

Of course, elevating this outspoken National Socialist and supporter of the Total War to a reference frame in supposedly progressive critical thought is nothing new. Jacques Derrida had offered a detailed reading of Schmitt in *Politics of Friendship*, interested in the logic of a "total enemy" and defending the leftist and deconstructivist attentions to Schmitt despite his "political commitments" which appear "more serious and more repugnant than those of Heidegger" because his thought is still deeply rooted in the "richest tradition" of European philosophical and legal thought. This defence only illustrates the ethical minefield into which notions of 'rootedness' can lead, making a shift in focus from earth to water even more urgent.

We have already seen that "[N]ot much about our behaviour in relation to the ecological crisis has been rational" (Plumwood 2002, 1); yet it is now time to enquire more deeply into the conditions that enable this derangement, to then disable and replace those same grievances. Val Plumwood here equally indicts the human 'derangement,' reflecting concerns about the apparent misfit between ecology and political action (when conceived on a systemic, not activist, scale). Her reproach of irrationality initially seems to mirror Gosh's desire-based critique of human inaction; responding to continued trends in architecture which favour "shiny, glass-and-metal-plated towers" despite being built in a period of accelerating carbon emissions, he asks what might be "the patterns of desire that are fed by these gestures" (Gosh 2017, 11) to criticize the consumerist desires which Western societies stand in thrall of, but which ecological issues cannot meet. His reference to the phallic and emphatically power-driven image of the office tower is evocative as a site of such a critique, particularly as the mantle of mastery surrounding such architecture had been shattered in the 9/11 attacks even as the downtown centres of precariously flood-and-hurricane prone cities, such as Mumbai or Manhattan, increasingly join the forefront of ecological upheaval. Yet while Gosh operates within a psychoanalytic framework of drives and desires, Plumwood offers a critique of this specific form of madness in a mode that lends itself more obviously to politization.

Plumwood's charge of unreason appraises how the dual split between nature and culture on the one hand, and mind and body on the other hand, has been equated with a nature versus reason dichotomy. This "centric and self-enclosed form of reason" (Plumwood 2002, 4) which operates on the idea of independence from embodiment or any material base disavows, according to Plumwood, the "counter-sphere of 'nature'" (Plumwood 2002, 4) because any acknowledgement of human implication or enmeshment in matters of nature would undermine the pure externality of reason. This self-destructively circular logic paradoxically serves human desires (to revert once more to Gosh's more psychoanalytical concepts) despite its death-drive into ecological breakdown, because it flatters the "sado-dispassionate" hubris of reason (Plumwood 2002, 2f) in the interests of the corporate decision-makers most likely to benefit from such delusions. Fostering "illusions of invincibility" and concealing "our real danger" (Plumwood 2002, 2f), rationalist culture claims distance from and control over non-human nature, disavows networks of dependency, hyperbolizes autonomy, and consequentially dismisses all non-human claims to mind, reason or ethics. Our current 'derangement' in relation to ecology is thus "a liability to survival" (Plumwood 2002, 5) not because reason itself is the problem, but because the notion of reason used to define human's place within ecologies is limited and ecologically unaware.

An ecological politics, thus, needs to question notions of human exclusivity as regards claims to agency, signification, and reason. By the way, before making his unfortunate move into promoting ecological politics as trials of force between the earthbound and the modern, Bruno Latour proposes a useful concept for thinking such dispersed political potencies: he suggests that the traditional agents of humanity and nature become "disaggregated" (2017, 121), which not only emphasizes the challenge of ditching the birds-eye view of looking at the world as a globe, implicitly seeing oneself as a God; he also uses this idea to turn the question of political agency on its head. Seeing as the human actors seem to be resigning themselves to haplessly play the role of "witless object" (2017, 74) when it comes to climate change, he questions how humans – not nature – can even be seen as a political actor in the true sense of the word in this context (2017, 140):

> to live in the epoch of the Anthropocene is to force oneself to redefine the political task par excellence: what people are you forming, with what cosmology, and on what territory? One thing is certain: these

actors who are making their stage debuts have never before played roles in a plot as dense and enigmatic as this one! We have to get used to it: we have entered irreversibly into an epoch that is at once post-natural, post-human, and post-epistemological!

(Latour 2017, 143f)

This is a challenge, as the mere projection of human patterns of speech or intentionality onto the non-human, for instance by unquestioningly promoting an animated world of mythological pantheism for the 21st century, would be both ethically misleading and logically incoherent. The polluted seascape surrounding Fukushima and the Great pacific garbage patch won't just start communicating in the manner of transformed Greek goddesses who lost their human shapes. Freya Mathews, in her plaidoyer for a panpsychism of the 21st century, calls on us to encounter a "reanimated" non-human world as a "subjectival matrix" (Mathews 2003, 4) in which matter is infused with mentality, thus breaking open the dualism which Plumwood prominently critiqued. Nonetheless, the dialogic and participatory relationships between human and non-human nature she envisages are characterised by a friction that is also always erotic, rather than a sense of shared and homogenous agency. Imbuing the non-human world with the kind of interiority and agency that can be politically potent, therefore, is a balancing act that can only be resolved when acknowledging that beings without speech, but with voices or other modes of significations, are political potencies, too. This question of speech is consequently the first and perhaps most fundamental precondition of politics I will explore in this chapter.

Voices Unbound

Jacques Rancière, in his 1999 study *Disagreement*, located the beginning of politics in the coming-into-being of the Athenian demos, which is simultaneously a coming-into-speech. Rancière's conception of politics is therefore premised on the logos as a specifically human form of signification which expresses the useful, harmful, just or unjust to a community, contrasting the pre-political (or possibly non-human, animal) voice which merely indicates its presence (Rancière 1999, 2). Politics originates in this coming-into-speech of a group, such as "the poor" (Rancière 1999, 11) when it begins to express itself, claiming – and this is another key premise for Rancière – a partition, an interruption in the "natural order of domination" by those who previously have had no part and who now introduce contention. Understood thus, politics necessarily relies on recognizing the equation of whole with the multiple as a "basic miscount" (Rancière 1999, 10) an equation which might satisfy the needs of a party when attempting to present itself as the whole community but would, if unchallenged, stifle the very nature of politics constituted in speech and disagreement.

This conception of politics widely resonates with current political practices. Nonetheless, how precisely a conception of politics premised on logos and partition fares in an ecological context remains very much an open question. Who, after all, is speaking up to be counted?

> I pass, like night, from land to land;
> I have strange power of speech;
> That moment that his face I see,
> I know the man that must hear me:
> To him my tale I teach.
> (Samuel Taylor Coleridge,
> "The Rime of the Ancient
> Mariner," 1834)

Samuel Taylor Coleridge's "Rime of the Ancient Mariner" is a tale of ecological enmeshment; having shot an albatross during his journey across icy seas, the Mariner is forced to suffer nature's retribution for this unwarranted killing. The albatross hung around his neck like a cross, he endures the drought of a dead calm, the fire of the sun and the powers of wind and ocean. This ballad is also typical of the ecological literature at the heart of this chapter in another sense: with its seeming distance from questions of politics, it illustrates how ecological literature rewires questions of politics in subtle yet decisive ways. Debbie Lee, for example, has shown how this seemingly otherworldly tale, with its pungent imagery of corpses rotting on a ship, can be linked to the politics of the slave trade, exposing the English population's undercurrents of guilt about their indirect participation in (and profits from) slavery (2002). Implication, in this sense, is both an ecological and political phenomenon, and the Mariner's tale exposes how both dimensions of life are entwined not where political content is concerned, but in the structure and conditions of their experience.

Ultimately, though, this ecological trauma becomes a testimonial challenge: haunted by a voice beyond him, the sailor is forced to tell his tale time after time again. He has become a mouthpiece for ecological destruction, lending human speech to the elemental powers of the wind, the sun and the sea that are holding him in their grip. Questions of speech and agency are thus closely entwined, casting doubt on humanity's illusion of being in control of either. The Mariner is, above all, someone who has experienced what is means to live in ecological relation, in an enmeshed web in which perhaps not everything is connected to everything else, but certainly all is connected to something else, for better or worse. Ultimately, however, the voice of nature here remains anthropocentric. Coleridge relies on a human as speaker, lending expression to a nature that is vital, impactful, and endowed with furious interiority – but remains numb. For nature to be politicized in the "Rime of the Ancient

Mariner," it appears in need of a human to be vocalized. While demoting the human from master over life and death to participant in an ecological world, but there is no doubt that such a logocentric focus simultaneously represses non-human, ecological modes of expression.

Interestingly, this does not change much even in 21st century adaptations of the tale. Nick Hayes' 2011 graphic narrative *The Rime of the Modern Mariner* features a capitalist mariner with a hankering for "dominoes made of whalebone," who presents as a blasé, money-driven, cigarette-smoking and suitably bearded hipster. Hayes uses this figure to expose complicity not in slavery, but in violence of another kind: the ocean which this 21st century ship crosses fills with the flotsam of plastic waste, into which the mariner adds his cigarette stubs upon killing the albatross as a momentary diversion – "its death seemed no great loss." Like Coleridge before him, Hayes here uses the power of literature to expose the unsaid and often unwitnessed breakdown, which is invisibly eroding the basis of human life, in what Zapf would call the literary ecology's culture-critical dimension.

However, even here the ocean's voice relies on an anthropomorphic figure capable of human speech. From the depths emerges a creature of the sea, a grotesque mermaid who toes the line between human and watery being. She lends nature her voice, accusing the mariner of his "hubristic human boast." This cosmic figure encompasses the elements – fire, rain and wind – as well as the depths of the ocean and the moons of the sky. While the albatross's body around the Mariner's neck decomposes into flesh, bones and the nylon gauze which the bird had incorporated into his own wounded body, this deranged and misbehaving sea goddess infuses the Mariner with her voice. Hayes visualizes the ocean whirls to symbolize the Mariner's ultimate recovery and transformation in both body and mind, but it is this cosmic voice that will speak through the Mariner's tale. His transformation, thus, is not a matter of a sudden moment of knowledge or recognition, but requires him to open himself to his connections with other bodies and non-human beings. Thus rendered porous, he speaks in a voice beyond his own body.

Both the 19th century "Rime of the Ancient Mariner" and its 21st century adaptation thus offer only a limited notion of ecological voices that remain reliant on de-centered, porous, but ultimately human(ized) mouthpieces. This poses a string of fundamental challenges: How could a politically potent voice that does not revert to such anthropomorphism be conceived? Is it non-human voices, unacknowledged because they cannot access the logos of human speech, that are today going miscounted? What does this dismissal entail for our understanding of the political potency of the ecological matters and materialities involved in tsunamis, glacial meltwater, or species extinction, even if this is not a fully-fledged, anthropocentric intentional agency? And how can a politics premised on disagreement be made responsive to the ways in which human life is enmeshed in the complex relationalities of ecological systems?

Ecological politics, therefore, revolves around the question of voice. If for Rancière, the being that can claim the space to express itself and to be heard is a political being, then dispersed political potencies can only fully come alive in a political sense if such 'speech' is equally de-centred and de-anthropized. It can thus come as no surprise that the language of 'authorship' pervades new materialism, particularly in its more political forms; Stacy Alaimo, for one, calls to end the view that actions need to conform to "unilateral 'authoring'" (Alaimo 2017, 102), and Donna Haraway makes the political impetus of this even more explicit when proposing that the "Capitalocene" can only be unmade in a relational manner, by connecting diverse "material-semiotic SF [string figuring] patterns and stories into something more livable" (Haraway 2016, 50). Literature offers as testing ground for such semiotic diversity, the precondition of a truly ecological politics.

Poetically, this requires a turn from autopoiesis to sympoiesis, from the figure of the narrative hero to dispersed and confluent narrative forces engaged in processes of "making with" (Haraway 2016, 58) ethically, politically and ecologically more viable worlds. Such co-creation might provide alternatives to "the thrall of the fantasy of the first beautiful words and weapons, of the first beautiful weapons as words and vice versa" (Haraway 2016, 118) which shape narratives of earth history according to trail of strength. Approaching narrative from the perspective of water breaks this tradition of approaching the word as sword and the world as one story with one tragic actor, effectively dismantling, too, the 'fix-it' approach to climate change which assumes that human political agency, having wrecked the planet, is now well placed and sufficient to heal it even without itself undergoing fundamental changes. Water is fundamentally transitional, evaporating above and flowing beneath the linear plot that tracks the conflicts and troubles of single protagonists who are now immersed in a "community of expressive agencies" (Abram 2010, 173). The visual language of discolouration affecting coral reef could thus be understood as a semiotic system that expresses and signifies, despite differing from logocentric speech. In its muddy, whirling, or torrential dimensions it undoes notions of purity and single purposes.

It is worth casting a second look at the example I started this chapter with, *The Shape of Water*, to approach what such dispersed expressive agencies might entail. Silence, after all, is a key theme in this movie, yet the apparently numb in this politically charged fictional world are simultaneously the most impactfully expressive. After all, the bonding between Eliza and the amphibian creature operates without logocentric language, as neither is able to speak, but via gesture, music and touch. Despite thus lacking the agency of speech, both enact a politically potent encounter. But for such speechlessness to actualize this political significance requires changed notions of narrative agency, including acknowledging the presence of non-human interlocutors and opening politics to the animal and vegetal world, of which Irigaray observes that it is "one of its teachings to show without saying" (Irigaray 2016, 6). I have already briefly mentioned that the merman's skin has semiotics of its own, lighting up in iridescently moving streams upon touch. It is through these currents that the merman can heal what he touches, offering a communication that is non-verbal but which signifies on both a material and symbolic level. These intra-actions between him and humans thus link discursive and embodied practices, not unlike Eliza's gestural speech; his skin exemplifies what Karen Barad proposes to be matter and meaning as "inextricably fused together [. . .] mattering is simultaneously a matter of substance and significance" (Barad 2007, 3). Acknowledging such signals as speech, thus, broadens the spectrum of politically impactful communication beyond the logocentrism of the human word to performative signs which lend the world "differential intelligibility" (Barad 2007, 335). Thus incorporating difference within speech describes a movement away from the idea of language as encoded messaging, or as expression that assumes the clarity of its message. This amphibian leads speech into murkier waters, but also into more inclusive ones.

This is not just a matter of characterization. Del Toro's narrative structure is itself to some extent diffractive, though loosely held together by a narrative voice which is always in self-doubt. Currents of water, though, run through each scene. Raindrops running with streaming traces along bus windows, drips from ceilings, flooding bathtubs or the murky laboratory tank offer a fluid sense of connectivity to the scenes. These shapes of water are what the narrative focus gravitates towards, and can be "read," as Iovino and Oppermann suggest, as "discursive formulations [. . .]" arising in coevolutionary landscapes of natures and signs" (Iovino and Oppermann 2014, 1).

The obscurity of the tank symbolizes both peril but also uncontainability, hinting at the military personnels' inability to see what is right in front of their eyes, limited as they are by abjection. The water that will eventually flood the cinema beneath Eliza's flat submerges the consumerist and visually oriented post-war society with elemental force, suggesting the fragility of such simulacral constructs as the commercials and movies shown in this space. The drops on the window, on the other hand, convey a sense of purpose and direction, moving Eliza, who traces their paths, towards taking action. In contrast, those seeking to control the narrative – the military figures – are actually devoid of any agency besides destructive violence, and even that runs into a dead end. They neither hold the plot nor shape it, while their acquired 'asset' runs through their fingers like water. In many ways this is a moderate version of a diffractive narrative compared to Linda Hogan's texts or even Virginia Woolf's *The Waves*, although the latter, too, questions power politics (in Woolf's case those of colonization) in her fluidly retracting and expanding narrative. Yet diffraction here does lead to civil disobedience when it acknowledges the agency of the silent. This is thus a narrative that seeks the "turning edge" (Moe 2019, 7) of a protean poetics, following lines of division, morphing and becoming rather than unilinear emplotment. Unlike the "expression" which Rancière observes in Athenian politics, this is closer to Barad's "diffraction" (2007, 381), reconfiguring connections, agencies and hierarchies through what Iovino and Oppermann have termed "interference patterns" (2014, 9). Water being the interfering matter here, submergence into water from the highly controlled and hierarchized environment of the lab suggests that both difference and freedom are possible only when the scientific and political 'purity' – a purity that is always exclusionary – is liquefied and submerged in the whirls of the flowing canals that mark the end of the movie. Driven by an ultimately more-than-human energy, it shows how non-human signifying forces can acquire political significance. If we therefore acknowledge that the "true dimension of matter is not a static being, but a generative becoming" (Zapf 2014, 52), then this is also a point of political change.

The semiotics of non-human voices are more akin to metaphorical thought, operating figuratively and opening towards a horizon of transformation and possibility instead of de-limiting the signifying patterns of language to the word as political or demagogical tool. A key point here is that referring to such figurative patterns is not a logocentric move. Wendy Wheeler argues that such metaphoric and metonymous strategies are not language-centred but, indeed, the "real means by which both natural and cultural semiosis drives natural and cultural evolution" (Wheeler 2014, 70). Such natural metaphors are biosemiotics and driven by the material world. Abduction in this context, therefore, requires an interpretive leap that brings together apparently separated domains. The unconscious reasoning, affective or intuitive components it entails, therefore, are not irrational but harbour potential for change. Water is a particularly potent semiotic carrier in this sense as it is transversal and thus inherently relational. As opposed to a political expression that stages opposition, we can therefore already see that it is connectivity, instead of a politics of disagreement, which such non-human voices provide and to which they call on us to respond. Such voices are process-oriented; rather than conceiving them in terms of substance – the fixed substance of the one who speaks, and the fixed content of what is spoken – they need to be thought in terms of emergence and relation.

Of course, in such gestural and affect-driven semiotics always inheres a quality of untranslatability, which I called unavailability when speaking about the amphibian creature in *The Shape of Water*. Yet this is not a negative dimension. To the contrary, like metaphor, it opens signification to virtual horizons of possibility. This 'more-than' quality inheres in the merman already, but is even more striking in Linda Hogan's opening scene to her 2008 novel *People of the Whale*. An octopus climbs up onto a shore to hide in a cave, amazing the "ocean people" who belong to a culture deeply rooted in its links to the sea but already caught between tribal and white US-American culture. Its eye resting on the humans, making them feel "each one seen" (Hogan 2008, 15) the octopus becomes a catalyst for the delicate negotiations between the entwined lives of humans and the sea. Its "potent meaning" (Hogan 2008, 16) scares the fishermen who want to contain it by killing it to use as bait, or the mother keeping back a child, claiming him as one of the "land dwellers" who is no "communicator or friend of any eight-legged sea creature" (Hogan 2008, 15). The octopus thus immediately introduces the narrative as "sympoetic" (Haraway 2016, 33) collaboration between humans and non-humans. It is the first embodiment of the novel's biosemiotic impulses, in which non-human matter emerges as a "web teeming with meanings" (Wendy Wheeler quoted in Iovino and Oppermann 2014; Wheeler 2014, 4). The active voice, though non-logocentric, here belongs to the octopus, making the humans "known" and "seen" and paling at the sight, foreshadowing the ocean-human conflict triggered by the issue of whale hunting that is too come. This paling, however, is also a moment of grief, as the new-born boy who emerges from his mother's womb on the same day the octopus walked across the beach will spend most of his adult life in traumatic paralysis, having survived the Vietnam War. Challenging anthropocentric notions of progress, the motif of a sea dweller climbing on land thus questions the evolutionary narrative which, as Donna Haraway has observed, traces development via links between tools, weapons and words. The octopus, able to sense human emotions and a shape-shifter at heart, is an ecological trickster who makes visible to human eyes the "fabric of matters" (Haraway 2016, 40) in which humans remain embedded. A creature of the "hypersea" (Mark and Dianna McMenamin 1996) in which life nests within other life, the octopus expresses a lateral view of evolution; change occurs transversally, not in a teleological manner, as the octopus traverses the beach to the cave and back again without showing any interest of reaching a different evolutionary 'stage.' Its potent meanings get passed along horizontally through the community, symbolically introducing the existence of a non-hierarchical, non-vertical organisation of life. It thus offers a horizon of alternative possibilities to the war-torn future awaiting the new-born at the beach, its arrival both primal and futuristic.

Meaning, thus, emerges from being implicated. When the octopus in *People of the Whale* continues to change colour, it becomes clear that it is a semiotic agent bearing a variety of meanings even if the humans struggle to translate them initially; the mysteriousness of the creature's "purpose" is possibly due to the fact that this mode of signification and agency is not bound to an individual body, eight-legged or otherwise, but emerges from the kind of interplay and interpretational patterns which Jesper Hoffmeyer observes to be the basis of genetic biosemiosis" (Hoffmeyer 2009, 131). Such tentacularity, therefore, is also a poetic project, responsive to Amitav Gosh's and Rob Nixon's sense that an ecological literary politics requires an equally patterned and dispersed narrative mode. The octopus's tentacles, after all, are not only sensory but move both individually and in rhythms, multilinear and open-ended.

If such biosemiotics are truly to open into the political, though, it is not only because of their dispersed and post-anthropocentically democratic nature but because they are more radically abstract than exclusionary language-based expression could allow. This claim seems paradoxical at first; after all, how can abstraction entail a greater political impulse, seeing as politics requires some sense of situatedness in material, economic, or ecological reality? Yet in the proto-political dimension that concerns us here, these tentacular and patterned 'voices' suffuse the narrative with "diagrammatic" potentials in Deleuze and Guattari's sense (1987). Such diagrams, or "abstract machines," are a constitutive part of any regime of signs and acknowledge what logocentric notions of political voices repress: enunciation and formalized expression are only one side of signification. The other side is constituted by matter and contents. However, as Deleuze and Guattari argue, these should not be thought of as objects of speech or fixed contents. A process-oriented view of language replaces such substance-based ideas with closer attention to what is to come. Like the octopus which presages the energies shaping Linda Hogan's narrative, these diagrams are inherently future-oriented. They do not seek to represent what is already given, but "rather construct[s] a real that is yet to come, a new type of reality" (Deleuze and Guattari 1987, 142). If the "abstract machine" is therefore "'much more' than language" (1987, 141), then this 'much more' is precisely the location of the horizons of change which push such apparent abstraction into a driver of the political. Made of matter, not substance, and seeking functions, not forms, this dimension of language thus inscribes change into the apparently closed-off worlds such as Del Toro's high-security labs. Non-human voices push humans, themselves too entangled in discourses of violence, into political openings, offering alternatives other than subservience to the powers that be.

What politics can such tentacular, diagrammatic voices suggest? Donna Haraway brings tentacularity into relation with "string figuring," a tripled process of following threads through a thick present, becoming attuned to both their semiotics and materiality, and passing on threads in relational movements of making and unmaking (Haraway 2016, 3). Instead of a politics that relies on voices expressing group-based concerns in opposition to others, this is a fundamentally transversal practice beyond a conflict-driven notion of politics. The space of these voices is not a parliamentary one, with factional seating and speaker's stages in which expression is a performance of persuasion.

Rather, it politicizes what Haraway calls the 'humus' and what, for Hogan in her water-bound poetics, is the ocean, in which myriad temporalities and spatialities form assemblages of the human, more-than-human and other-than human. Described as a "timeplace for learning to stay with the trouble of living and dying in response-ability on a damaged earth" (Haraway 2016, 2), this is simultaneously a poetic, political and ecological project. Not utopian in the stricter sense because it describes not a different place but current terrestrial realities, it asks for humans to immerse themselves in "multicritter humus" (Haraway 2016, 2); this, however, is neither harmonious nor static, nor nostalgic for a lost Garden of Eden. Haraway's nature, like Hogan's octopus, signifies, performs and unsettles. She suggests that the tentacular "chthonic ones" are monsters in the double sense of the word: they de-monstr-ate and perform material meaning-making, yet seek neither safety nor belonging, preferring to "writhe and luxuriate in manifold forms and manifold names in all the airs, waters, and places of earth" (Haraway 2016, 2). This trouble-making thus is an ecological form of politics, unsettling the "sky-gazing homo" (Haraway 2016, 2) and any notions of human singularity, particularly because their embeddedness means they demonstrate not only their being but the consequences of any action within their shared humus. It thus requires a political expression that acknowledges enmeshment, submergence and, in particular, the consequences of speech. Hogan's octopus signals to the humans in order to aid them to better inhabit an ecosystem which both the tentacular and the human ones share and shape. Instead of the exclusionary signals of a logocentric politics, such dispersal of diverse voices can help create notions of political communication not as persuasion or manipulation, but as a gesture towards articulating visions for a sustainable and shared future.

Immersed Agencies Along Thresholds of Sustainability

We have seen that literary texts – despite their language-based nature – suggest the de-centring of politically potent voices beyond the human. Yet Linda Hogan's tentacular opening to *People of the Whale* immediately entwines questions of speaking with the challenge of acting. Strikingly it is the octopus who holds the active voice, though non-logocentric, making the humans 'known' and 'seen' and paling at the sight, foreshadowing the ocean-human conflict triggered by the issue of whalehunting that is too come. Humans, thus, are passive here, syntactically dethroned from the status of sole agent over a world supposedly filled with force and energy, yet not with the kind of intentionality that agency requires. "Something else makes me do it" (Hogan 2008, 38) the protagonist Ruth's son Marco exclaims when diving for so long that his mother fears for his life. The gilled and webbed hybrid beings of this novel are attuned to being called upon by the ocean, thus exposing notions of free agency and purely individual intentionality to be illusory. "Planetarity," as Neimanis argues, "is the species to which water belongs. This 'of me yet beyond me' is the unknowability to which water asks that I attend" (2017, 145). Suggesting intimacy and an alterity not derived from human being, water in Hogan's novel takes precedence over the humans who inhabit it when it comes to questions of agency. The second precondition of politics I would like to explore is therefore, evocatively and inevitably, that of agency. This raises a string of questions about the territory in which such agency might be located, its effects in a context of power, or its ultimate purpose. All these, however, are based on preconditions which an ecological politics must challenge, namely the anthropocentric exceptionalism that assumes singular and individually acting human subjects and non-human objects; this is what Linda Hogan subverts.

Yet merely role-switching the actors and the acted-upon is equally a dead end. Rosi Braidotti's posthuman philosophy offers a valid departure point from this, as she promotes a "recasting" of political agency per se, "in the direction of transversal alliances and relational ontology" (Braidotti 2017, 24). Her "cartographic method" (2017, 15) is based on an understanding of the human actor as both embodied and embedded in complex relations of power as well as complex ecologies. This cartography, for Braidotti, is initially conceptual, seeking to reject closed systems of thought, undoing human exceptionalism, and re-thinking posthuman subject formations as they are embedded in capitalist de-territorialisations. This is evocative here as it shows how deeply entwined questions of ecology are with power relations. Her "Zoe-centred egalitarianism" (2017, 22) takes the post-anthropocentric subject in its relations to nonhuman, vital forces of life as its starting point. It therefore envisages an actor who is already immersed, implicated, and relational, doing away with the myth of the detached puppet master enacting of freely willed choices. What Braidotti calls "a materialist, secular, grounded and unsentimental response to the opportunistic trans-species commodification of Life" (2017, 22) is therefore in no sense de-politicised or was ever prior to politics. It originates in the power relations of advanced capitalism and advocates a vital politics that departs from its conventional identity-and singular-subject-bound grounding.

Human subjects, in such a view, are inherently transversal as they resonate to complex flows of forces; yet this resonance is active, as "multiple mechanisms of capture engender multiple forms of resistance" (Braidotti 2017, 22f). In our context here, there are some caveats to this approach. Her "politics of location" (2017, 24) reach their limits when faced with watery habitats that are as de-territorialized as the capitalist patterns she rightly critiques. Ecological de-territorialisation, though, is of a different nature from the forced capital and migration flows she references. Oceanic beings like the octopus are immersed and situated yet simultaneously nomadic, offering visions of embeddedness beyond location alone. Power, and the agencies and potentialities which can form such resistances, are thus transversal. An ecological notion of political agency not only distributes the ability to affect to non-human players. It is also situated in a forcefield that is not operated single-mindedly or with a single purpose. Reading such agencies thus requires tracing power along lines of sedimentation and flight.

In this project, semantics continue to matter, and I am here reverting to the terms 'potentiality' and 'potency' instead of 'agency' intentionally when referring to non-human matters, in order to emphasize the heterogeneity of such political forces. The claims in new materialism which assign 'agency' to all materialities, after all, are essential when working towards a vision which acknowledges "entanglements and interactions between humans and the nonhuman world," stressing interactivity and dispersal of material agencies which might be "nearly impossible to trace, delimit, or scientifically capture" (Alaimo 2017, 101). Agency, however, comes with connotations of conscious intentionality, and I am not sure how a concept so deeply entwined with enlightenment ideas of the free will and bound subjecthood translates to the nonhuman – and whether there is really any worth in even attempting this. That such distinctions are necessary, however, does not entail hierarchies of worth or impact; just because non-human potentialities are not identical to human agency does not mean they are inferior, or not there at all. Dispersal remains linked to difference, though on a transversal, transformative plane.

In Linda Hogan's *People of the Whale*, such matters of agency and power span both sides of the Pacific; Ruth, a fisher and weaver born with gills, lives with her A'atsika tribe on the north-Pacific coast of the U.S.A. She is a woman of two elements, whose son swims from her body with webbed feet and who was herself born more fish than human, forced into the element of air when a doctor stitched up her gill slits after birth. Like Eliza, this liminal being gives her a sense of both immersion and alignment with the elements, so that the Pacific, with its "mind of water" (Hogan 2008, 83), becomes her communication line to her husband Thomas, the baby whose birth the octopus seemed to guard, when he serves in the Vietnam War only to disappear there for years. Her life bound up with the violence of the allegedly 'Cold' War, it is the ocean – disobedient to any attempt to be cut into spheres of influence – that informs both her outlook and her activism when she sides with the ocean's whales and against the males of her own tribe.

Yet her tribe's relation to the sea is generally submerged in a present thickened with both past inheritances and future possibilities, thus encompassing both the threat and opportunity of constant change and transformation. It contains both the memories of ancient houses covered shells, and of the slow violence of industrial whale fishing and influenza epidemics brought in by white settlers. The ocean's nature might be animated in a mythological sense as its black rocks give rise to tales of sea monsters, but it is a place of turbulence, where rivers conjoin in a "muddy rush" (Hogan 2008, 10), a place not of clarity but of intermingling and immersion. This "thickness of life" (Hogan 2008, 160) engenders disobedience, or 'trouble-making,' to stay with Haraway's lexicon. Despite being steeped in her tribe's traditions of whale-hunting, Ruth turns to activist politics against whaling when she realizes that the men's efforts to revive it are driven by a desire for profit, thus emptying the sustainability and respectfulness of tribal traditions of their core. By aligning with the whales and against her own tribe, she attracts the hatred of the only people she has spent her life with along with unwanted media attention, who, sympathetic to the apparent traditionalism of the whale hunt, flock to the reservation. The men's impulses, however, remain driven by a "need to fill themselves up" (Hogan 2008, 90) with superficial actions, not deeper alignment with their ecological surroundings; while the women grieve for their fellow creatures, feeling the loss "from the body of the ocean" (Hogan 2008, 91), the men hunt like they did in Vietnam, stunted by their own weaponization on behalf of the US government. For the war veterans seeking solace in identity politics, "the alive world is unfelt" (Hogan 2008, 128). The whale hunt ends with a dead whale washed back into the sea and the murder of Marco, Ruth's son, who had embodied the traditional tribal life of kinship with the elements.

Yet it is not only her entry into this openly activist realm that politicises her. An ecological politics in the truest sense requires humans to replace notions of free will – only thinkable when assuming a bounded identity removed from its material basis – with questions of diffractive and possibly rebounding consequences. If interventions cause ripples, then bodies of water are not immune to the whirls they cause either. Her immersed being is the precondition of her activism, and thus needs to be understood as political in itself, along with the natural forces which align with her. Rancière's politics is not just about claiming a voice, but also a space. Ruth's very mode of being on her fishing boat is such a claim of space, not in order to disagree, but in order to inhabit and contribute to the material mesh of nature. The difference of her ecological politics is that it claims a porous space within the world, not a territory, and is ready to bear the consequences. She fights against what Wheeler constates to be the "randomness and meaninglessness of nature" as well as the idea that humans are "thrown" (Wheeler 2014, 73) into the world; yet her existence also exposes how active her gills-driven submergence truly is.

As an amphibian activist, Ruth thus negotiates the "thresholds of sustainability" (Braidotti 2017, 26) that mark an ecologically conceived posthuman politics. She advocates non-profit modes of being and acts in the interest of the collective, both human and oceanic, to which she is so keenly attuned. Her continued affinity to meshed figurations, be it in her son's webbed feet, the fishing nets she mends or the baskets she weaves, demonstrates how her activism emerges from a relationality that always has an element of the 'more-than:' she herself is unaware of the potency of her own body, symbolized by her gills, until late in life, just as the octopus returns in human form as a *deus ex machina* figure to help her end the post-whale hunt drought that threatens the ecology she inhabits. The moment of radical agency, however, is her disloyalty to her own species, or to be more precise, to the male group that assumes power in her own generation. After all, her disidentification is an act in the interest of the future generations or her tribe as well as of the whales.

Yet Ruth's activism, seemingly failed, is fulfilled when the ocean itself withdraws in an extreme weather condition of draught and constant low tide. The sense that the "ocean is mourning" (Hogan 2008, 136) endows it with interiority, as the tide of public opinion turns against the tribal whale hunters, too. The whale hunt thus symbolizes a larger ecological disconnect, a microcosm of the attitudes that, on a global scale, caused climate change. As the ocean aligns with Ruth, a complex landscape of forces emerges which, though not necessarily intentionally political, are politically potent. The politicization of this "distributive agency" (Bennett 2009, 31) thus foregrounds the core characteristic of watery bodies: they are porous and will suffer the consequences of the toxins, metaphorical and real, which they themselves set free. "It is quite arduous for humans to declare their agentic independence in a hybrid, vibrant, and living world" (2014, 30), as Iovino and Oppermann argue, yet in Hogan's novel it is also suicidal. Dwight, the main driver behind the whale hunt, ends as an outcast from his tribe while others, when setting the forest on fire in order to cause Ruth's arrest, burn themselves.

If Ruth thus demonstrates the possibilities of agency and resistance that come from being de-territorialized in an oceanic and ecologically immersed sense, her husband Thomas exposes the virulent violence of an uprooting forced by nation-state politics. This Pacific ocean, after all, is also a pathway of power, carrying colonizer's ships and crossed by the military planes of the Vietnam War. While Ruth's activism is literally driven by ecological concerns, this implicatedness equally changes notions of action and resistance in political conflicts that are not driven by nature. Across the ocean, the novel exposes the violence of landmines and chemical warfare in Vietnam. Yet despite being in constant tension with his own oceanic being, it is Thomas' impulses of ecological immersion in the war in Vietnam which allow him to survive; he becomes one with the jungle, digging himself underground and navigating as a sensate being in a darkness in which "his body had eyes. His back had eyes. His fingers had eyes. But so did the trees, the leaves, the moss and stone" (Hogan 2008, 172). He thus navigates his way through the war zone by becoming animal and vegetal, and it is precisely this entanglement that makes him first resist his comrade's cruelties against the civilian population, until he chooses to shoot other soldiers in order to prevent them massacring the local population. "I became the earth" (Hogan 2008, 122), is what he ascribes his own survival to, yet as his Vietnamese wife gets killed by the landmines he reluctantly helped to hide, he experiences both sides of this immersion. Years before. his own decision to re-define his tribal identity as that of a "warrior" (Hogan 2008, 161) had driven his decision to enter into the war.

Instead of the oceanic alignment sought by ancestors like his grandfather Witka and predicated at his birth by the octopus, this decision marks his change to a politics of disagreement. It brings about his own emotional and spiritual numbing, which he tries to hide behind the psychological and physical walls he builds around himself. "He wants a wall" so that he "can't see the eyes of the ocean watching him" (Hogan 2008, 113); such walls would protect him from bearing the consequences of his own actions, including his implication in the deaths of his wife and son. Within a political context that sought precisely such cordoning off – of tribal reservations, or through the iron curtain – the ocean remains in protest against the very idea of a wall, insisting, instead, on facing the full extent of the ecological and political immersion of the human animal.

Ecological being is not a passive endeavour, but an activist's choice. Bodies of water thus are linked to responsibility. They seek insurgence, which in its conventionally political sense surfaces in moments of civil disobedience or more broadly organised activism. The responsibility they advocate, though, is dispersed and not easy to locate, but – as Neimanis cautions – that does not mean it does not exist. An ecological politics calls on humans to acknowledge their own implication, making it necessary to re-align politics with this ecological complexity. The hybrid bodies in both *The Shape of Water* and *People of the Whale* are intrinsically politicised. Impacted by and subverting the objectifying impact of racist politics or military hierarchy, watery bodies offer a conceptual angle for an ecological politics that foregrounds the planetary instead of seeking solace in a misguidedly territorial earthbound nostalgia. Countering the "natural prioritisation of humans and human interests over those of other species on the earth" which Graham Huggan and Helen Tiffin, in their postcolonial ecocriticism, rightly interpret to be "generating and repeating the racist ideologies of imperialism on a planetary scale" (2015, 6), this global angle is essential because of the scale of the political challenge. If the exploitation of nature thus aligns with human-on-human violence, the ecological thinking, with its potential for transformation, offers a horizon of alternatives.

Monstrous Freedom

Ed, a seasonal worker on the island of Hiddensee in 1989, grapples with the notion of the borderline. The island's off-shore coastline, heavily patrolled, surveyed and policed, marks the iron curtain. Yet on a map his friend Kruso shows him, the eponymous figure of Lutz Seiler's 2014 novel, the issue of the borderline presents itself in a different light:

> The slender shape of their own island, the seahorse with the sledgehammer muzzle. The animal floated upright, its swollen head turned to the east – half in black, half in red. [. . .] The red between the southern and northern shores was covered with a network of barely discernible geometric links, dotted and continuous lines that intersected wildly.
>
> (Seiler 2017, 150)

This erosion of a non-traversable border is a key theme in the novel, and is ecologically driven. The location of the slightly shady restaurant where Ed and Kruso have been hired as dishwashers already liquefies the apparent solidity of this watery line between East and West. Ed's and Kruso's jobs as dishwashers at the "Klausner" situates them within a space that is triply eroding: "the flow conditions [. . .] the constant breaking off and slow drift of the coastline," "the gradual, inexorable disappearance of the island into the expanse of the Baltic Sea" (Seiler 2017, 39) is an ecological fact that literally pulls the ground from underneath their feet, and this is only enforced by the Radiation Institute, a secret research lab for radiation not unlike the setting of *The Shape of Water*, which pollutes the local ecosystem. Yet this also turns the Klausner into a metaphor for the state of the GDR itself, which – as the kitchen radio continues to proclaim – is itself literally crumbling under the streams of refugees attempting to cross the border. Thirdly, though, this erosion is also a literal dying of both human and animals, who either perish from toxic water or drown in the Baltic Sea when attempting to swim across the border. To Ed Bendler, the stowaway on this ship of cheap meat cuts, ice cream and cockroaches, the place seems like a cadaver about to be returned to the sea, crumbling to the force of the water. And disintegrate the Klausner does, parallel to the end of the DDR and the dissolution of the Soviet Union in the autumn of 1989.

Despite the sense of distance from the state – "the mainland was nothing more than a backdrop that slowly blurred and faded away in the sea's continuous roar. What, then was *the state*?" (Seiler 2017, 156) – this is by no means a depoliticized space. His whole being shaped by the sea, Kruso leads a double life, and operates as a nocturnal underground activist, hiding and helping migrants attempting to cross the border into the West by swimming from Hiddensee to Denmark. The interplay of life and death in the motif of watery bodies, thus, is no coincidence. Hiddensee, after all, is highly politicized territory. Patterned as much by the rhythms of the tides as the pulsating searchlights of the border patrols, Kruso's maps show the watery pathways of the dead cutting through the official lines. Through those lines and colours, the sea-horse-shape of Hiddensee is grotesquely deformed, its skull swollen and its mouth frayed. The refugee's desire for freedom, however, is not programmatically or ideologically charged, but treated by Seiler and his activist protagonists as a precondition of the political existence of humans. At stake in the sea-horse map is a proto- (and protean) politics unsettling notions of territory and borderline.

Kruso's map at first sight suggest an ecological grotesque. The deformed seahorse is transversed, broken open and de-limited, suggesting an impulse of freedom that always also includes the possibility of death. Such entwined dualities of life and death, freedom and violent capture, is a key feature of the grotesque, which Bakhtin defines as a phenomenon of de-limitation (1968). Featuring chimerical creatures between the human and the non-human, the grotesque epitomizes the principle of border transgression itself, and does so in a deeply embodied, material manner. Its figures subvert clear dichotomies as they merge contraries and emphasize metamorphosis and change, so that it is not by accident that one of the most notorious examples of the grotesque is the image of pregnant death, which dilutes the most fundamental boundary as decay and fertility merge into one. Its significance here, however, lies in its potential to link the material world to politics. Not only does it open the world onto a state of estrangement and delirium, though this is certainly at work in the world of *Kruso*, but it can also present the possibility of metamorphosis, change and fertility. The grotesque turns the spheres of power upside down, humiliating the king in front of the elevated peasant. Therefore anti-hierarchical in nature, the Bakhtinian grotesque celebrates the acts of eating, drinking, defecating and sexual intercourse where Bakhtin sees the principles of merging, change and fertility most clearly. The grotesque, understood thus, is a phenomenon that is sustained by eternal change. It is a world-in-becoming, and even more so as it integrates even the most fundamental oppositions. It laughs at power, but this laughter is not necessarily always triumphant; it is also born out of torn and open bodies. In arresting attention whilst defying understanding, the grotesque, as Geoffrey Galt Harpham suggests, has the potential to question our categories of the world and to thus provide breakthrough intervals towards (Harpham 1982, 15). This rupture is precisely what Kruso seeks to share with the "castaways" (Seiler 2017, 159) as he calls the migrants, whom he sees as creatures long lost to the solidity of land. This liberty, shot through with death, is the ultimate resistance to state control but as a political impulse emerges from the nature of the island which is not only "hidden," as its name suggests, but ex-centric in the sense of the grotesque. The grotesque, therefore, becomes the mode in which the marginalized is able to answer back in an ecologically embedded form of activism.

The disfigured seahorse, thus, is only one symptom of the deeper energies shaping political activities in this novel, which – set in a one-party context which forbids disagreement – take place under cover. This grotesqueness of the island, not merely its liminal location, is the reason why it is truly uncontainable to state power. The novel navigates between a variety of such transgressive spaces. The "Man of the Baltic Waves" (Seiler 2017, 33) appears to the narrator Ed as an embodiment of the Baltic Sea, a figure about to dissolve in steam but just lingering long enough to reveal his teeth rotting with algae and mussels. That night Ed also develops a friendship with a fox, who inhabits a cave at the beach and whom Ed frequently visits to share his deepest thoughts and feelings. This feline interlocutor dies, though this will not end Ed's visits to his "old rascal" (Seiler 2017, 138). Poisoned by a toxic well, his fur teems with green insects which fly into Ed's face, his body greying and flattening against the rock and sand. This moribund companion is responsive with his whole gory being to Ed's most traumatic memory, of his girlfriend run over by a tram, lying dead with "her bare legs sticking out" (Seiler 2017, 138). Placed on a beach of skeletal trees which resembles a battlefield, the fox inhabits a liminal space where life and death merge in rocks appearing as "skulls with algae for hair" (Seiler 2017, 108) on an island like a "corpse," "returning to the sea" (Seiler 2017, 108). Such grotesque figurations make the island itself a trickster figure, a phenomenon of disobedience but also of material life. They initiate the novel's responsiveness to a politics that is less logocentric, not driven by speech, but experienced in the wounded and dead bodies washed up on shore.

However, the grotesque, while certainly subversive to power, cannot fully explain the ecological politics of the borderline here, contained as it is (both conceptually and temporally) in the ephemeral space of the folk carnival. The deeper significance of the lines traversing the sea horse shape on the map lies in their opening of the border to a logic of the transversal. The criss-crossing, disobedient, broken and breaking lines suggest a de-territorialisation which calls into question the idea of a national border per se. The lines describe actual and potential watery paths, and are thus much more attuned to proposing horizons of possibility than to obeying any mimetic logic. When Hester Blum notices that Oceanic Studies has precisely such a focus on border transgressions, as it "unmoors planetarity from the nation state" (Blum 2015, 26), then this is certainly the case here. These lines gesture towards the "unrest of a world in becoming" (Massumi 2011, 2), suffusing the borderline with the virtual potential of a world-in-becoming uncontainable by borderlines drawn on a map. This island is "not a grab-bag of things. It is an always-in-germ" (Massumi 2011, 6). Such unfolding is the shape that the liquefication of the borderline here takes. Kruso's activism can therefore best be described in Massumi's sense as the "first stirrings of the political, flush with the felt intensities of life" (Massumi 2015, ix), seeking to engulf political realities in change rather than requiring programmatic de-limitation in a programmatic sense. Kruso's anti-border wall activism is thus moulded to the ecological transgressiveness of this place between land and water. He celebrates the island in a pseudo-mythologizing way as a place of illumination, which imbues the soul with a liberty untouchable by the powers of the state.

The bodies that relate to such politics are, in Guattari and Deleuze's sense, without organs and thus akin to posthuman corporealities. Both the sea-horse on the map, traversed by lines of flight, and the dead fox on the beach, flooded with water and opened by green flies, subvert and re-define any possibility of de-limitation from the inside out. They re-imagine the human body as a field of waves, vibrations, migrations and thresholds – a "zone of intensity" (Deleuze and Guattari 1983, 156). Though the body without organs screams out at the idea of being a unitary organism, "They've wrongfully folded me!" (Deleuze and Guattari 1983, 159), it does so not because it disdains corporeal being. What it fears, not unlike the activists and refugees in *Kruso*, is being a subject, "nailed down" (Deleuze and Guattari 1983, 159). Such transversal embodiment, therefore, is the precondition for political freedom.

This *bios*-based politics of the borderline is nowhere as apparent as in a very particular amphibian figure which Kruso and Ed encounter and bury with care. Babbling a quiet symphony of doubt, "why else, why else, why else on earth are you here?" (Seiler 2017, 93), Ed is crouching naked on the greasy floor of the dishwashing station, letting the cool water run over his back. Suddenly he notices feet protruding from one of the sinks, legs "immobile as a dead man's limbs" (Seiler 2017, 93), until the whole figure emerges as Kruso.

> A second later, the man who belonged to the legs was standing in front of Ed, as naked as he was, a bushman, powerful and gleaming with streaks of moisture. In his right hand, he held his machete, a large kitchen knife. [. . .] A trickle of blood ran down his arm; a disgusting stench filled the room [. . .] The creature was tapered towards its tail and ended in a thin grey rivulet. [. . .] The plait creature must have been heavy; it trembled lightly at the end of Kruso's arm. Kruso's arm trembled. The thing looked like an amphibian [. . .] Only then did Ed notice the myriad long, apparently human hairs that ran through the creature like veins, similar to the web of blood vessels on the surface of a newly exposed organ.
> (Seiler 2017, 94–96)

This creature, more than four months old as Kruso explains, exudes an unbearable stench. Weighing down Krusos' s arm when he holds it up high with a hunter's pride, it only gradually reveals its nature: it is a knot of human hair and soggy kitchen waste, shaped to form in the water-pipes. Akin to the greyish veins of a freshly bared organ, these hairs give it a sense of being alive. Kruso explains the care he takes with this waste product, treating it as a living being, by referring to the original, common roots of human and non-human nature. Yet it also embodies his own activism; according to a ritual of his own creation, each 'shipwrecked' person he helps to feed and accommodate is bathed in the large sinks of the Klausner. The amphibian, thus, is the material memory of those who have left and who might already have lost their lives at sea whilst trying to swim across the border. It is quite literally a "material 'mesh' of meanings, properties and processes" (Iovino and Oppermann 2014, 1f) in which human and non-human matter come to co-signify. A matter of distributed semiotic agency, this amphibian body without organs here performs the vulnerability and tenacity of sympoetic systems in which meaning is co-produced. Without self-defined spatial or temporal boundaries, and distributing both information and control across various components, such systems are evolutionary, and, as Haraway argues, "have the potential for surprising change" (Haraway 2016, 33). Kruso is aware of this transformative potential in this seemingly dead body, and uses it to nourish his fight against state violence.

Kate Rigby points out that "the natural world is the dynamic enabling condition of all cultural production, which in turn bears the trace of more-than-human genesis" (2004, 4). What emerges when one specifies this production to the political is that bodies matter more ferociously when de-limited. An ecological literary politics of the border thus suggests not an undifferentiated world without borders, just as the body without organs is not without skin. Yet it does promote porosity, reciprocity and transversality in these borders, constituting them in order to gesture beyond. The border of a literary ecology, thus, does not mark off territories. Instead, it performs a process of limitation and transgression, seeking encounters that engulf human and non-human subjects in constant transformation.

Watery Politics as Queering?

> There is no longer man or animal, since each deterritorializes the other, in a conjunction of flux, in a continuum of reversible intensities. [. . .] Furthermore, there is no longer a subject of the enunciation, nor a subject of the statement. [. . .] Rather, there is a circuit of states that forms a mutual becoming, in the heart of a necessarily multiple and collective assemblage.
> (Deleuze and Guattari 1986, 22)

What does it mean to think politics not as disagreement, but as whirl? The politics of ecological fictions teems with monstrous creatures which have no track with the equally whirl-based, vorticist militarism of a century ago. We have seen that without exception, these authors employ hybrid beings, be it amphibian humans or animalized matter, as their political agents and activists in watery worlds. In her 2015 novel *Tentacle*, Rita

Indiana brings this tendency to the point. In a post-apocalyptic Santo Domingo, the young transsexual Acilde is anointed son of Olokun, deity of the Ocean, by the sting of a miraculously surviving anemone and a gender-transitioning 'Rainbow' injection, giving the prostitute-turned-maid the male body she had desired even without these pantheistic features. A 21st century trickster par excellence, s/he has all the streetsmarts her integrated data plans could teach her; but as son of the Ocean, s/he inhabits several bodies across time, including that of a 17th century buccaneer, in order to unravel the events that led to the species extinction which had turned the Caribbean into an uninhabitable, smouldering, epidemic-infested mass.

Water, thus, queers ecological politics. It is, after all, an element of hermaphrodites, a quality which Linda Hogan's or del Toro's hybrid figures are particularly attuned to. These hybrids are all akin to Rob Nixon's ecological picaros or Donna Haraway's monstrous chthonic creatures, with little patience for the limitations of apocalyptic cynicism. While Ursula Heise deplored in 2008 that ecocriticism has not quite caught up with the idea that identities are fragmented, mixed and dispersed -"or that precisely these mixtures might be crucial for constituting "identities" politically as "subjects" (Heise 2008, 43) – these bodies of water demonstrate how ecological hybrids are agents beyond (and mostly disinterested in) identity politics. They uproot politics and the human bodies driving it, offering a vision of transversing and transversed voices, agency, and borderlines. Their mode is darkly comedic rather than tragic, with all the transformative potential for change this entails. As mer-human hybrid they expose the "fragile states where man strays on the territories of animal" (Nixon 2011, 55), unsettling the illusion of distance between nature and human being. The effect, depending on perspective, can be uncanny or liberating, but Nixon links such creatures to Kristeva's concept of abjection in order to further emphasize its state of being "cast off," not just uncannily doubled or defamiliarized.

This is also a political question, as these bodies of water challenge the consensus that underpins the socio-political order – mostly a white, cis-gendered and largely male, territorialized structure of hierarchies. Abjection, however, has a decidedly psychoanalytical frame and is closely linked to notions of disgust, acknowledging the need to re-erect any borders of the self which the abject creature might have punctured. Val Plumwood, on the other hand, suggests that such figures offer the "gift of meaning and communication from the world" (Plumwood 2002, 228), yet the disobedient agency of these erotically driven and spiritual beings goes beyond the idea of the gift. Tricksters require humans to become more open to the unexpected, providing a body endowed with subjectivity to channel nature's forces into agency.

These hybrid agents ensure that such a politics does not revert to a nostalgia for prelapsarian mythological beginnings. Indeed, water as an element is closely linked to mythological origins, though its fertility and life-giving nature make it the site of the kind of creation which liberates its creatures, "letting be" (Irigaray 2016, 30) instead of seeking control. Astrida Neimanis' argument that this mythological base does not (and should not) easily transfer to a 21st century context is particularly relevant here, replacing the search for all-encompassing meaning with an interest in dispersal and porosity (2017, 117). Whether conceiving it as a pre-human elemental womb for creation or as an undifferentiated force of obscurity and chaos, origin tales, after all, differ from 21st century narratives in seeking to provide holistic meaning. In this sense water offers opportunities to refract origin stories, in itself a political project considering these tend to operate on the logic of weaponry, so poignant in a Cold War context. Breaking this evolutionary link between weapon and word is a key precondition of the watery politics of contemporary literature. Neimanis thus employs the idea of humans as "bodies of water" in the sense of "evolutionary carrier bags" (Neimanis 2017, 122), interpreting humans not as weapon-bearing mammals, but as gestational milieus in which the new can proliferate. This potential for change is in itself political, yet its politics is of a kind different to that of disagreement.

Contrary to any notion of nostalgia for watery beginnings, this is where its future-bound potential originates; indeed, Joan Roughgarden suggests in her study on queerness in aquatic life that the particular abundance of genderqueer lives in aquatic environments might indicate not an earlier, primitive evolutionary stage but a higher one (2004, 41). Politics conceived through and with water, thus, encourage a "re-activism" (Cohen and Duckert 2015, 6) and not reactive moves, seeking to renew (non) human ethical enmeshment and immersion in ways that are responsive to the ideas of water as both life-giving and deadly, but ultimately future-driven and fully situated in specific sociohistorical contexts. In particular, these texts emphasize the need to not immediately dismiss the search for different ways of being as apolitical, just because they do not adhere to the operations of disagreement.

In an era of "insistent, inescapable continuities, animated by forces that are nothing if not inconceivably vast," (Gosh 2017, 62) water offers particularly potent meanings, connecting planetary submergence with conjoint movements of signification and action. It becomes the shifting new ground for a more resilient imagination of resistance, which is necessary when one acknowledges the subtle ways in which different forms of natural exploitation and cultural subjugation are interrelated. The potency of water in each of these texts subverts the alleged power of a dominant nation or narrative, whether this relates to (post)colonial, national, or cultural mastery. It questions notions of authority through its ephemeral and shifting shapes, which communicate its continuous and irrevocable, life-giving energy. Yet its fluidity not only informs the narrative structure of these texts, engendering a textuality of flux; it is also linked to notions of eros when understood in Freya Mathew's sense, as not a necessarily sexual experience but a sensation of interconnection, of friction and tenderness between human and non-human bodies. Eliza in *The Shape of Water* is particularly responsive to this dimension, which needs to be understood as a precondition for her ensuing sabotage of the Cold War weapons complex, too.

Perhaps the principle of di- and re-fraction most aptly sums up the political impact of watery being, particularly when set against the rigidity of Cold War ideologies. As a poetic principle, it encourages a style of reading that cherishes interferences, interleaving the natural and the material with each other. Yet if world and text form such an "agentic entanglement" (Iovino and Oppermann 2014, 10), this changes the preconditions of our politics, too, which we have seen to be ecologically destructive precisely because such diffractions are intentionally obscured.

"Forget the knife-cuts, the chalk-line partitions," Luce Irigaray asks in her *Marine Lover of Friedrich Nietzsche* (1991, 21); "realize that a solid plane is never just a solid plane" but "rests on subterranean and submarine life" (Irigaray 1991, 20), stirring this seeming solidity ceaselessly. Water's "liquid ground" (Irigaray 1991, 37) refracts partitioning certainties. The fierce vulnerability of these desirous and ecological writings thus shows how a more manifold language can come into being to topple, from the groundwater up, the partitions and hierarchies of the Anthropocene.

References

Abram, David. 2010. *Becoming Animal: An Earthly Cosmology*. London: Penguin Random House.
Alaimo, Stacy. 2010. *Bodily Natures. Science, Environment, and the Material Self*. Bloomington, IN: Indiana University Press.
Alaimo, Stacy. 2017. "Your Shell on Acid: Material Immersion, Anthropocene Dissolves." In *Anthropocene Feminism*, edited by Richard Grusin, 89–120. Minneapolis: University of Minnesota Press.
Bakhtin, Mikhail. 1968. *Rabelais and His World*. Cambridge, MA: MIT Press.
Barad, Karen. 2007. *Meeting the Universe Halfway: Quantum Physics and the Entanglement of Matter and Meaning*. Durham, NC: Duke University Press.
Bennett, Jane. 2009. *Vibrant Matter: A Political Ecology of Things*. Durham, NC: Duke University Press.
Blum, Hester. 2015. "Terraqueuous Planet. The Case for Oceanic Studies." In *The Planetary Turn. Relationality and Geoaesthetics in the Twenty-First Century*, edited by Amy J. Elias and Christian Moraru, 25–36. Chicago: Northwestern University Press.
Braidotti, Rosi. 2017. "Posthuman Critical Theory." *Journal of Posthuman Studies* 1 (1): 9–25.
Cohen, Jeffrey Jerome. 2014. "Foreword." In *Material Ecocriticism*, edited by Serenella Iovina and Serpil Oppermann, ix–xii. Bloomington and Indianapolis: Indiana University Press.

Cohen, Jeffrey Jerome, and Lowell Duckert, eds. 2015. *Elemental Ecocriticism: Thinking with Earth, Air, Water and Fire*. Minneapolis: University of Minnesota Press.

Deleuze, Gilles, and Félix Guattari. 1983. *Anti-Oedipus: Capitalism and Schizophrenia*. Translated by Robert Hurley, Mark Seem, and Helen R. Lane. Minneapolis: University of Minnesota Press.

Deleuze, Gilles, and Félix Guattari. 1986. *Kafka: Toward a Minor Literature*. Translated by Dana Polan. Minneapolis: University of Minnesota Press.

Deleuze, Gilles, and Félix Guattari. 1987. *A Thousand Plateaus: Capitalism and Schizophrenia*. Translated and edited by Brian Massumi. Minneapolis: University of Minnesota Press.

Derrida, Jacques. 2005. *Politics of Friendship*. Translated by George Collins. London: Verso.

Gosh, Amitav. 2017. *The Great Derangement: Climate Change and the Unthinkable*. Chicago and London: The University of Chicago Press.

Haraway, Donna. 2016. *Staying with the Trouble: Making Kin in the Chthulucene*. Durham, NC: Duke University Press.

Harpham, Geoffrey Galt. 1982. *On the Grotesque: Strategies on Contradiction in Art and Literature*. Princeton, NJ: Princeton University Press.

Hayes, Nick. 2011. *The Rime of the Modern Mariner*. London: Random House.

Heise, Ursula K. 2008. *Sense of Place and Sense of Planet: The Environmental Imagination of the Global*. Oxford: Oxford University Press.

Hoffmeyer, Jesper. 2009. *Biosemiotics: An Examination into the Signs of Life and the Life of Signs*. Scranton, PA: University of Scranton Press.

Hogan, Linda, 2008. *People of the Whale*. New York and London: W.W. Norton & Company.

Huggan, Graham, and Helen Tiffin. 2015. *Postcolonial Ecocriticism: Literature, Animals, Environment*. London and New York: Routledge.

Indiana, Rita. 2015. *Tentacle*. Translated by Achy Obejas. Sheffield: And Other Stories.

Iovina, Serenella, and Serpil Oppermann, eds. 2014. *Material Ecocriticism*. Bloomington and Indianapolis: Indiana University Press.

Irigaray, Luce. 1991. *Marine Lover of Friedrich Nietzsche*. Translated by Gillian C. Gill. New York: Columbia University Press.

Irigaray, Luce. 2017. *To Be Born: Genesis of a New Human Being*. London: Palgrave Macmillan.

Irigaray, Luce, and Michael Marder. 2016. *Through Vegetal Being*. New York: Columbia University Press.

Latour, Bruno. 2004. *Politics of Nature: How to Bring the Sciences into Democracy*. Translated by Catherine Porter. Cambridge, MA: Harvard University Press.

Latour, Bruno. 2017. *Facing Gaia: Eight Lectures on the New Climatic Regime*. Translated by Catherine Porter. Cambridge: Polity Press.

Lee, Debbie. 2002. *Slavery and the Romantic Imagination*. Philadelphia: University of Pennsylvania Press.

Linton, Jamie. 2010. *What Is Water? The History of a Modern Abstraction*. Vancouver and Toronto: UBC Press.

Massumi, Brian. 2011. *Semblance and Event: Activist Philosophy and the Occurrent Arts*. Cambridge, MA and London: MIT Press.

Massumi, Brian. 2015. *Politics of Affect*. Cambridge and Malden, MA: Polity Press.
Mathews, Freya. 2003. *For Love of Matter: A Contemporary Panpsychism*. Albany, NY: State University of New York Press.
McMenamin, Mark, and Dianna McMenamin. 1996. *Hypersea: Life on Land*. New York: Columbia University Press.
Moe, Aaron M. 2019. *Ecocriticism and the Poiesis of Form: Holding on to Proteus*. London and New York: Routledge.
Morton, Timothy. 2013. *Hyperobjects: Philosophy and Ecology After the End of the World*. Minneapolis and London: University of Minnesota Press.
Morton, Timothy. 2017. *Humankind: Solidarity with Nonhuman People*. London and New York: Verso.
Neimanis, Astrida. 2017. *Bodies of Water: Posthuman Feminist Phenomenology*. London: Bloomsbury.
Nixon, Rob. 2011. *Slow Violence and the Environmentalism of the Poor*. Cambridge, MA: Harvard University Press.
Plato. 1997. *The Republic*. Ware: Wordsworth.
Plumwood, Val. 2002. *Environmental Culture: The Ecological Crisis of Reason*. London and New York: Routledge.
Rancière, Jacques. 1995. *On the Shores of Politics*. Translated by Liz Heron. London: Verso.
Rancière, Jacques. 1999. *Disagreement: Politics and Philosophy*. Translated by Julie Rose. Minneapolis: University of Minnesota Press.
Rigby, Kate. 2004. *Topographies of the Sacred*. Charlottesville, VA: University of Virginia Press.
Roughgarden, Joan. 2004. *Evolution's Rainbow: Diversity, Gender, and Sexuality in Nature and People*. Oakland, CA: University of California Press.
Seiler, Lutz. 2017. *Kruso*. Translated by Tess Lewis. Melbourne and London: Scribe.
Wheeler, Wendy. 2014. "Natural Play, Natural Metaphor, and Natural Stories: Biosemiotic Realism." In *Material Ecocriticism*, edited by Serenella Iovina and Serpil Oppermann, 67–79. Bloomington and Indianapolis: Indiana University Press.
Zapf, Hubert. 2014. "Creative Matter and Creative Mind. Cultural Ecology and Literary Creativity." In *Material Ecocriticism*, edited by Serenella Iovina and Serpil Oppermann, 51–66. Bloomington and Indianapolis: Indiana University Press.
Zapf, Hubert. 2016. *Literature as Cultural Ecology: Sustainable Texts*. London: Bloomsbury Academic.

5 Unravelling the Nation State

Openwork Lives in Migrant Graphic Narratives

A fine mesh of intricate lacework opens Kate Evans' *Threads*, a work of graphic journalism immersed in the Calais refugee camps which were made notorious as a 'jungle' by the right-wing media. Yet the fragile, floral openwork for which the French city had been famed in the 19th century is twisted and turned in the 21st; it has slid from the lace makers' nimble fingers, the dance of their bobbins straightened and petrified into a razor-wired wall snaking through a desolate port landscape. The visual paradox of soft threads turned into harsh steel is an apt metaphor for the clash between seemingly irreconcilable modes of inhabiting the globe: on the one hand, endowed with political, socio-economic and bio-power, a nation-state order premised on fixed boundaries and exclusive citizenries; on the other hand, an ever-increasing number of lives in precarious movement, who mark out spaces on their cross-border passages but have no place in the fixed reality of parceled-out territories. Speaking from deep within the mass displacements of the second World War, Bert Brecht noted with bitter irony in 1941 that the passport, the "most distinguished part of the human being," is defined by its solidity. Not as recklessly conceived as an ephemeral human life, the passport is guaranteed to be valid whilst a human being will go devalued without it. It is this rigidity that is troublesome, rendering absolute a notion of human worth tethered to arbitrary and changeable notions of citizenship. In a 21st century world that is becoming less sedentary by the hour, and currently home to over 70 million forcibly displaced persons and 258 million international migrants, such a system is not only unjust but out of touch with reality. The literary politics of the graphic narratives at the center of this chapter therefore respond to Braidotti's call to "reintegrate [. . .] with worldly actuality," developing a vision in which the world is not "divided, administered, plundered," as humanity is "thrust into pigeon-holes, by which 'we' are 'human' and 'they' are not" (2016, quoting Edward Said 2004, 26).

Imaginaries of fragile threads woven and interlaced provide the key impulses in this chapter to address this disconnect. I am not interested in promoting a glorified rootlessness, which, after all, is most often unchosen and would mislead us into a binary choice: an either-or between the 'citizens of nowhere' on the one hand and rooted lives securely contained in national boundaries on the other hand. To the contrary, it is the toxic illusion that such a choice did exist and would describe lived alternatives that I am setting out to challenge. I am interested in a different thought experiment: what politics emerges when we imagine global space not as a pre-given set of territorial lines, but constantly created in the threads-being-woven of human passages and relations? This is a Diatopian question, not a utopian one, as migrant paths are already re-defining and traversing the spaces so carefully territorialized by post-war diplomats and so diligently measured by their cartographers. And it is a necessary question when seeking to re-inscribe change and movement into the core of human life, so that being uprooted will not entail your expulsion into a 'jungle' of de-humanization and disenfranchisement.

The politics inherent in literatures of movement and migration, therefore, gains its edge not because it is the voice of an 'Other' – even though giving voice to the voiceless is certainly an impulse behind all fictions discussed in this chapter – but because it calls for a new humanism. An alternative to what Rosi Braidotti and Paul Gilroy describe as the "double imperative of bio-genetic productivity on the one hand and security on the other" (2016, 2), Kate Evans' lace threads weave their way beneath and beyond the wall they are forced to construct. A mesh of those who "don't count" (Evans 2017) caught up in impermanence, Evans' refugee camp is defined by the interactions of "life's threads crossing" (Evans 2017). Coming into being as it is being inhabited, the makeshift city is an entangled world. Yet the fine webs of yarn go up in the smoke of Russian bomber planes over Syria and return in the prison bars of police van windows, deporting those whom the State holds to be illegal. The woven openwork does not indicate a harmonious world; it is too much defined by breaks and holes, the darkness between the tender threads and the sharp needle points, to promise painlessness. But it does suggest the possibility of a new horizon which does not constantly succumb to the desire for extermination. Processes of weaving move neither along a border, nor acknowledge an Other, but seek relation in their knots and twists. This chapter therefore proposes the politics of migrant literature to emerge from relation, be it in gestures, crossovers or rhizomes. This is not a reactive move, and is not articulated against or counter to singular roots or spaces striated in borderlines. Diatopian weaving rather describes a political and lived reality of a different order, a "borderlessness that attends to borders" (Spivak 2016, 47) defined by personal relations, bodies or the locality of the current moment.

Édouard Glissant diagnoses such a "repulsion of sharing the being-of-the-world" as the result of the "terror of having to abdicate the exclusivity of one's wealth" (1997, 23). This observation, though first articulated in 1969, remains poignant into the young millennium. Indicating why

weaving offers such a potent imagery in this bitterly contested political context, the movements of the weaving threads are politically significant as an alternative to rootedness. After all, what screams from deep within the backlash against lives lived on the move is the anger at being interwoven, implicated, and entangled in webs of history that are too complex – and too potent – for walls to hold. While Kate Evans entwines threads of arms sales with personal histories of forced expulsion and searches for the interstices between police violence and the smoldering disregard for suffering on twitter, the refugee camp is razed to the ground by the authorities. The purity of national identity, as Homi Bhabha suggests, can only be achieved "through the death, literal and figurative, of the complex interweavings of history" (1994, 5). This death, however, is not a final erasure. Complex histories, global ecologies and precarious lives keep mattering, calling for a "changed basis for making international connections" (Bhabha 1994, 6).

In such a Diatopian reading of the politics of interweaving, the material side to this mattering is key. Bhabha, writing at the end of the 20th century, had remained indebted to a notion of borderlines that is primarily discursive and has duly been criticized for its "disembodiment" of translocal theory (Moslund 2015, 206). Weaving, on the other hand, is tactile; it shares a deep sense of bodily being with the graphic mode that I will focus on. This does not make it opposed to metaphoric dimensions, as the translocal and transcultural intertextual enmeshments of migrant fiction show. Yet like Kate Evans' lace, such networks remain not only distinctly human-made but also immersed in the broken skin and dirt paths of actual passages. They are akin to Mona Hatoum's *Keffieh* fabric; she interweaves human hair and cotton to create the patterned headscarf symbolic of Palestine. The shed, silky curls move in multiple directions, disobedient to the straight lines of the cotton pattern. Thus hybridized, the fabric opens up its symbolic dimensions, too, infused with questions not only of displacement but also of lived gender roles, both provocative and alluring.

Weaving as Diatopian Metaphor

Besides etymological links associating 'text' itself to the art of *texere*, weaving has a long and rich history as metaphor for textuality; Ulysses' faithful wife Penelope, Arachne, or indeed Virginia Woolf's dictum that "Fiction is like a spider's web" are commonly evoked touchpoints for a metaphoric tradition evoking domesticity, harmony and loyal wifehood. At first glance, therefore, the 21st century graphic narratives of migration and flight seem worlds apart from a critical tradition for which weaving means "to unite, to interlace, to bind: the act is so straightforward that it requires no explanation" (Scheid and Svenbro 1996, 10). Glissant's shared being-in-the-world and Kate Evans' lacework are certainly not straightforward acts, and neither do they aim to create an end product of homogeneity in any "unified, harmonious textile" (Scheid and Svenbro 1996, 12), which would only, again, symbolize how movement is arrested and a pregiven, 'natural' order restored. Shot through with difference, these migrant embroideries emphasize gestures of relation in entwining nodes and the continuous movement of the threads; and while a peacemaking moment remains, this is shot through with difference. In the end, one needs to read the metaphoric tradition against the grain to get closer to the core of the matter. Beneath the wifely surface, Penelope and Arachne's threads move with impulses of resistance, making weaving a political art that has been wrongfully domesticated.

It is an act of unravelling which lies at the heart of Penelope's power. Threatened and beleaguered by predatory suitors in her own house, weaving a pall for the hero Laertes serves as a pretense to keep them at bay, which is why Penelope diligently undoes her daily work at night. Commonly read as the epitome of loyalty to her husband Ulysses, who is presumed dead, I am more interested in how Penelope uses the art of weaving as a strategy to undermine the patriarchal entitlement of the suitors beleaguering her. Even more to the point, Marie-Louise Nosch has shown the weaver's shuttle to be materially akin to Ulysses' ship. Not only are textiles the material for the ship's engine, the sail (Nosch 2016, 112); she also traces the similarity in shape and matter between loom-weight and anchor, embedded in the fluid and repetitive movements of weaving and rowing (2016, 118). When she notes that loom and mast are both called 'histos' in Greek, whilst the weaver is the 'histeus,' weaving begins to emerge not as the feminine negation of travel in a confined homely life, but to the contrary, the loom infuses her chamber with unhomely travel to distant shores. The act of completion, forced upon Penelope by her own maids, is thus an act of violence as it arrests movement and dooms her to acquiesce again to her fixed, exploitable status in society.

Disobedience against overwhelming power is at the heart of Arachne's weaving, too. In his *Metamorphoses*, Ovid tells of this master craftswoman who challenged Pallas Athena to a weaving contest. Yet this is no simple act of hubris, and Arachne is no Icarus tempted to fly too close to the sun. She undoes the sheen of the Gods by crafting images testifying to acts of exploitation and rape; while Athena exults in the lofty thrones and regal grace of the Pantheon, Arachne's fabric exposes the blood running underneath the appearance of splendor. Her images of Greek gods assuming human form to rape and kidnap women, forcing them to bear their children, undo Athena's smooth narrative of lustrous and divine glory. Enraged, Athena transforms Arachne into a spider.

Like a sheet of paper, such textiles convey meaning. Though (not untypically) ignored by Deleuze and Guattari in favor of metalwork, such weaving is an art of "nomadic writing" (Deleuze and Guattari 1987,

402), which merges borrowed traditions of pattern and abstraction into systems of meaning-making. The tendency towards graphic schematization and visual encoding is already a hint for why this tradition offers such rich reference for current graphic artists. Cloth, of course, is a more vulnerable artefact than metal, as Kathryn Sullivan Kruger points out. Yet this makes the act of women weavers, "transforming their domestic activity of making textiles into one of making texts by inscribing their cloths with both personal and political messages" (Sullivan Kruger 2001, 13), more, not less, politically potent. Sullivan Kruger calls out how this deeply gendered tradition of textile making has been tamed, exposing instead how women worked from the margins of society to infuse their tapestries with "what is forbidden by their society, what is abject" (Sullivan Kruger 2001, 44).

Understood in this sense, weaving makes personal life political. Its motions, materials and metaphors deeply entwined with travel, the act of weaving might rub particles of the weaver's skin into the fabric, immersing the textile in bodily being. Emergent from crossings of the transversal shuttle, created in layers and from twists and turns of multiple thread, woven texts and textiles are heteroglossic, infused with the threads of multiple voices. It would be too easy, however, to read this heterogeneity as expression of a diaspora. As Paul Gilroy cautions, the word diaspora "comes closely associated with the idea of sowing seed" (Gilroy 2000, 125), to be traced back to "indistinguishable peas lodged in the protective pods of closed kinship and subspecies being" (2000, 125). The roots of woven threads, however, grow in multiple soils and originate from the fur of animals grazing on different leaves of grass. Steeped in different colorings, these threads suggest roots in various locations, thus creating a fabric that is rhizomatic rather than yearning for an original root. If weaving is thus understood as a metapoetic device, too, then it tells of the difficulty of crafting a narrative of multi-centered and centripetal velocities. Weaving, therefore, can be motivated to express challenges to power and to subvert lives constraint, whether such restriction of movement be the corners of a women's chamber or nation-state borderlines. Insurgent with movement, it seeks to unravel a fossilized order of power with its continuous rhythms of exchange, each thread a missive back and forth, driven by a desire to express and to feel that has nothing in common with the twitter rants of those most vocally defending the nation-state borders of the Western world.

Unfixability: Migrant Graphic Narratives

> A major, or established, literature follows a vector that goes from content to expression. [. . .] But a minor, or revolutionary, literature begins by expressing itself and doesn't conceptualize until afterward [. . .] Expression must break forms, encourage ruptures and new sproutings.
>
> (Deleuze and Guattari 1986, 28)

That the graphic narrative is the genre directly at the forefront of registering such movements is hardly surprising. Weaving does not follow a linear vector, and neither does graphic art, the apparent "sequentiality" (Eisner 2008) of which is often superseded, undermined and crossed by processes of reading that entwine and braid together visuals and text. After all, graphic narrative does not stop with the superhero comic. Since the 1960s, countercultural 'comix' art – with the ' – x' "marking off distance from more conventional comics" (Sabin 1996, 92) – has openly aligned itself with the 'x-rated,' or taboo, in society. Immersed in the underbelly of the non-normative, taboo or disenfranchised, this is perhaps the most explicitly political literary genre, "smashing formal and stylistic, as well as cultural and political, taboos" (Spiegelman and Mouly 1987). Indeed, its "virtues of unfixability" (2005, xiii) and "habit of questioning" (Hatfield 2005, 65) make it peculiarly suited to the political poetics of movement I am interested in here. Graphic artists, particularly in the Middle East, are energizing this long-dismissed genre as the minor literature of the 21st century. Revolutionary in the sense introduced by Gilles Deleuze and Felix Guattari above, these graphic artists work from within lived realities that are often violent and always disrupted, disjunct, deformed but desirous of new connections and vital immersions. Their expression, therefore, is gestural in nature: its 'sprouting' cannot be contained in pre-given formats and does not have any pre-articulated paths to follow; as each line is being drawn, it defines its own spaces to shape an innovative artistic and political reality. It is a method that propels ideas into diversified orders, shaping artistic spaces that function according to a completely different logic from that of the nation state boundaries with which these narratives take issue.

In their work on Kafka, Deleuze and Guattari argue that such minor literature can function as a "relay for a revolutionary machine-to-come," not because it describes an ideology but because, as the people's concern, it can "fill the conditions of a collective enunciation" (Deleuze and Guattari 1986, 18) otherwise lacking. Such motioning from the figure on the page towards a broader collective is, indeed, a key concern of graphic art. Speaking from the context of Lebanese comic art, Ghenwa Hayek argues that "comics not only passively imagine communities, but they also actively form them through the very medium itself" (2014, 177); Hillary Chute and Marianne Dekoven infuse this impulse towards collectivity with a sense of deliberation when they, too, argue for the strong reader-orientation in graphic art, making it a "deliberate form of communication that aims to involve readers and produce some kind of response in them, be it compassion, understanding, respect, or simply entertainment" (2006, 767).

Particularly in the context of refugee art, this communal gesture is a key moment and emerges from the complex triadic splits performed by graphic artists: in combining figural abstraction, immersion in lived reality and gestures of empathy, graphic art can avoid the voyeuristically exploitative moment which Susan Sontag cautioned against in *Regarding the Pain of Others*: "when we look at photos of great pain, we are complicit, we become voyeurs, whether or not we mean to be" (2003, 42). The perspective of graphic art, conversely, differs fundamentally from such asymmetry between photographer (or reader) and the object of his or her gaze. Responsive to what Deleuze and Guattari postulate as the absence of the "master" in a literature that produces an "active solidarity in spite of skepticism" (Deleuze and Guattari 1986, 17), the graphic genre de-centers the self. What comics show is not the object of our gaze, an individual fixed and therefore at risk of becoming abject, but a process of misrecognition in which we as humans do find not ourselves, but a humanity figured as changed, deformed or in transformation.

Yet minor literature is not only characterized by its tendency to make the individual space political, very much in Lena Merhej's sense; in a 2017 interview, the co-founder of *Samandal* (a Beirut-based volunteer collective using the genre of comic art to explore art, society and politics) constates that it is impossible to "separate the politics from the social at this point." It also de-territorializes. While Deleuze and Guattari make this point from a linguistic point of view, their proposition that minor "language is affected with a high coefficient of deterritorialization" (Deleuze and Guattari 1986, 16) returns in a more hybrid form in the comic genre. Kate Evans' threadwork creates a web between anti-refugee posts on twitter, various activists and refugee voices, but this de-territorialisation can – and often is – a more profound intertextual movement entwining pictorial traditions and comic styles.

The spaces of comics, after all, are disobedient to territorialisation as such. Rather than forcing the reader into linearity, they encourage reading as relation. In his influential work on comic art, Thierry Groensteen renounces any attempt break down comics into signifying units, and proposes the concept of "braiding" (Groensteen 2007, 22) as an alternative: The systems of relation of comic art, he argues, are made of gaps, fragmentation, and co-existing icons (Groensteen 2007, 6). His recourse to textile art – 'braiding' – is striking in such an undomesticated genre but is an apt descriptor for a process of reading that is translinear, dialogic and reciprocal. Comic art is not a sum of text and image, but a transformative process. Each unit, though perhaps initially perceived to be framed as a unified whole, is immediately destabilized when the reader puts it into relation with other units of their own choice. In this back-and-forth reading movement that does not just direct one frame to the next but moves across the page and the whole work in a multilinear fashion, each allegedly fixed unit continuously metamorphoses in a play of relations. As minor literature, comic art thus gestures towards impulses which might be termed revolutionary, yet this political momentum is primarily driven by relation. As in Penelope's ruse, each unified and territorial single frame

Unravelling the Nation State 145

is immediately deconstructed and undone. This undoing is at the heart of Kate Evan's lace-based response to the impact of border walls. It returns, in intertextual patterns and other lines of flight, in work by Marjane Satrapi, Shaun Tan, and Hamid Sulaiman.

"We are the granddaughters of the witches that you could not burn": Embroidery as Rhizomatically Rooted Feminism

Ghada Amer, an artist originally from Cairo but moving between New York and Paris, too – thus "always out of place," as Laura Auricchio suggests with a tone of bitterness (2001, 32) – is one of the most influential pioneers in using embroidery as the art form of a feminism with multiple, moving and metamorphosing roots. "We are the granddaughters of the witches that you could not burn" is the slogan stitched in large letters across a turmoil of thread and acrylic paint in her 2015 *Sindy in Pink*, turning embroidery into an utterly undomesticated art. I am interested in how migrant artists who resist categorization in terms of their national and cultural origins use the craft of embroidery, which like weaving is only seemingly contained in the close confines of domestic female spaces, to simultaneously oppose restrictive gender identifications and misleading notions of singular origins. After all, the triumphant clarity of Amer's message is only the surface appearance of how she uses this craft to subvert patriarchal patterns which span across cultures and countries. Despite the fact that "to impose categories on artists who resist categorization is, of course, a contradiction in terms" (Daftari 2016, 10), Fereshteh Daftari is not alone in noting that, particularly as regards so-called 'Islamic' art, the convention to identify artists in terms of their origins is still common currency. Shirana Shabazi expresses equal frustration with the expectation that she should represent a specific culture:

> I wasn't trying to define my roots or my identity or whatever because I'm very clear about it . . . I don't have any problems with living between borders and so on. Then people come with their difficulties trying to define who you are, where your work comes from . . . and they get into trouble because they can't put you in very simple terms. East vs West is very simplistic.
>
> (quoted in Bhabha 2016, 32)

Yet what is the role of slower traditions of manufacture, such as weaving and embroidery, as monolithical notions of national and cultural belonging are failing? Homi Bhabha suggests that the emphasis on the process of making itself disrupts the "global reach of digital immediacy" (2016, 30); from a political point of view, this is an interesting perspective as making implies agency, endowing the material of threads, fabric or dye with intention. Such mattering agency is at the heart of the multiple-rooted, feminist motif of embroidery. It performs the silenced reality of female sensuality, choice and hybridity, endowing the threads of fabric and narrative with friction and resistance to being tamed. Weaving and embroidery, however, are also layered and transitional processes; they open up spaces to articulate the artists' experiences of displacement and belonging which are not separate from, but deeply entwined with the propensity of patriarchal structures to un-home female lives.

Marjane Satrapi elevated the motif of embroidery to the title and poetic principle of her 2003 graphic narrative *Embroideries*, offering a different angle on her use of graphic narrative as hybrid art. *Persepolis*, Marjane Satrapi's best known work, had shown her migrant younger self to be performing the splits: one leg rooted in the Tehran of her birth, the other anchored in the Europe she moved to as a young student, her body was caught in what Homi Bhabha would call 'hybrid hyphenations' (Bhabha 1994, 219). Writing in the late 20th century, "the moment of transit where space and time cross to produce complex figures of difference and identity, past and present, inside and outside, inclusion and exclusion" (1994, 1), Bhabha worked against the notion of identity as unified root and energized the migrant subject into a new sense of empowerment who, like Satrapi's figure, was seemingly paralyzed by the splits of being French-Iranian-Austrian simultaneously. I would like to raise the question, though, if the splits and its discursive equivalent – the hyphen – really remain the most valent descriptors of lifes lived on the move. Such concepts, after all, remain mired in incommensurability and therefore inadvertently reify dualisms, operations of difference and exclusion. Along with other postcolonial theorists, Bhabha certainly enabled the body-in-splits to move again, transforming identity into an oscillating process instead of fixing it as a root cause. This remains articulated, nevertheless, from a perspective of difference which always implies a prior state of unadulterated purity before things got hybrid, mixed and messy.

Satrapi's *Embroideries*, on the other hand, grows out of a space that is interstitial in the most literal sense. A needle stitches together the threads of an after-dinner conversation as the female guests retire, to clean up the dirty dishes but also to poke holes into the patriarchal sheen. Like Kate Evans' threads, this embroidery is an act of relation, as the line of the needle moves in between each woman, entwining their stories around shared themes of marriage, intimacy, independence and migration. Its sharp prick, however, is manifold. The first thing it slices is a testicle. Passed from the hand of one young woman to another in the Grandmother's anecdote, the needle becomes a means of keeping up the pretense of virginity by producing the necessary drop of blood on the wedding sheets. The plan goes awry, as the non-virginal bride, in the heat of the moment, accidentally attacks her betrothed's intimate parts instead of her own. "Misled about the merchandise," the young husband decides against making this scandal public, fearing his own name to be made ridiculous. This anecdote, shot through with irony, immediately foreshadows Satrapi's unique take on the embroidery theme. The women's shared laughter celebrates how the alleged signs of domesticity become undomesticated tools for disobedient women whose role as dutiful wife, their husband's 'merchandise,' makes up only part of a multiple life.

Such multiplicity, indeed, is at the core of Satrapi's embroidery, which does not aim to express or represent, but to unsettle. Even before the needle is introduced, Satrapi creates a double-page spread in which sensual emancipation and cross-stich homely domesticity are juxtaposed. The dainty embroidery frame on the right, with its floral pattern and lace aesthetic, can barely contain the figure on the left: in an abstracted black-and-white style that evokes a European, turn-of-the-century Art-Deco style, Marjane's aunt sensuously sipping tea, the glass held elegantly in her manicured fingers. A former child bride who had successfully escaped a husband 56 years her senior, this woman's conversational thread entwines polygamous sexual experience with years spent independently abroad. The self, in this narrative, is inherently multiple, driven by a search for intimacy that has liberated itself from the narratives of romantic love and marriage. Thus propelled by desire, it is akin to Frantz Fanon's postulation that

> As soon as I *desire* I am asking to be considered. I am not merely here-and-now, sealed into thingness. I am for somewhere else and for something else. [. . .] I should constantly remind myself that the real *leap* consists in introducing invention into existence. In the world in which I travel, I am endlessly creating myself.
>
> (1986, 218, 229)

Satrapi's characters live such desire not in the discursive forms which Fanon (and certainly Bhabha) privilege, but as an embodied, material practice. They thus operate in two different dimensions. Yet Fanon's desirous subject who is inventing, gesturing and creating itself into a different existence, across borders both literal and figurative, offers an intriguing entry point into the selfhood which Satrapi creates. The motions of embroidering here are not reactions to a contest with a Goddess, as in Arachne's case, and neither are they defensive moves against Penelope's suitors. Satrapi's more metaphorical movements of needle and threat infuse apparently objectified wifehood with a desire for relation with the other women, but also with the world beyond domesticity. They expose the centrifugal forces which are barely contained in the after-dinner living room, there to ensure adequate "ventilation of the heart," opening to currents of air in a stuffy world.

I must concede, of course, that this conversation could very easily be read in Bahbha's sense, and indeed, he also notes how Marjane Satrapi herself combines text and image as "device shared with the illustrated manuscripts of Islamic art" (Daftari 2016, 21) while being equally inspired by Art Spiegelman. This hybridity, however, does not take the form of the split, because it is so enmeshed as to become invisible in Satrapi's signature black-and-white style. It is a feature of the genre that graphic narratives perform in-between spaces as terrain for pronouncing innovative forms of human identity, contesting and collaborating on ideas of human society. Even more poignantly, because the women's 'embroidery' session is ultimately about sex, with all its dimensions of sensuality, power and desire, the notion of incommensurability just does not have any traction here. Like any weaving imagery, and typical for the graphic genre, embodiment knows more of processual becoming and relation than difference. What Satrapi achieves in *Embroideries*, therefore, is to expose an otherwise hidden dimension of reality in which relation is already lived in its most subversive forms. Like the threaded, enforced nomadism in Kate Evans' refugee narratives, interwoven existence is already a fact of life. It is now calling to be legitimized and empowered in open articulation.

The multiple voices entwined in *Embroideries* have already passed the stage where the experience of migration is made explicit; in contrast to *Persepolis*, movement and hybridity have become implicit as the baseline of authorial perspective here. This is why, politically, *Embroideries* develops concepts of being-in-relation despite not offering an explicit migrant narrative of moving from one place to another; nor is it about cultural displacement. Its "unhomeliness" is not set in contrast with alleged "roots" (Bhabha 1994, 9), and is not about "extra-territorial and cross-cultural initiations" (Bhabha 1994, 9). It is charged with feminist impulses, and at first sight more akin to Spivak's idea of the subaltern (1999). The women in Satrapi's narrative, not unlike Spivak's silenced colonized women, seem to not be able to speak. Within their own homes they have to retreat from the official patriarchal space, which they are obliged to uphold by marking their respect when, for instance, they address their husbands by their last names. It might thus not be a different language which they are forced to employ, but the discursive rules of a patriarchal system designed to suppress them. In the context of postcolonialism, Spivak would encourage women in such situations to interrupt the colonizer's monologue in order to create their own voices. In Satrapi's women's 'embroidery' session, such an intervention takes the shape of literal and metaphorical needles pricking into the smooth surface of patriarchal power, which, in the women's' stories, had more often than not been established in forced and disappointed movements across cultures and countries.

We have already seen that Satrapi's desirous embodiment inhabits a different dimension to Fanon's or Bahbha's discursively doubled selves. It is now time to explore this corporeal impact, which escapes the male focus on the colonized and post-enlightenment 'man' of these theorists.

Embroidery, in Satrapi's narrative, has a double meaning: it metapoetically refers to this entwined narrative of multiple voices and gestures; yet it also inspires the bodies of these women, who are objectified to the point of being married only for the sales value of their wedding gifts, with a processual quality that escapes such thingness. Having a 'full embroidery,' as the aunts explain to an interested young Marjane, describes an operation which restores your vagina to a seemingly virginal state to keep up appearances in a patriarchal marriage market without giving up any actual sexual freedom. As regards feminist politics, this is controversial for its obvious links with the kind of cosmetic surgery aimed at pleasing the male gaze, which is a core theme of this 'ventilation of the heart' session. The embroidery needle, therefore, is also a surgeon's knife, making embroidery not a domestic craft for pure young girls waiting marriage, but a cutting bodily practice. The subversive impact of this becomes more apparent when the conversation moves on to partial 'embroideries,' restoring the vagina to its former elasticity after child birth. Inherently opened and much more radically in process than other human bodies because of its ability to give birth, the female body thus becomes an elastically evolving matter, with 'embroidery' acting as a code word for a sense of control. In the case of partial 'embroideries' in particular, this means taking control and assuming the right to sexual pleasure; the lexicon of domestic craft thus offers a language for a subject otherwise silenced, and a practice driven by desire for both sensuality and survival in a hostile society. As Roszika Parker pointed out in *The Subversive Stitch*,

> Embroidery has provided a source of power and pleasure for women, while being indissolubly linked to their powerlessness. Paradoxically, while embroidery was employed to inculcate femininity into women, it also enabled them to negotiate the constraints of femininity.
>
> (2012, 11)

'Negotiations', however, is a cautious term for such practices. The open sensuality of Satrapi's work re-emerges, radicalized, in Ghada Amer's unapologetic embroideries of female sexuality. Laura Auricchio unearthed the complex visual references of Amer's work, with blotches of thread and drips of paint echoing the abstract expressionism of Jackson Pollock or Clyfford Still. But in works such as *Gray Lisa*, these hybrid gestures only serve to infuse these painters' brash masculinity with a subversive layer, as the seemingly abstract stitches evolve to reveal fondling, seducing and masturbating female figures.

The motif of embroidery, thus, re-imagines hybrid identities as relational bodies engaged in processes of making and unmaking. Their impact is not merely a disruption of the discursive space, but a call for acknowledging the complexity of lived realities, parts of which are being disavowed and sacrificed in the name of what Shirana Shahbazi has called the 'simple terms' of unitary cultural belonging. Refusing any homogenization, these artists' "multivocal polyphony" (Daftari 2003, 175) seeks expression in the processes of becoming-matter of fabric crafts.

Woven Voices: Intertextual Patterns of Disorientation

In Hamid Sulaiman's *Freedom Hospital* (2017), the figures of Henri Matisse's *La Danse* form a joyful circle above an anti-regime demonstration in Syria in 2012. Springing from the dreams of the demonstrators, their joyous movements of renewal and hope infuse the stark black-and-white aesthetic of Sulaiman's graphic narrative with fluidity, promising renewal and change. Such intertextual gestures across space and time break through any presumptions of territorial or cultural specificity, rendering porous the harsh reality of civil war. Weaving, after all, can also be a stylistic principle. In graphic narratives documenting conditions of violence and flight, this polyvocality surges against the idea that identity, culture or voice could ever be monolithic. Intertextuality knows no Other, only lines of difference and thresholds of articulation to become entwined with, changing and metamorphosing in the process.

Non-fictional graphic narratives about refuge and migration, therefore, do not merely document a reality of bloodshed and disorder. Their main political potential is not re-presentative, fulfilled in the sharing of stories and witnessing injustice, but performative: like Donna Haraway's string figures, their intertextual patterns pass the threads of various aesthetic traditions along, enmeshing each in one shared reality in the process. To displace the torture in Syrian prisons or the Somalian climate emergency by 'othering' it thus becomes impossible; once entangled, the nationalist illusion that these are brutal, yet somehow contained realities which leave the West safe and neither complicit nor contaminated is exposed to be the xenophobic lie it is. Intertextual strings "propose and enact patterns for participants to inhabit, somehow, a vulnerable and wounded earth" (Haraway 2016, 10); participation instead of gazing at a distance, and inhabiting rather than territorialising, are the political modes of being responsive to such intertextual gestures. They acknowledge the world to be a political, cultural and ecological system which, once wounded, touches all. After all, Henri Matisse's dancers are already sensing the shadow of World War One, echoing the impending doom of the protest movement which Hamid Sulaiman, at this particular moment in the narrative, still infuses with such hope. The politics of such interwoven intertextuality can thus be understood as the aesthetic equivalent of Haraway's "Terrapolis": an n-dimensional niche space defined by entangled time and chimeric becoming-with (Haraway 2016, 11). To continue the "old art of terraforming" (2016, 11), this space is one of "always-too-much connection," calling for a "response-ability" (2016, 11) that acknowledges the impossibility of disconnection. Embroiled, intimate and ensnared, such narratives perform what is means to be-with and become-with via their intertextual knots, ties, relays and returns. Beyond the charitable gestures of compassion, they expose a world of connection in which violence is relayed as much as desire.

The graphic form lends itself particularly organically to such relational realities. Even Joe Sacco's more conceptionally documentary graphic journalism, which opts for a sense of realism in its figurative style over the abstraction practiced, for instance, by Satrapi, attempts the polyvocal; his 2009 *Footnotes in Gaza* balance the outsider narrator's perspective with the insider Abed's focalization, jumping between multiple angles and settings to create a sense of multiplicity. The truly decentering effects of the intertextual graphic narrative, however, emerges from work that embeds the journalistic gaze's search for orientation in an authorial process that is steeped in the realities it represents.

A collaboration between design students and refugees in the Southern German city of Augsburg in 2015 is only one example of many similar projects experimenting with this form. For the collection *Geschichten aus dem Grandhotel* ('Stories from the Grandhotel,', edited by Mike Loos in 2016), students paired up with refugees, lending their drawing skills to enable the new arrivals to share their stories without being hindered by language barriers. This co-authoring de-centered the autobiographic self, transforming it into a non-unitary, open and porous form of subjecthood. Immersed in the refugees' vulnerability through this relation, the graphic narratives perform the act of being affected by the experiences of another as much as they bear witness to the brutality of flight. Authorship, thus, becomes an act of relation. Such collaborations radicalize the generic features of autobiographical graphic narratives per se, which always demand a distancing from the self, to be presented in the third person as if from the outside. This stepping beyond the self, un-homing and exposing it, is a fundamental gesture of such intertextual and relational creation. The other implied consequence, of course, is the impossibility of absolute truth: the clarity of the birds-eye view is abandoned whilst navigating disorientation, and perhaps even exposed to be a dangerous illusion given the implicated nature of human life. The documentary value of these non-fiction narratives, thus, is always relational and perspectival, in-becoming rather than pre-given to be unearthed and represented. It is the act of an encounter in a world to be co-inhabited and to be collaboratively shaped that is at the heart of these short narratives.

Sulaiman's *Freedom Hospital*, too, braids its deeply immersed and situated emplotment into a visual language that is transversal. At its core, the narrative traces a young woman's attempt to maintain a hospital in the fictional town of Houria ('Freedom') during the Civil War in Bashar al-Assad's Syria. The seeds of Yasmin's idealism, however, soon evaporate as the region descends into a cataclysmic conflict. The petals of spring flowers with which the narrative opens soon give way to checkpoints reflected in the still water of rivers; in the stark black-and-white aesthetic, the panels begin to emanate disorientation as a blinding effect sets in; harsh contours emerging from the dark create a sense of sudden assault; any light ever only illuminates a partial view, and remains streaked by shadow. Bombardments increase, but as footage of the town in ruins emerges online on YouTube, outlines become even more broad-brushed. "Look at this," a survivor demands in one of the youtube panels, yet Sulaiman makes it impossible to see him, so bleary are the figures on this page. The gaze of detachment in a doubled mediation – from youtube to comic – reveals less than the visceral close-ups of bodies torn apart. The motifs awarded whole-page spreads of white on black create a vortex of seemingly irreconcilable dimensions of the hospital inhabitants' reality; a body pierced by bullets, a couple making love, and an amputated limb expose a reality so ruptured as to make the search for orientation futile. Nevertheless, this is no simple tale of heroes and villains, of freedom fighters fitted against an inhumane regime. Sulaiman's critique is multi-faceted and complex, tracing shifting conflict lines in a war defined by confusions, shifting allegiances, and porous passages from resistance to complicity.

At first sight, this seems an aesthetic shot through by fissures. Beneath the rupture, though, deeper connectivities emerge in a comic noir style interweaving apparently disparate visual languages. Sulaiman's black-and-white visuals, often deformed and abstracted, evoke the woodcut aesthetic employed a century ago and a continent apart by Käthe Kollwitz. Focusing on those left behind – mothers, women and children – she employed the aesthetic of the woodcut to develop a war series of seven prints which, in a letter to a friend, she described as an attempt to grasp four years which flee comprehension. The woodcut, in her work, is a craft both radical and rooted, passed on through the centuries. Each shape a cutting in the most literal sense, the woodblock bears the scars of the sharp knife, creating an image both visceral and abstracted enough to create universally legible gestures of the horrors of war. Despite the frequent references to 21st century mass and social media, Sulaiman's visual language employs these gestures and echoes the cuts of Kollwitz's blocks. The hospitalized child crying for his mother lies on his back, his face rift in stark lines, as her figure of a widow did in the previous century's war. Gesturing across dividing lines of time, space and language, Sulaiman therefore articulates his Syrian story on the basis of a fundamentally transversal visual formula.

However, this gesture is not a mere return to a modernist tradition. Sulaiman's aesthetic also nods towards Frank Miller's noir style; counter-intuitive as it might seem to braid Kollwitz into the visual language of the *Sin City* postmodern crime comics, these multidirectional stylistic threads create the multi-dimensional friction which defines *Freedom Hospital*. Whereas Kollwitz employs the uncompromised figural focus of her woodcuts to expose grief in its relentless despair, the radical disorientation lived and breathed by the inhabitants of Miller's crime-infested world seems bitter reality in Sulaiman's Syrian story. Indeed, in *Freedom Hospital*, a close-up of the face of a dead friend in a body bag alternates with perspectival shifts which unsettle the sniper ranges and frontlines of this continuously shapeshifting and morphing war. This intertextual polyvocality threads deep and compassionate humanity into a splatter reality; the impact is unbearably grim. Its key gesture, however, is to undermine the idea that a refugee artist bears witness to help others imagine a reality that is, somehow, other. However deeply immersed his graphic reality is in the local situation in Syria, shot through with visual memories of European Wars and US-American comic book violence, it is also a global one from the start.

Weaving Tails: Fantastical Migrations Through Folded Space

The migrant protagonist in Shaun Tan's 2006 wordless graphic novel *The Arrival* flees a reality shot through with seemingly disparate forces. Dragon-like tails weave through the grid of city streets which he leaves behind, casting their shadows on his family's life. Yet once he arrives, stepping from an airborne doorway into a fantastical new reality, tailed creatures already wait for the encounter. This species, though, is friendly. A little tailed beast becomes the migrant's friend, guiding him through a world shaped by the creatures almost more than by the humans. As the migrant begins settling in, his experience of forced flight becomes interwoven with the narratives of other migrants, telling of death marches, bone-filled killing fields, and realities rendered as harsh blocks, towering above the minuscule humans in threatening geometries of dark boulders and concrete quadrants. The fantastical world that has become the migrant's destination, in contrast, is an intricate network of circular patterns, with pathways spiraling through the air. Laden with entwined singularities, this world offers an alternative to the strict grids and gothic towers of the migrants' despotic, life-threatening origin worlds. Curvilinear and inhabited on multiple levels and by multiple species, it offers a space for encounter.

Nomad thought, as all the migrants' backstories and all the narratives in this chapter expose, strives for connection but is not an originally peaceful thought. To the contrary, in Gilles Deleuze and Felix Guattari's *A Thousand Plateaus*, nomad thought emerges from the war machine. It is "of another species, another nature, another origin than the State apparatus," (Deleuze and Guattari 1987, 352), propelled by "incredible velocity, a catapulting force" (1987, 356). In the war machine, the formation of stable power is an impossibility. Favoring a "fabric of immanent relations" (1987, 358) between packs, gangs, "groups of the rhizome tribe," the war machine is an alternative to the "arborescent" (1987, 358) type of organization that centers around organs of power. Without organs, the war machine is a milieu of exteriority. In it, feelings turn to affects, utilizable as "weapons of war" (1987, 356). The self, de-subjectified into a "vortical body in nomad space" (1987, 366) in these affective currents which "transpierce the body like arrows" (1987, 356), has to navigate time in a new rhythm. No linear arrow but "an endless succession of catatonic episodes or fainting spells, and flashes or rushes" (1987, 356), such time creates a relayed space. It cannot fall back on the idea of identity, and neither can it seek reproduction. The war machine prefers metamorphosis, creating a hydraulic, curvilinear dimension of vortices and spirals in which no being is stable, but always transforming in response to their conditions. In it, one is "a foreigner in one's tongue," seeking to "bring something incomprehensible into the world" (1987, 378).

Nomad thought, therefore, is a visceral thing. Its dynamic conception challenges the State, which seeks to make it sedentary, with "counterthoughts, which are violent in their acts and discontinuous in their appearances, and whose existence is mobile in history" (1987, 376). Yet nevertheless, it is beyond question that Deleuze and Guattari's opposition between the State and the war machine offers a succinct metaphor for the seeming incompatibility between migrant lives of velocity on the one hand, and the territorial powers of nation-states on the other hand. Shaun Tan's seemingly dream-like world is created along such rhizomatic lines. Laid out in a space that spirals and curves around multiple centers, this is no war machine in the literal sense of the word, as it knows no violence. Yet it is a version of a war machine in that it interprets nomad thought for the post-war state, understood in terms of its underlying vortical forces, transformative instability, and curvilinear spaces that are ongoing sites of creation.

It is significant in this context that the new arrivals land in this world through doorways carried by wings. A similar trope returns in Mohsin Hamid's 2017 novel *Exit West*, which describes a world on the move and perpetually on the brink of violent and ecological collapse. Hamid envisions door that transform into virtual openings across space, enabling refugees to appear, seemingly re-born into a new existence, in another country's bedrooms, bars and occupied houses. Such openings transform space itself. Not merely a relay, as in Deleuze and Guattari's nomad space, these doorways redo the geography of the world by folding it, stitching it together in places and tearing it apart in others. Space, thus, becomes a fabric, but not in the sense of a smooth, well-ordered and flat plane. Such sudden connections between places hundreds of kilometers apart make it necessary for the fabric to be folded together at will, the doorway functioning as a stitch, threading together in momentary intimacy that which, on a level plane, would be worlds apart. Such a processual geography is shaped by disappearance and reappearance. It creates a world in relation, in which the borderlines of a territorial state simply lose their traction.

Conclusion: Processual Space, Relational Politics

> [W]hen our landscape combines cleanly with the lines of a country we suddenly discover to be ours, then (the vow fulfilled, the impatience dried up, the silence and leisure of the work ideal offered up), the dream of the One, formerly abandoned, gathers us once more into its tyranny.
>
> (Glissant 1997, 10)

There are two modes of looking at the world: one is the bird's-eye view, preferred position of colonial powers or victorious alliances divvying up newly conquered territories between themselves. This perspective continuous to be at the heart of global mapping, as atlases align space with power and infuse our dreams, as Glissant suggests, with a tyranny of the One. This dream of cleanly delineated unity is exposing its blood-soaked underside in the abused child migrants detained at the US-Mexican border and in the depths of the Mediterranean, a sea turned graveyard. Woven cartographies, stretching, contracting and flowing with lives lived in movement, are not only disobedient to this spatial politics; they suggest a different reality altogether, one which is more responsive to "process geography" (Madera 2015, 16) than to the men charting territories on drawing tables.

This leap from resistance onto the construction of altogether "[O]ther geographies than those determined by sociopolitical or identity-political interests" (Moslund 2015, 10f) is key to the spatial politics of relation which emerge from these graphic narratives; this is because it allows us to acknowledge how literary language activates existent, lived spaces beyond the drawing-board powers, energizing realities that are in the best case casually ignored and in the worst case violently repressed. Instead of resulting from the violence of the trenches, process space is generated through participation; whereas bird's eye cartographies operate on normative codes of ethnic exclusivity, economic profitability or military strategy, which are hidden beneath the apparent clarity of the borderline, woven maps dismantle such codes.

However distinct and unique they are, the graphic narratives by Tan, Satrapi, Evans and Sulaiman suggest that such a cartography of participation in the 21st century operates on three core principles: firstly, it traces space through corridors and via passages, not borderlines. In his philosophy of relation, Edouard Glissant had suggested the archipelago as emplaced model for such tentative, moving thought. In contrast to a continental thought which envisages the world in blocks, archipelago thought runs with the river currents, becoming diffracted, polluted in the process. Passages are not mere movements from one side of the border and its lived reality to another, but are the constitutive feature shaping archipelago space (Glissant 1990, 58). Yet the openwork of refugee paths which Kate Evans traces already indicate that this archipelago thought, in the 21st century, is stretching across continents, too. Hamid Sulaiman's Syria has itself become an archipelago in which the logic of pre-defined, fixed territories has ceased its hold on reality. Now defined by passages and routes which, opening and foreclosing in unforeseeable intervals, shape an embattled space, this creates a violent and anarchist side to Glissant's archipelago pacifism. Passage space is not necessarily more peaceful or harmonious than borderline space. What is does allow, however, is the opening-up of "spaces of dissension" (Madera 2015, 4) such as the Freedom Hospital itself; these are not peripheral but at the very center of the passage-geography, as mobile roots which can transfer through and transgress space to re-emerge – in the hospital's case – in the refugee camp. Working in the context of African American fiction, Madera argues that such spaces are creative, not reactive, emergent "fields of invention that mediate different worlds" (2015, 4). A geography of passage therefore departs from its complicity with the powerful, but does not simply side with the powerless. Beyond any such duality, it traces the complex webs of living and moving relation.

Secondly, such passages entwine in nodal relays to move back and onwards in other directions, each transformed through new relations and re-energized with the heteroglossia of other linguistic or visual signifying systems, becoming attached in the friction like particles of yarn. The cycle of receiving welcome, learning and then giving welcome to others in Tan's immigrant narrative shows such relays to be processes of self-transformation, "knowing that that which is not destined to a relation to the other is worthless" (Glissant 1990, 16). Rather than being caught in a hyphenated in-between of migrant-citizen as described by Homi Bhabha, nodal identities do not oscillate between the two dimensions of origin and destination, but are in perpetual movement, continuously being spun into different relations in webs of narrative encounters. If indeed "[T]he End is relay," (Glissant 1990, 18), then this end is a series of moments, continuously transforming into expression. The heteroglossic web of intertextual references which Sulaiman weaves and Satrapi navigates, after all, are open-ended; they cannot be fixed in terms of misconceived East-West influences, but are cat's cradles in which each gesture offering a thread changes the network before and the web to come, moving and complexifying the nodes. These relays, like the points in Deleuze and Guattari's nomad space, are "strictly subordinated to the paths they determine" (1987, 380). Each doorway opening is not an ultimate arrival, not a settling back into a sedentary order; it transforms the self, just as the Sin-City inspired comic noir style changes Sulaiman's narrative, only to continue weaving towards other arrival relays and merging with other visual patterns. Making the relay the end, therefore, implies a perpetual processuality; it ensures that no identity can be sublimated only to become tyrannical, no space can be elevated as ultimate territory to be fenced and defended.

Both these dimensions – passages and transformative nodal relays – are driven by the final and perhaps most fundamental aspect, that of emplaced velocity. Movement and emplacement are not mutually exclusive, unless one pay credence to the discourse of the far-right that posits migrants as fundamentally uprooted; emplaced movement originates in a different kind of root, one that has detached itself from the toxic anchor between the 'racine' and race, and has become mobile and unhomely. This emplacement is all the more important as what Sten Pultz Moslund terms "imperial relations to reality" (2015, 11) suppress the sensing, material body. At the beginning of this chapter, I already noted how weaving entwines the worker's shed skin with the fabric, making this a deeply embodied practice. Instead of a rationalized geopolitics focused on cost-benefit calculations, flows of data, money or economic transaction, this makes "place-language-body" (Moslund 2015, 10) the defining geocritical triad. In resisting disembodiment, Moslund hopes that "sensuous geographies in migration literature may work as a force of resistance that [. . .] resists coloniality/modernity as the underlying logic of imperialism" (2015, 206). Like the threads spun on a loom, such a geocritical moment always entails a doubling of figuration and bodily immersion. It is through this doubled insurgence of matter and sign that a sensory, participatory geography can step outside the predominantly abstracted, disembodied geopolitical patterns of power, and return to critique to create alternative modes of inhabiting global space.

How can such moving roots be grasped? It is tempting to revert to the rhizome, as Édouard Glissant does in his Poetics of Relation; too apparent is the potential of this root that does not seek any unified origin but, skeptical of any "racine totalitaire" (Glissant 1990, 23), grows and flourishes as a mesh of threads, thresholds and lines of flight. As such, it liberates the self into relation, transforming identity into a nodal relay of sprouts and offshoots. However, is the nomad not, as Glissant then asks, also determined by the conditions of their existence (1990, 24)? Is nomadism truly a "jouissance de liberté" or rather a product of adversary contingencies (1990, 24)? Certainly, being in flight dooms the devastating desire for sedentariness (1990, 24) along with the passion to define oneself (1990, 26). Conventional rootedness and identity thus shattered, liberation can follow but – more often than not – so does searing pain.

Yet literature is not psychotherapy; its fictional relation to emotional and geopolitical realities is more complex. If literatures "rompent *contre*" (Glissant 2009, 42) the iron law of singular origins, then this is not a utopian aim of joyful liberation. A Diatopian moment, this is steeped in the knowledge that this trembling world remains unknowable; immersed in movement, it offers no summary overview and retains no secure core of selfhood. What it offers is the possibility to think differently, envisaging a mode of being human in which the desire for one place and one root has become redundant. The pain of uprooting, after all, is all the more scathing because it seems to cut the very umbilical cord that gives legitimacy to a life lived as worthwhile and deserving of respect. Nodal networks of woven threads, however, affect this very root, making it possible to be human whilst being in movement. Ultimately, this opening is what migrant graphic fiction offers; instead of binding human life in the constant dread of an originary lack, the relays of nodal selfhood suggest that being human means to be driven by the desire for encounter and for change. Whether propelled by conditions of violence or by curiosity, this is perhaps the only mode of being that is too entwined with other lives to revert into the tyranny of the One.

References

Auricchio, Laura. 2001. "Works in Translation: Ghada Amer's Hybrid Pleasures." *Art Journal* 60 (4): 27–37.

Bhabha, Homi K. 1994. *The Location of Culture*. London and New York: Routledge.

Bhabha, Homi K. 2016. "Another Country." In *Without Boundary: Seventeen Ways of Looking*, edited by Fereshteh Daftari, 30–35. New York: The Museum of Modern Art.

Braidotti, Rosi. 2016. "The Contested Posthumanities." In *Conflicting Humanities*, edited by Rosi Braidotti and Paul Gilroy, 9–45. London: Bloomsbury Academic.

Braidotti, Rosi, and Paul Gilroy. 2016. "Introduction." In *Conflicting Humanities*, edited by Rosi Braidotti and Paul Gilroy, 1–7. London: Bloomsbury Academic.

Chute, Hillary, and Marianne Dekoven. 2006. "Introduction." *Graphic Narrative: MFS Modern Fiction Studies* 52 (4): 767–82.

Daftari, Fereshteh. 2003. "Beyond Islamic Roots: Beyond Modernism." *Islamic Arts* 43: 175–86.

Daftari, Fereshteh, ed. 2016. *Without Boundary: Seventeen Ways of Looking*. New York: The Museum of Modern Art.

Deleuze, Gilles, and Félix Guattari. 1986. *Kafka: Toward a Minor Literature*. Translated by Dana Polan. Minneapolis: University of Minnesota Press.

Deleuze, Gilles, and Félix Guattari. 1987. *A Thousand Plateaus: Capitalism and Schizophrenia*. Edited and translated by Brian Massumi. Minneapolis: University of Minnesota Press.

Eisner, Will. 2008. *Comics and Sequentiality: Principles and Practices from the Legendary Cartoonist*. New York: W.W. Norton & Company.

Evans, Kate. 2017. *Threads from the Refugee Crisis*. London: Verso.

Fanon, Frantz. 1986. *Black Skin, White Masks*. London: Pluto.

Gilroy, Paul. 2000. *Between Camps: Race. Identity and Nationalism at the End of the Color Line*. London: Allen Lane, The Penguin Press.

Glissant, Édouard. 1990. *Poétique de la Relation*. Paris: Éditions Gallimard.
Glissant, Édouard. 1997. *Poetic Intention*. Translated by Nathalie Stephens. Callicoon, NY: Nightboat Books.
Glissant, Édouard. 2009. *Philosophie de la Relation. Poésie en Étendue*. Paris: Éditions Gallimard.
Groensteen, Thierry. 2007. *The System of Comics*. Translated by Bart Beaty and Nick Nguyen. Jackson: University Press of Mississippi.
Hamid, Mohsin. 2017. *Exit West*. London: Penguin.
Haraway, Donna. 2016. *Staying with the Trouble: Making Kin in the Chthulucene*. Durham, NC: Duke University Press.
Hatfield, Charles. 2005. *Alternative Comics: An Emerging Literature*. Jackson: University Press of Mississippi.
Hayek, Ghenwa. 2014. *Beirut, Imagining the City: Space and Place in Lebanese Literature*. London: Bloomsbury.
Loos, Mike, ed. 2016. *Geschichten aus dem Grandhotel: Comic-Reportagen von Augsburger Design-Studierenden*. Augsburg: Wißner Verlag.
Madera, Judith. 2015. *Black Atlas: Geography and Flow in Nineteenth-Century African American Literature*. Durham, NC and London: Duke University Press.
Moslund, Sten Pultz. 2015. *Literature's Sensuous Geographies: Postcolonial Matters of Place*. New York: Palgrave Macmillan.
Nosch, Marie-Louise. 2016. "The Loom and the Ship in Ancient Greece: Shared Knowledge, Shared Terminology, Cross-Crafts, or Cognitive Maritime-Textile Archaeology?" In *Weben und Gewebe in der Antike. Materialität – Repräsentation – Episteme – Metapoetik*, edited by Henriette Harich-Schwarzbauer, 109–32. Oxford and Philadelphia: Oxbow Books.
Parker, Roszika. 2012. *The Subversive Stitch: Embroidery and the Making of the Feminine*. London: I B Tauris & Co Ltd.
Sabin, Roger. 1996. *Comics, Comix and Graphic Novels; A History of Comic Art*. London: Phaidon.
Sacco, Joe. 2009. *Footnotes in Gaza*. London: Jonathan Cape.
Said, Edward. 2004. *Power, Politics and Culture: Interviews with Edward W. Said*, edited by Gauri Viswanathan. London: Bloomsbury.
Satrapi, Marjane. 2003. *Embroideries*. London: Jonathan Cape.
Scheid, John, and Jesper Svenbro. 1996. *The Craft of Zeus: Myths of Weaving and Fabric*. Translated by Carol Volk. Cambridge, MA: Harvard University Press.
Sontag, Susan. 2003. *Regarding the Pain of Others*. New York: Farrar, Straus and Giroux.
Spiegelman, Art, and Françoise Mouly. 1987. *Introduction to Read Yourself RAW; Pages from the Rare First 3 Issues of the Comics Magazine for Damned Intellectuals!* Edited by Art Spiegelman and Françoise Mouly. New York: Pantheon.
Spivak, Gayatri Chakravorty. 1999. *A Critique of Postcolonial Reason: Toward a History of the Vanishing Present*. Cambridge, MA: Harvard University Press.
Spivak, Gayatri Chakravorty. 2016. "A Borderless World?" In *Conflicting Humanities*, edited by Rosi Braidotti and Paul Gilroy, 47–74. London: Bloomsbury Academic.

Sulaiman, Hamid. 2017. *Freedom Hospital: A Syrian Story*. London: Jonathan Cape.

Sullivan Kruger, Kathryn. 2001. *Weaving the Word: The Metaphorics of Weaving and Female Textual Production*. London: Rosemont Publishing & Printing Corp.

Tan, Shaun. 2006. *The Arrival*. Sydney: Hachette Australia.

Index

abduction 119
Adorno, Theodor W. 8, 22, 32, 36–38, 44
Amazing Spiderman, The 71–72
Amberstone, Celu 63
Amer, Ghada 145, 149
Anthropocene 103, 113, 135, 158
Arachne 140–141, 147
Arendt, Hannah 3, 9, 25
Atwood, Margaret 3, 9, 20

Bakhtin, Mikhail 129
Barad, Karen 62, 107, 118–119
Baudrillard, Jacques 31, 76, 84
becoming-with 11, 27, 33, 150
Benjamin, Walter 30–32
Brecht, Bertolt 6, 72, 138
Bhabha, Homi 140, 145–148, 156
biopolitics 12, 43–46, 54, 56–58
biotechnology 12, 47–48, 61
Bladerunner 47–51, 58, 61, 63, 67
Bloch, Ernst 30–32, 38
body without organs 36, 54, 56, 65, 131–132
Bowling, Frank 70–71
Braidotti, Rosi 45, 63, 123, 125, 138–139
Butler, Judith 27, 46, 73–75, 77, 80, 98
Butler, Octavia 20, 64–65

"Capitalocene" 38, 43, 117
Caruth, Cathy 72, 77
Coleridge, Samuel Taylor 115–116
comix 143
cyberpunk 12, 48, 58–59
cyborg 44–45, 50–55, 57, 59–64, 66

Deleuze, Gilles 3, 7, 10, 15, 28, 35–36, 44, 54, 56, 62, 64–65, 67, 83, 88, 91, 93–96, 121, 131–132, 141, 143–144, 153–154
del Toro, Guillermo 102, 104, 107, 121, 133
Denkbild 30–32, 35
de-territorialization 36, 75, 83, 106, 123, 126, 130, 144
diagram 20, 25, 94, 121
diffraction 104, 107, 119, 135
Dimock, Wai Chee 33, 91, 93–94
DuBois, W. E. B. 26
dystopia 8–10, 23, 25, 43, 48, 52, 109

Eagleton, Terry 2, 21, 34
Esposito, Roberto 22, 56–59, 64, 67
Evans, Kate 138–140, 146, 148, 155–156

Felski, Rita 14
"Fold, The" (Gilles Deleuze) 95–98, 154
Foucault, Michel 43, 46
Freud, Sigmund 55, 73–74, 75, 77, 93, 97–98

Gaia 111–112
Gibson, William 52–53, 55, 57, 75, 97
Gilroy, Paul 139, 142
Glissant, Édouard 139–140, 155–157
Gosh, Amitav 107–108, 112–113, 134
'Great American novel' 29–30
grievability 77, 83
Groensteen, Thierry 144

Index

grotesque 47, 76, 87, 116, 128–130
Guattari, Félix 7, 10, 15, 18–19, 23–25, 28, 35–36, 54–55, 65, 131, 141–144, 153–154

Hamid, Mohsin 154
Haraway, Donna 3, 10, 15, 27–28, 50–52, 55, 58, 60–62, 64, 66, 102, 117, 120–122, 125, 132, 150
Hassan, Ihab 41
Hayles, Katherine 45
Heise, Ursula 133
heteroglossia 33, 62, 156
Hogan, Linda 13, 118–127, 133
Holzer, Jenny 79
humanism 41, 62, 64, 66, 139
'hypersea' 120

ideology 6–7, 10, 18, 21, 24–25, 31, 112
immunity 22
Indiana, Rita 133–134
insurgence 13, 107, 109, 127, 157
Irigaray, Luce 13, 103–106, 108, 134–135

Jameson, Fredric 20, 45, 51, 66

Kearney, Douglas 11, 23, 32–33, 37–38
Kollwitz, Käthe 152

Lai, Larissa 58–62
Latour, Bruno 102, 111–112
Laub, Dori 73, 92–93
LeGuin, Ursula 20
Levitas, Ruth 6, 9–10
Loy, Mina 66
Lukács, Georg 6, 31–32

Mannheim, Karl 20–21
Major, Devorah 64
Massumi, Brian 82–84, 92–93, 95
materialism, new 117, 124
Miller, Frank 152–153
minor literature 15, 143–144
Moravec, Hans 44–45, 54, 65
More, Thomas 9–10, 19
Morrison, Toni 3, 14
Morton, Timothy 103

Neimanis, Astrida 106–107, 127, 134
neoliberalism 11, 20, 24, 44, 52, 65–66, 86–87

Nixon, Rob 13, 19, 107–110, 121, 133
nomad thought 153–154
nomad writing 141
Nussbaum, Martha 14

oceanic studies 106, 130
Ozeki, Ruth 75–76, 90–91, 94–97

panpsychism 114
Penelope 140–141, 144, 147
Perry, Grayson 9
Plumwood, Val 13, 103, 110, 112–114, 133
process geography 155
prose fragment 30, 32, 36
Pynchon, Thomas 76, 85–89

Rancière, Jacques 5, 7, 105, 114, 117, 119, 125
Rankine, Claudia 11, 18, 23–30, 32–33, 36–37
Redfield, Marc 72, 85, 87
replicant 48–54, 58, 63, 67
resistance, literature as 14–15, 16, 18, 23–25, 27, 35, 43, 45, 55, 59, 66, 81, 83, 104–105, 123–124, 134, 155
"response-ability" 26–28, 55, 66, 122, 150
rhizome 4, 10, 35–36, 64, 139, 154, 157
Ricœur, Paul 9–10, 19, 20–21, 25
Rothberg, Michael 70, 74, 81, 97
Rushdie, Salman 74

Sacco, Joe 151
Satrapi, Marjane 13, 145–149, 155–156
sequentiality 143
Shamsi, Kamila 75–77, 80–85
slow violence 19, 109–110, 124
Sontag, Susan 144
Spiegelman, Art 72, 92, 143, 148
Spivak, Gayatri 84, 139, 148
subjecthood, implicated 12, 55–56, 74–75, 87, 97
submergence 109, 119, 122, 125, 134
Sulaiman, Hamid 145, 150–153, 155–156
'superpower syndrome' 84
sympoiesis 27, 117

Tan, Shaun 145, 153–155
temporality: forked 58, 97; as gyre 91, 97; pre-emptive 92–93, 95, 97–98
territory 7, 11, 19, 102, 113, 123, 125, 128–129, 157
transcorporeality 57, 61, 63
transhumanism 41, 44, 46–47, 54, 57, 62, 65
transversality 11, 16, 22–24, 26–29, 33, 54–57, 66, 73, 75, 77, 80, 119–121, 123–124, 130–132, 142, 151–152
trauma: multidirectional 81; national 71–72, 74; of spectatorship 78; virtual 87
trickster 34, 63, 105, 120, 130, 133

utopia 8–12, 16, 19–21, 24–25, 28–29, 33–36, 45

V 25

Wheeler, Wendy 119–120
Whitehead, Colson 11, 24, 34–36, 41–43, 45–47

Zapf, Hubert 5, 16, 109–110, 116, 119
Žižek, Slavoj 20–21, 24, 85
zombie 24, 41–43, 45–47, 96
zoon politicon 11

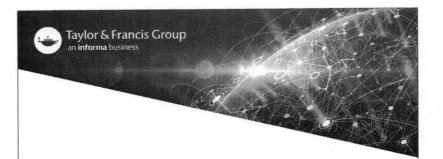